THALIA WINKS

THALIA WINKS

HUMOR, COMEDY, & DEEP THOUGHT

E.M. SCHORB

HILL HOUSE　　　　**NEW YORK**

ISBN: 978-0-578-87618-4
Cover Design: Selah Bunzey
Cover Cartoon "Guru Frappé" by the Author

ACKNOWLEDGEMENTS

Grateful acknowledgement is given to the following publications
in which some of these stories and poems first appeared:

Antioch Review, The Bangalore Review (IN), Best American Fan-
tasy 2007, Blue Ridge Literary Services, Blue Unicorn, Brooklyn
Review, The Carolina Quarterly, The Chariton Review, Chatta-
hoochee Review, Chelsea, Clark Street Review, Coe Review, The
Dark Horse, Eclectica Magazine, Futures Trading, Ginosko Liter-
ary Journal, Haight Ashbury Literary Journal, The Hudson Re-
view, The Kit Cat Review, Light: A Quarterly of Light Verse, The
Lyric, Measure, The Mississippi Review, Off Course Literary
Journal, Oxford Poetry (Magdalen College, UK), Pennsylvania
Review, *Phoenix Rising from the Ashes* (Anthology, Canada),
Plainsongs Poetry Magazine, Poetry Salzburg Review, (AT), *The
Prose Poem* (Anthology, edited by Steve Wilson), S N Review,
Sparrow 62, Spoon River Poetry Review, Spring: A Journal of the
E.E. Cummings Society, The Road Not Taken: A Journal of For-
mal Poetry, Trinacria, Wascana Review (CA), Willow Review,
WordWrights! Magazine, and Xavier Review.

"The Girl Upstairs," " An Actor Prepares," and "The Sandal Shop"
are excerpted from the Eric Hoffer award winning novel, *A Portable Chaos.* "Marijuana at Monticello" was produced by M.T.
Pockets Theatre Company, Morgantown, West Virginia. "Resurgius," originally published by Rainy Day Reads and subsequently
by Hill House New York as *R&R: A Sex Comedy* was winner of
the Beverly Hills Book Award for Humor. Cartoons originally appeared in *Moon for the Misbegotten?* by the author.

And with thanks for grants from the Provincetown Fine Arts
Work Center, the North Carolina Arts Council, and Robert
Rauschenberg's Change, Inc.

Comedy is the abundance of life.

Patrick Kavanagh

Dying is easy, comedy is hard.

Edmund Kean

FOREWORD

In THALIA WINKS you are getting the unique humor of E M SCHORB in poetry, short stories, novels, and, more importantly, in his "deep thoughts." But you also get his love of the human condition. In my mind, this work should be titled: *Humor, Comedy, Deep Thought, and Love.* The work opens with a sonnet expressing his love for his wife, Patricia, and ends in a sonnet to his first agent, a love and (maybe hate) relationship. His drawings are deftly dropped into places that make you sit back and think deeply. They are extracted from his book, *Moon for the Misbegotten?* Borrowed from Eugene O'Neill, one might expect to enter the dysfunctional world of the Tyrone/O'Neills. Far from it. This is a title borrowed with respect. Just as O'Neill plumbed the human frailty of his own family, Schorb plumbs the frailty and mystery of the human condition with his drawings. To me it is not a book of cartoons. It is a book of poetic artistry whose slender lines and suggestive curves delve into the foibles and idiosyncrasies of being human, a condition that he sees as inseparable from the birds, bees, flowers, and imaginary creatures we might conjure up to explain ourselves. The excerpts from *RESURGIUS* (*R&R: A Sex Comedy*) should inspire you to read the work itself. I did and it engulfed me with laughter. It's deadly funny. Visions of Gloria Steinem, Betty Friedan, Helen Gurley Brown flashed through my head. The sexual revolution was at its zenith. E M Schorb has created a satirical homage to the time. "The Girl Upstairs," "An Actor Prepares," and "The Sandal Shop," are excerpts from his Eric Hoffer award winning novel, *A Portable Chaos.* They should whet your appetite for the novel. I recommend that you get it. It is an historical novel that brings to life the transformation of the United States from the conforming Fifties to the volcanic social eruptions of the "swinging Sixties." It is a great American novel set against that chaotic and transformative period of American history. We follow eighteen-year-old Jimmy Whistler, from the bottom rung of America's social ladder, to his time in the Marines in Hawaii, where he meets Leilani, a girl destined to be the love of his life. Discharged, he returns to New York, a city churning with the chaos of the Sixties. Jimmy mines the very heart of that New York as an actor and a writer, one who sees himself as a poet. He hangs out with the denizens of the theatre and the hippies who seek the extremes of the chaos. This is a bitter-sweet story, one that charts the uncertainty of life in America today and attests to the myth portrayed in the Norman Rockwell covers. But don't read this book for any of these reasons. Read it to be captured by characters who are brought to life better than any you've ever encountered. Read it to be enthralled by dialogue so real that you are taken inside the life of each. Read it to experience what it's like to be a voyeur and an eavesdropper on every page. Read it to feel the poetic resonance of the language. Read it to experience E M Schorb, a writer who will, from now on, stand at the top of your reading list.

—Pat Mullan
Poet, Novelist, Essayist
Member, International Thriller Writers

SONNET TO MY MUSE

Poe wrote a riddling good acrostic once.
  D**A**vies turned trick into a feeling tribute
Be**Th** could take pride in. Well, I'm not a dunce.
  You**R** servant, you will find, is a glib brute,
ma'am. *I* am able, any time I choose,
  to do a**C**rostics cleverer than theirs,
Presto! **It** is the nature of my muse,
  Patrici**A**—money as to millionaires.

Now here i**S** what to look for: scan the page—
  then, if you **C**an't see anything, try counting
inward, from **H**igh to low. Soon a presage
  of what is to c**O**me, love, will form, this mounting
as you proceed. **R**emember, it's a name.
Patricia Schor**B**? You *got* it! Here's to fame!

CONTENTS

MOVIE MONEY

Aunt Gertrude had had no education—had been, due to the poverty and ignorance of her family, virtually a waif—but possessed noticeable innate intelligence. She kept several sets of account books, some of dubious public record and some honest, illegal, and secret. The house of her dominion may have been a rooming house in a Newark slum, but it was papered green with numbers racket hundred dollar bills that had to be accounted for.

She had been a buxom girl who had swollen into an enormous woman and subsequently shrunk back to a two-hundred and fifty pound mere shadow of her former self, leaving her sallow, inelastic skin loose and hanging. Jimmy's earliest memory of her—he was about four or five—was of that enormous middle-aged woman of sixty.

She sat across from him and his mother in a restaurant booth and he counted her seven ballooning chins. Tactlessly, he asked about them, though he was just as fascinated by the even larger balloons that rested side by side on the table top, that were deep-trenched and powdered and seemed to roll about of their own volition.

Of the chins, Aunt Gertrude told him that each represented a daughter and that, collectively, they indicated that she was the seventh daughter of a seventh daughter and was therefore possessed of magical powers, such as the gift of the evil eye.

Later, his mother told him that Aunt Gertrude had been stolen by Gypsies as a little girl—actually, farmed-out as a helper—and had lived in a Gypsy camp somewhere in the Watchung mountains of New Jersey for over a year, when finally her father had—reluctantly, for she had been a demonic child even before being "kidnapped," and some said that she had been given away—gone to retrieve her. Into her early sixties, she had developed ghostly cataracts that added impact when she gave you the evil eye, which she often did, and either had or feigned to have a heart ailment. By now, this doubtful heart condition had been present for as long as anyone could remember with no more dire consequence than that if anyone crossed her she would go spinning off across the room like a top on her little horny feet, her great, low bulk knocking a swath in the furnishings, and dive into a possum faint. This was called "swooning," and Jimmy's mother said that Aunt Gertrude had "swooned" or was about to "swoon." In truth, it was difficult to tell if her heart or her temper was the true culprit. She took—suitably—nitroglycerin for this condition, and smelling salts were always advisable. The smelling salts were carried in the pocket of another enormous, though much younger, woman, named Charity. Charity was Aunt Gertrude's flunky. She had culled Charity and Charity's husband, Donald, from the mildly-challenged ward at the mental institution at Vineland, New Jersey. Charity and Donald lived, as it were, by Aunt Gertrude's leave. Charity was a low, wide three-hundred pounds; Donald a high, narrow one-twenty-five. This couple existed upstairs and would plummet down a back stairwell at Aunt Gertrude's ear-splitting behest. Charity did all of Aunt Gertrude's domestic chores, more or less ran the roominghouse, including keeping in supplies—slow or not, she was a sharp bargainer—and Donald did the toting and fixing. They were well content, and even protective of Aunt Gertrude, who needed protection no more than did her favorite wrestler, Gorgeous George. Far from the least important member of this odd ménage was a canine. Wiggles was a very old bitch with tumorous, pendulous breasts. Aunt Gertrude, who had been at various times in an otherwise amoral career immoral on a professional basis, had been unable to have children, and had always felt the lack of a daughter. Wiggles served her as such. Jimmy took it that there had been other doggy-

2

daughters before the obscene Wiggles, but for as long as he could remember Wiggles had been about, door-scratching and spitting horrid barks at any intruder, himself included, being dragged back and shushed, and traipsing off down the hall ahead of the menagerie, like an old woman who has just given a salesman an earful, nails clicking, upright stubby tail stiff, broad hindquarters naked, unappetizing. Jimmy was a fastidious little boy and Wiggles deeply disturbed him. She sat at table, wrapped in a bib, and ate from a dinner plate. Because she was an old dog and couldn't chew, all were subjected to the spectacle of Aunt Gertrude, or sometimes Charity, masticating morsels before placing them in Wiggles' worn-down chops. And often, not being content with her own portion, Wiggles would heave her clattering bulk to the floor and beg Jimmy's, which he must forfeit or incur Aunt Gertrude's wrath.

"Isn't she a sugarball? Give her some of your meat. Don't forget to chew it for her!"

Friday was the big day of the week. Fridays, Aunt Gertrude prepared to go to Long Branch, New Jersey, where she would be met by her paramour and dominant partner, Tony "Ice Pick" Scarpia, a nearly four-foot tall man with a twisted spine, her "little giant," who ostensibly sold live bait, hence, "Ice Pick," to the fishermen on the pier there, but who was actually a mob-sponsored bookie and runner with the need of getting large sums of money out of his possession and back to Newark, to the roominghouse he owned and which existed under the absolute dominion of Aunt Gertrude.

*　　*　　*

When Jimmy's nervous mother rang the doorbell on Fridays, sending Wiggles into a conniption fit, Aunt Gertrude would usually be applying a sulphur-based solution, which she used instead of a razor, to her jowls and chins and pulpy, varicosed legs, of which, no pun intended, she was very vain, and every recess of the house would reek of sulphur, like a brimstone pit. Jimmy's mother would adjust herself to the powerful, rotten-egg fumes while Wiggles was being calmed and sent on her haughty way. On recovering from the spinning heart-seizure his mother's entry had caused, Aunt Gertrude would tell her to get herself some breakfast (coffee would suffice for Jimmy's mother in such an atmosphere); then Aunt Gertrude would carry on with her toilet like Susannah herself, if sans Susannah's everything including the intrigued elders. If Jimmy's mother could manage to be pleasantly helpful during the course of the day on Friday, and Jimmy could join her after school, and do the same, Aunt Gertrude might give them the money to go to a movie and buy some popcorn.

What was required was that they take her to the station and wait with her until train time. Jimmy would carry her bags and his mother would make chitchat, larding her comments with compliments.

"What a lovely dress, Aunt Gertrude!"

"I don't care for it that much!"

"Don't you?"

"No!

"Well, maybe it is a bit . . ."

"A bit what? Don't you like it? You just said you did!"

"I *do*!"

"Well—" Huff-puff!

Jimmy invariably arrived at a crucial moment, for with Aunt Gertrude there were no non-crucial moments. By now her beard and leg-hair would have been peeled heart-attackingly off with the sulphurous pancake crusts that had mummified various parts of her anatomy, her top-hair would have been freshly dyed—this was Jimmy's mother's specialty—either jet-black or fire-engine red, as Aunt Gertrude's mood would have it, her too-small shoes force-fed by horn her horny feet, and, corseted, frocked, and fully decorated, she would look like a Woolworth's Christmas tree. But

4

Wiggles would have to be left in the care of Charity and Donald, whom Aunt Gertrude did not trust to do right by her doggy daughter while she was away (albeit so in awe of her magic were the poor serfs of her household, that she had little to fear), and therefore had to be bathed and prepared for the weekend before Aunt Gertrude could take her leave in confidence. The galvanized tub would be on the kitchen table and Charity would be turning Wiggles fatly and stiff-leggedly about in it, soaping and scrubbing her under Aunt Gertrude's close scrutiny. Jimmy's mother would answer the door, lead little Jimmy back into the kitchen, and stand aside, eager to please, afraid to offend, baffled and thwarted, it being understood that she was not competent to be involved in this splashy task.

"Is there anything to eat?" Jimmy asked.

"Not now," his mother said, meaning of course not that there wasn't anything to eat but that Jimmy should keep quiet. Aunt Gertrude shrieked, grabbed her fat-buried heart, and fell back, knocking pots and pans from the stove. Charity had lost her soapy grip on Wiggles and the ungainly animal had slopped about in the bubbles.

"I thought she'd drown," cried Aunt Gertrude. "For God's sake, Charity, be careful with her!"

Jimmy sniggered.

"And just what do you think is so funny?"

One ghostly evil eye was on him, the other tightly shut.

His mother pinched him.

"Nothing, Aunt Gertrude."

"I should hope not!"

Charity got Wiggles rinsed, spread a bathtowel out on the table, patted her dry, turned her over, powdered her tumorous breasts, and put a nice clean jockstrap on her. These jockstraps served as double-D doggie brassieres, holding Wiggles' pendulous powdered breasts in place. There were several other elongated jockstraps hanging about

5

the kitchen on towel racks, drying. Wiggles stood upright now, a small whale on four toothpicks, jockstrap at sway. Charity sweatered, harnessed and leashed her.

This was where Jimmy came in. He could not fathom what gave Aunt Gertrude the idea, but she was firm in her conviction that it was good for Wiggles to be walked after her bath, and it was his delightful duty to walk her, and not just in front of the house, where he would frowningly skulk, if he were not urged on, but all the way up to Broad Street and under the Lackawanna overpass, where the bus stop was, and many people were, and back. If not conscious, was it subconscious sadism that compelled Aunt Gertrude to force Jimmy to do this? On more than one occasion people had laughed out loud at the sight of the red-faced, embarrassed little boy in short pants and the enormously overweight, pendulously jock-strapped dog that seemed in charge of their direction. It happened again on this particular Friday, and one woman even pointed at them from a passing bus. Jimmy's face burned red as a tomato, and tears of shame and temper rolled down his cheeks. But Jimmy consoled himself with the prospect of the movie that lay ahead—maybe.

They couldn't be sure. Aunt Gertrude was capable of not coming through on her part of the unspoken bargain, just to show them. There had been sad times when they left the station with empty pockets and had had to be satisfied with just looking at the bright marquees, to imagine how good it might have been to see the pictures and to talk about how much they would have enjoyed them. Then they would go home cursing Aunt Gertrude a little but mostly laughing about the mishaps of Wiggles and Aunt Gertrude's swoons. Later, they would listen to the evening radio programs and look forward to next week, the eternal optimists—for, after all, being dirt poor, they had no choice.

Aunt Gertrude loved gin rummy and Jimmy was the only soldier in her small army who knew how to play it. But she had a method. She would set up the card table next to the television set, then a relatively new device with a huge, rabbit-eared antenna, and turn on wrestling, which she loved—Jimmy noted her adoration of Gorgeous George—and then, when in trouble with her cards, would shout for him to look at what was happening in the ring, and, while his attention was diverted, would cheat by changing cards or stealing extras. One time he caught her at it, though he had suspected her of cheating before this. Boldly, he accused her, and she accused him of being a thankless ingrate like his no-good drunken father. Jimmy sat fuming, about eight years old, then charged across the room like a little bull, goring her with his cowlick horns. She was terrifically strong, even then, and he could believe the family tales told of her by nieces and nephews whom she had lifted into the air in her lustier youth and thrown clean across rooms. This time she easily finessed him into a half-nelson, boxed his ears red, whirled, and, having subdued him, promptly fainted. Charity brought out the smelling salts while Wiggles and Jimmy's mother had hysterical fits of their own. No one was concerned with the crushed, defeated little heap under her—Jimmy. That Friday they did not get their movie money.

So Jimmy's eyes sucked back his tears and he held himself in and brought Wiggles back to the house.

"What did Wiggles do?"

"Sniffed at things."

"Was she cute?"

"Yes, Aunt Gertrude."

"Did she pee or poop?"

"No."

Thank God! That would have required removing the jockstrap in public and replacing it afterwards (he was always required to take extras along). It had happened before and was perhaps worst of all.

7

"Well, we are all ready to go then. Charity, get my pocket book! Donald, get my bags!"

When they took a taxi, the trip to the station wasn't so bad. Then it was just a question of stuffing Aunt Gertrude, her bags, and themselves into the back seat and setting forth. But sometimes she couldn't get a cab to come to the house at the right time; or else, for other reasons, preferred to take a bus. Jimmy thought she preferred to take the bus sometimes so that the passengers could get a load of her, all dolled up and, as she no doubt believed, dazzling. But this bus ride with Aunt Gertrude was nearly as much of an embarrassment to him as were the afterbath walks with Wiggles. Indeed, Wiggles and Aunt Gertrude had much in common. Aunt Gertrude's legs, however, were of stouter stuff than those of her doggy daughter. Jimmy watched her now, as they climbed the great wide ramp that led to the trains; and, though he could scarcely drag the suitcases that were attached to his weakening hands and weight-sloped shoulders, he giggled to see the bowed, varicosed, mouth-down megaphones of her legs triumph over the upgrade. Side to side she heaved, as if the whole station, and the whole world, were tilting.

As usual, she had bought them chicken salad sandwiches and coffee in the lunchroom down the ramp behind them, where everyone had seen them before, for many Fridays. As usual, she had complained about the expense. As usual, she had been rude to everyone, and as usual Jimmy felt a little sick. But it was a good sign. It showed that she was in a giving mood. Perhaps she was in a good mood because she was looking forward to making love to her little "Hot Pepper." He loved her, they all knew that, if not why. Perhaps because she seemed oblivious to his deformity. Perhaps because she only heard his deep voice or saw his handsome head. But then, there was the gambling money she would be bringing back from Long Branch to Newark on Monday, and perhaps she feigned her obliviousness to his deformity, and her orgasms, which were occasionally overheard and commented upon by the horror-struck tenants of the roominghouse, as she feigned her heart attacks. Who knew?

They boarded the train with her, as was their practice, and sat with her, waiting for the train to show signs of life. Jimmy wondered if she would give them their movie money, which he felt they had earned, and if it would be enough, and if they would be able to get off the train in time, and not be swept off with her, away from the many glittering marquees of Newark, while she strung it out, cat and mouse. She bullied. His mother strained to be dutiful. He perspired. Aunt Gertrude's perfume was dizzying. The train jerked with coupling. Steam hissed.

"We'd better get off, Aunt Gertrude," his mother said.

"You have plenty of time. You're awfully anxious to get away. Where are you going?"

"Nowhere," said his mother, cowed.

"Well, then, sit still! Oh, by the way, here are a couple of dollars. Why don't you go to a movie? 'Gone With the Wind' is playing at the Adams on Branford Place." But she did not hand over the bills.

"All off!" cried the conductor.

Aunt Gertrude sighed, and handed the bills to Jimmy's mother.

They kissed her and got off the train. Now they must stand and dutifully wave until the heavily laden train puffed out of sight. If they did not stand long enough, she would call them on it next Friday, and they would not get their movie money then. Finally, the train completely disappeared, and they could leave the station and walk back to the center of Newark and study the other worlds of the magical marquees. In those days you really had a choice.

Or so it seemed.

THE FINE ART OF HAUNTING

I

"Watch how," my teacher said, "when I tug, she tugs
right back, annoyed. She thinks she's caught on something,
then wonders, when she sees that nothing's there,
how she got caught—on what, on where? And now
she's baffled, for there's nothing near her sleeve,
no furniture nearby, no hooking chair.

II

And now she speaks to him. I think he's here, she says.
He thinks she's suffering guilt—There's no one here.
He pours champagne. She pulls her glass away.
She tells him that she feels your presence in the room.
Don't ruin the occasion, he tells her.
We've got his house and all his money and each other.

III

Yes, haunting is an art," my teacher said.
"You mustn't be too obvious, too crude.
They'll think it's all a trick, or caused
by natural tremors, earthquakes and the like,
and what you want above all other things
is to be certain that they know it's you."

RESURGIUS

*. . . to see one-half of the human race
excluded by the other from all partici-
pation in government was a political
phenomenon that, according to abstract
principles, it was impossible to explain.*

A Vindication of the Rights of Woman
—Mary Wollstonecraft

1

To Serge Bering-Strait, young ward of five aggressive, progressive, and, to him, oppressive, women, the phrase "Swinging Sixties," meant, at this moment, swinging like Tarzan from a subway strap.

But he was no Tarzan. His mother and four aunties had forced *him*, a *poet*, out of his Greenwich Village attic sanctuary and into the struggle for survival here among the *poloi*, where he felt in imminent danger of being crushed, which partly accounted for the look of angst he wore. But what really depressed Serge was that he had already missed a whole half-hour of reading from his beloved Plutarch's *Parallel Lives*, which he gripped under his free arm, and which was being pressed painfully into his ribs by a grubby fellow traveler. The "lumpen mob" was just too thick this morning, too thick to hold up his book—so thick, in fact, that he was not sure if he had missed his stop.

There were no signs in prominent display, the windows were painted gaily over with spray paint, and the terrific, ear-splitting cough made by the loud-speaker hadn't served in the least to clear things up. Serge decided to get out.

12

The train doors shut just as he stepped through them, smudging the shoulders of his new London Fog, a twenty-third birthday gift from his Auntie Janet Hoover, and knocking his copy of Plutarch's *Lives* from his grasp. The book was kicked ahead of him into obscurity by the mob's stampeding hooves. The train reopened its doors with a snort, shot them shut behind him, and pulled away.

It was the wrong station. Well, it was a natural enough mistake. He had not had time to develop that sixth sense about subway stops that comes with practice. He had only been on the job for a few weeks, his Auntie Janet Hoover having procured his position as staff writer for him through her connection with the boss, the lady editor Bettina Battle, who sometimes worked for Auntie Hoover as a speech writer. Auntie Hoover was in politics, an assistant to Mayor Dimwiddy.

This was not his first job. His first job was being a poet, which he had been since his prodigious graduation from New York University some five years before, at eighteen. But Auntie Hoover thought that it was high time that the little "genius-boy" got out of the house. She thought his life up in his garret room was very unnatural.

When the crowd thinned, Serge found his battered Plutarch near the turnstile. He could have cried for the thousand indifferent kicks it had received. A tasteless modern world had no respect for the classics.

A train roared in, with a long, shrill, metallic scream of the sort he imagined Jurassic raptors might have used to indicate their ravenousness.

Pressed into the center of the crushed subway crowd, which held him upright, levitated, feet adrift in space, arms bound to his sides, his Plutarch bruising his ribs, he could still get a sniff of fetid hot air from above; but the air-conditioning blew his inherently wild red hair askew and, when he opened his spectacled eyes, he was forced to look at the advertising

13

signs over the windows. HEMORRHOIDS? one asked, distastefully. TAMPONS? another invited. UNDERARM ODOR? another challenged. JOCK ITCH! another asserted. THE NAKED TRUTH another—wait!

THE NAKED TRUTH?

Ah ha! The bureaucrats at the Poetry in Motion office had finally got around to putting up his subway poem—

THE NAKED TRUTH

The naked truth will lie.
I don't believe in facts.
What's in the inner eye
Is what the outer lacks.

The night's an Arab's sheet
Of swirling blue and black.
The earth is at his feet.
The stars are at his back.

And even love is true
If we should make it so.
O, lover, love me too!
O, lover, let me go!

by Serge Bering- . . .

The lights in the car flickered, went out. Serge thought of his loss of time. It seemed hours till they got started again, but it turned out to be only twelve minutes when he could read his watch.

The light turned green in Serge's favor and he stepped out from the curb, preoccupied with thoughts of his dreary, poetry-corrupting writing job, his guilty tardiness, when a taxi swerved in front of him with a screech, blasting its horn, the driver, a woman who looked as mean as Auntie Hoover, cursing him with words even more raffish than passages from

14

Allen Ginsburg's horrible "Howl." As his eyes rolled back in his head, Mother Nature's eternal blue highway shone between the tall, artificial escarpments of skyscrapers, still, surprisingly, possessing the magic of modernity—and he saw, high above him, in that blue wonder, an airship shaped like a Frankfurter. It was the Quaint Wiener Balloon, the inescapable red hot dog that he saw in every store, at every stand; but this one was gigantic, so big that it outloomed the skyscrapers, seemed to even outloom the Goodyear *dirigible*!

QUAINT WIENERS

was written on its side, plain as day. And then, it floated out of sight, banned from the sky by the behemoth buildings it sailed over.

He entered the revolving door of the American Rubber Climax Building and was shot up sixty-nine floors to the offices of *Women's Omnibus* magazine. He got to work just on time but was immediately assaulted.

"Your 'food-on-a-stick' article is très—and I do mean *très*—putrid, " cried Serge's editor, Bettina Battle, sometimes known as the Battle of Britain, having arrived at *Women's Omnibus* from *Swinging London*, the magazine as well as the city.

"What's wrong with it?" Serge was shaking out his London Fog. He hung it on the clothes tree that took up valuable foot space in his cubicle. It was a sad, dripping sight. His Auntie Janet would sting with the insult of it. But then, Auntie Janet Hoover was always prepared to sting. He wiped his face and dried his glasses with tissue, superficially listening to Bettina Battle's cockney-inclined locutions while inwardly bemoaning the condition of his battered Plutarch. He had to pee.

"What's wrong with it?" Bettina Battle cried. "That's old shit! We want something new! We want new concepts! On the ball, Bering-Strait! On the ball!"

Serge could scarcely keep his eyes open. He'd been awake since two a.m. when the burglar alarm went off at Schlock's Delicatessen down the street from his mother's house. Since his air conditioner was on the blink, and his window wide open, he'd heard the alarm full blast. "New concepts," he ruminated. "Food-on-a-stick, just heat and eat."

"What's that?" cried Bettina Battle.

"What do you mean 'new concepts'?" asked Serge. "The stuff's a lot of dreck. Who'd eat it?"

"Bering-Strait, what are you saying?"

The din of electric Selectric typewriters and office machines seemed particularly intense. His head ached, and he had to pee, badly. He took a bottle of aspirins from his desk and walked to the water cooler with Bettina Battle in pestering pursuit. She eyed him ruefully as he choked down two aspirins.

"This is serious business, Bering-Strait," she said, while he strangled on the aspirins, repeatedly flushing them down with paper cup after paper cup of water. It was business, Serge admitted to himself, and the money involved made it serious, he supposed; but it was disgusting, nonetheless. He yearned for the classics. He even yearned for Jane Austen. If only Bettina Battle spoke to him like a character out of Jane Austen instead of sounding like the screeching flower girl in "My Fair Lady."

"You see, Bering-Strait, the mashed potatoes, ground beef, and peas are all smooshed up together into a ball, like a lollipop, and frozen on a stick. Then you pop it in the oven, and there it is, ready to eat! A quick meal for busy women in a busy women's world." Bettina beamed. "Isn't it wonderful? It's a new concept!" Now Bettina frowned.

16

"You've got to get serious, Bering-Strait. Magazines are in stiff competition with—I can hardly bear to say it—the telly, TV, the tube, say-screen, or whatever you want to call that monster."

"Say-screen?"

"Whatever—call the monster what you will—it's ruining our circulation. That's why we need new concepts."

"Won't it fall off when it's heated?"

"Won't what fall off?"

"The food off the stick! Won't it fall off when it's heated?"

Bettina looked at him, hard. "Uuum. You look beat, Bering-Strait. What's the matter, not getting enough sleep?"

"No, I'm *not* getting enough sleep," Serge said, yawning, "I was up all night. First a faulty alarm went off and woke me and my air conditioner's on the blink, and then I couldn't stop thinking about a novel I want to write."

"Novels are dead! Flicks and the Say-screen have already killed them. Do you want the monster to kill *Women's Omnibus* as well? Here, we need people who can think on their feet around here—think original thoughts, new concepts," Bettina summed up. She stood looking at him, arms akimbo, waiting like a drill sergeant for a response from a recruit.

"Something like Amanda Quaint's idea for sky-mirrors?" Serge asked insinuatingly. Amanda Quaint wrote for a competitor of *Women's Omnibus, Ladies' Day,* and her recent article had caused a great stir among the New York magazine set. Leo Lerman had called her a genius.

"Quite, Bering-Strait, that's quite it! Think of it— constant daylight—'round the clock selling! Business would double. The world would have to run three shifts. Then too, it'd create a whole new market—sleeping aids; ear-plugs; sleeping pills; eye shades; black window curtains! Think of

17

that, Bering-Strait! New concepts! By the way, I want you to get started on researching the new UNIVAC machine."

"The great computer that's going to revolutionize life as we know it?"

"I want the angle on what it'll do for women—help free them from low-paying office drudgery—"

Serge saw himself in his cubicle, wetting his pants.

"—elevate them to technical personnel, programmers and the like. See what you can bring out of the tin. I want some stats on women—proving their oppression. Up till now we've only had deductive reasoning to go by—observation. Now, with this UNIVAC III, we can get statistics to prove scientifically what we've believed all along, that we women are nothing but drudges and slaves for you men. The UNIVAC III will set women free!"

Serge asked, "Won't it just increase production, rather than freeing any workers?"

Bettina didn't approve of Serge's obvious lack of enthusiasm. "I've got my eye on you, Bering-Strait." She turned and marched off on stiletto heels.

Serge could not run to the lavatory, for fear of losing urinary control, but he got there as soon as he could. All the urinals were vacant, but Serge was urinal-averse. He went into a booth, sat down, and peed. His mother and aunties had trained him from a toddler to sit down when he peed in order to reduce splashing and mistargeting, or so they told him, taught him, and now it was impossible for him to stand and shoot. He washed his hands and went back to the office.

Serge spent most of the afternoon acquainting himself with his new assignment. He'd have to figure out the female angle on the Univac III. What would it mean to readers of *Women's Omnibus*?

At four-thirty, Serge begged to be unhanded by Bettina, who dragged him from his cubicle—where he had been racking his brains—and into her glassed-in corner office.

18

"Sir Gay . . ." she began, lighting a Virginia Slim, sinking into her swivel chair, and putting her amazingly long and shapely legs on her desk, spike-heels spindling articles that covered every aspect of women's life from hair-dos to toenail polish, from gourmet cooking to commodity investments ("How Women Can Make a Million in Pork Bellies").

"Serge!" he corrected. "Why do you always call me Sir Gay? You know that my name is pronounced 'surge' like the surge of the sea."

"Whatsum," Bettina said. "Thing is, I've had my eye on you for some time."

"So you said," said Serge, with a snip in his voice.

"You're a presentable young man in a pouffy sort of way, and I'd like you to escort me to a meeting of the Lunar Society in Greenwich Village tonight. *I* live in the Village and *you* live in the Village, so, after the meeting, you can see me home . . . or should I see *you* home? It'll be getting dark by then. I have a black belt in Karate, so you have no need to fear the mean streets of the Village after sundown."

Serge understood her sarcasm. The infamous nymphomaniac had been trying to get into his virginal pants since his first day on the job, but he had thus far managed to fend her off. She had gone from merely chiding him to outright bitchy persecution. Clearly, however, she was going to have another try tonight, taking a different tack. It was not that her beauty did not appeal to him, but that she had none of the sweetness his embarrassed virginity would require in his first lover. Her beauty was controlled by a harsh machine, a soulless battery, that energized a force field. In other words, she turned him off, but good!

"What's the Lunar Society?" he asked, trying to show polite interest.

"The Lunar Society is an association of professional women who meet monthly, and I am surprised, your mother

19

and aunties being who they are, that you have not heard of it. *Our Mother is the Moon!* Doesn't that ring a bell?"

It did, faintly. A tiny tinkle. But, for as long as he could remember, he had been dragged to all sorts of meetings, conventions, and gatherings, yet, somehow, had managed, maybe, to have missed this particular one; or perhaps had actually slept through an earlier meeting of the Lunar Society, as he often slept through meetings, even sometimes snored through them. Sometimes all he had to show for a meeting was a bruised rib cage, where female elbows had poked him awake. His ribs were tender as a bird's.

"Why me?" he asked. "You can get anybody you want to escort you." But he already knew the answer. She wanted something new. Even a new disease would do for Bettina.

"Why must we go?" he asked.

"Because everyone who's anyone in the Women's Movement will be there. Don't you want to get somewhere in the magazine business? Well, you have to be inside. It's called networking. Besides, your whole family will be there. Now, no buts about it. Meet me at my limo out in front at five-thirty sharp. I have no more bloody time to spend on you. Not now. But I have something of great importance to tell you on the drive downtown." She pointed a long, ensanguined talon toward his cubicle, over the bobbing heads of busy, quietly desperate plebes. "Go!" she ordered, and closed the valves of her attention, as Emily Dickinson might have done.

At five-thirty sharp, Serge stood, like a reactionary lemming, a few feet in front of the revolving art deco door of the American Rubber Climax Building and refused to be moved by the outflowing crowd. Curiosity kept him in place. What was this thing of "great importance" that Bettina had waved before him like a carrot? And could he avoid the stick?

In the limo, a breathless Bettina Battle told him that she would be leaving *Women's Omnibus* poste-haste, for a better

20

job, and that he might very well be her replacement as editor of the magazine. Her contract allowed her final choice for the editorship and her eye was on him, she said. "Yes, my eye is on *you*," she repeated, squeezing his thigh.

He giggled, squirming. Her thumb had plucked a funny string in his leg.

"Gawd!" she exclaimed. "You're skinny. I hope there is something a bit more hefty in that region. Shall we see?" She reached out again, her fingers dancing like red-tipped spider legs.

"Yipes!"

To Serge, her offer of promotion seemed far-fetched, but curiosity kept him listening, as well as patiently struggling, almost arm-wrestling. But there was this little problem, eh? And so began a battle for Serge's honor in the back seat of Bettina Battle's limousine. His red suspenders were no match for her black belt. Putting a purr in her otherwise harsh voice, she whispered, "I hate these big macho muscle men. It's you cute little cuddly guys like Woody Allen I go for in a big way. You remind me of him."

She twirled his red and white polka-dot bow tie, and lifted her short skirt up to her creamy hip to show that she wore no knickers. There was a growling British lion tattooed on her hip with some writing under it. She started to lower the skirt but Serge stopped her.

"Wait!" he said. "What's that say?" And then he was able to read the legend: I'LL EAT YOU ALIVE.

"Good heavens!" Serge cried. He was appalled. He felt that any kind of tattoo or body-piercing was primitive, déclassé; simultaneously transfixing and stomach-turning.

"Hurry the bloody hell up," she cried, releasing her skirt to the grip of gravity. "It's a long dull drive downtown. Let's ball, baby!"

Her focus on the mechanics of unjamming his zipper had caused her not to realize that they had already arrived at the

Village home of Hettie Freed, renowned author of *Men: The Feminine Mistake.*

Before Bettina could find a way to get his pants down, she found it necessary to make herself presentable. As she dabbed at her makeup, she said, "I never wear knickers, myself. I'm like the Boy Scouts—always prepared. I strongly suggest you heed my example next time. Get a pair of pants with buttons that button up. I can bite off a button."

She was miffed, but it wasn't his fault that she couldn't get his pants down, except for the struggling induced by his animal instinct for survival. He pulled his zipper up, then down, then up again, and it was free, and so was he. Silently, he thanked the jammed zipper heartily for protecting his terrified pee-pee, which seemed to shrink an inch back into his body at every touch of her long red talons. He pulled up his off-the-shoulder suspenders, got back into the jacket and London Fog she had fairly ripped from his back, stuck his Plutarch under his arm, and followed the Amazonian Bettina like a small, neurotic mutt on an umbilical leash.

The words "Hurry up, *Sir Gay*!" wafted over her shoulder on an ill wind, seeming to come from her tall French twist, as she climbed the steps of Hettie Freed's brownstone on Horatio Street, toward the networking delights of the Lunar Society's monthly meeting.

"My name is Serge, sounds like a *surge* of the sea!" he called after Bettina Battle, but she was not listening. The door swung open and she feinted a kiss on each dangling jowl of Hettie Freed, who asked who her little companion was. "This is Sir Gay Bering-Strait. You probably know his mother, Dagmar Bering-Strait—"

"—who invented bra-burning? Yes, of course I know Dagmar. She's here. I'm surprised I haven't met Sir Gay before this."

"My name is Serge. Like the *surge* of the sea," he insisted.

"*Gay* is quite an imaginative writer," said Bettina Battle. "He just finished a wonderful piece for *Women's Omnibus* on food-on-a-stick, and is even now researching the UNIVAC III machine for an article on its impact on the lives of women. He is a gifted journalist, so gifted that he should never do anything else, and I'm quite sure he has no thought of changing to another line of work. He says he wants to write a novel, though. Am I right, Gay?"

Serge nodded in defeat.

"Sounds brilliant, darling!" said Hettie, patting Serge on the head. Out of politeness, he tried to wag his tail a bit.

"And you know who else is here tonight?" Hettie's grey jowls brightened with the blood of excitement. "That delightful new discovery who wrote the piece in your competitor's magazine about sky-mirrors—you know, so that no one can sleep. Oh, what is she called?"

"Amanda Quaint—yes," said Bettina, "I'm anxious to meet her."

Had Serge's mother introduced him to Hettie Freed, he'd have become the subject of a dissertation. Dagmar would have regaled Hettie with her favorite explanation for Serge's existence. "He was conceived," his mother would have claimed, "in a public swimming pool, and is the ward of the State of New York. Floating semen, you see. . ." And she would have gone into the long legal battle she had with the State.

The truth was that his father, Charles Bering-Strait, was dead, having died in a wine-soaked cardboard box behind the Port Authority Bus Terminal. His mother had rid herself of the "loathsome sex maniac" at an early stage of their marriage. Serge had once read a letter from his father to his mother that bore the salutation "Dear Furious," so he had some ideas of his own about their marriage.

He was certain that he had been named by his mother, not his father. He thought of the torment of his school days.

23

Even the progressive schools that she had sent him to were torture chambers if you bore such a name as "Serge" and had been taught to sit down like a girl when you peed.

He followed Bettina Battle and Hettie Freed into the cavernous living room, acquired a glass of Dom Pérignon with little stars rising in it, and took two of the "Rosebud" wafers topped with darling little pink vaginas—someone mentioned that they had been baked by the up-and-coming feminist sculptor Judy Chicago—pregnant with Beluga, that he was offered, and from thence tried to become a wall-flower in a room full of aggressive kudzu—professional women of every size and shape.

From somewhere across the room, above the general uproar, he heard his mother's voice, a dentist's drill hitting metal, saying, "It makes me furious to think what these old-boy networks get away with. Look at the Masters in Augusta! No women allowed, my ass! Why, that mighty woman athlete, the great Babe Didrickson Zaharias could've whipped every one of those fat-assed, pot-bellied, dong-brained, male chauvinist pigs at golf or anything else. She could kick ass! It simply infuriates me. No women! They'll rue the day!"

Along with the Champagne and cookies, Serge had somehow acquired a flyer stating the purpose of this gathering. ". . . to make the old-boy networks rue the day. . ." he read, glancingly, " . . . to pay tribute to the Great Tallulah Bankhead, our Lunar Mother of the Month, who went about naked in the Twenties, fearlessly, sweeping men underfoot like so much trash . . ."

Occasionally, the donkey-eyed head of a male feminist floated by as if on a pike, wearing an enthusiastic rictus for a smile. Like himself, these poor souls no doubt belonged to some powerhouse of a woman. Then someone started chanting "Women power! Women power!" Serge recognized the plangent voice of his Auntie Hoover, "She-Who-Must-Be-Obeyed," she who subjected Serge's attic room, or garret, as

24

he preferred to think of it, to random searches for any indicators of masculine mischief, such as "Playboy" magazines, jockstraps, or condoms, she who had driven him from his secret meditations, from his poetry, and out into the cruel world—a basso profundo whose notability in any crowd could only be outdone by his mother's cry of "FURIOUS!" *Her* voice was even more irritating to him than Auntie Hoover's. He could feel his heart screaming in his chest every time he heard it.

His mother, Hettie Freed, and Bettina Battle gathered around the gleaming pink piano—an extraordinary instrument, Serge now noticed, because its three carved wooden legs were those of a woman in high heels.

Hettie Freed asked for the crowd's attention. She told them that Janet Hoover had a few words for them.

"Clear the way!" Bettina cried, making a path to the piano for Auntie Hoover. Bettina liked to be close to power—her motto was: "It's valuable to have a wise companion, and wiser to have a valuable one"—and Auntie Hoover was a valuable companion.

Bettina had thrown her arm over Auntie Hoover's shoulder and was reluctant to release her, but was forced to do so as Auntie Hoover, tank-like, ground her way up the piano stool and onto the piano to address the room from the mount, so to speak. She stood like a mighty Maillol, arms akimbo, and waited for the crowd to recognize her position of authority. One member of the crowd did, immediately, and shouted, "O mighty woman, empower us all!"

"At each of our monthlies we gather to pay tribute to a mighty woman of the past. Tonight we are going to honor the great actress and free spirit, the late great Tallulah Bankhead. Hand me that poster," Auntie Hoover ordered, and a life-sized cardboard cutout with a bracing flap was passed up to her from the crowd. She stood it next to her, stood at attention, and saluted it. It was a cutout of the naked Tallulah, done in

25

the style of Augustus John, wearing only a string of pearls, along with other natural products of womankind.

"Some of you younger members of the Lunar Society might not know the great Tallulah, but for those of us who have battled long and hard for women's rights, this ballsy, outspoken dame, inventor of camp itself, has long been an inspiration."

"The naked truth," a female voice whispered in Serge's ear. He looked around but recognized no one in the crowd.

Serge leaned on a pedestal that held a bronze statuette of Atalanta determinedly piercing a boar. He squinted at the little face of the boar and thought that it resembled himself in its agony. Then his agoraphobic narcolepsy overcame him.

He fell asleep until his ribs were poked. How long he had slept he had no idea, but he woke to the tune of "The Battle Hymn of the Republic," only the words were those of the "Women's Anthem."

Glory, Glory, Hail Tallulah!
Glory, Glory, Hail Tallulah!
Glory, Glory, Hail Tallulah!
Her Truth comes marching on.

"Hip, Hip, Hooray!" shouted the crowd, which was uproarious now with inspiration and Champagne.

Auntie Hoover addressed the gathering, saying, "We must adopt Sheila Michaels's suggestion that we refer to ourselves as 'Ms.' No more prissy 'Miss' or downtrodden 'Mrs.'" She beamed to the applause this inspired.

"How do you say that?" someone called. "I see it here in the flyer. But it hasn't got a vowel."

"Screw the vowel movement," roared Auntie Hoover. "That's just a lot of masculine crap. Just shout 'Mizzzzzzzzz' for all the world to hear and take notice."

"What would be the plural, do you think?" the voice asked. "Mize?"

"Screw plural!" shouted Auntie Hoover. "Screw vowels! Just don't screw men." She whooped and the others joined in.

"I saw by the look on your face that 'The Women's Anthem' inspired you," purred the same soft voice that had whispered "the naked truth" in Serge's ear. "You looked so lonely, standing over here by yourself, I thought I'd bring you a fresh glass of Champagne. My name's Amanda Quaint. I know who you are. You're Serge Bering-Strait, the writer. I've read a couple of your pieces in *Women's Omnibus*."

She was a foot taller than he and wore a Mary Quant mini-skirt; but, somehow, she didn't frighten him. Most of the women he knew did. Amanda Quaint's voice was soft, forgiving.

He took the stemmed glass from her fingers—such pretty, well-manicured fingernails, such a nice shade of pink—and looked up at her; but he only had two hands and found himself awkwardly in possession of two glasses, the flyer, and his Plutarch, all of which he began to shuffle, or, more nearly, juggle.

Amanda Quaint said, "Here, let me take that. Why are you reading Plutarch? Are you taking a course?"

"Of course not." He blushed at his timid, almost inadvertent pun. "Everyone should know the lives of these extraordinary Greeks and Romans. Their parallel lives. The Anabasis and Katabasis—"

"Yes, I know all about that," she said. "I think that's Xenophon."

"You do?" His admiration for her lifted another notch. She took the empty glass and the flyer from him and managed to make them disappear while keeping her big violet eyes fixed on him. Her grace amazed him, her beauty gave him palpitations. "My name is Serge," he said.

"Yes, I know," she said.

"You're Amanda Quaint," he said.

27

"Yes, I know," she said.

"I'm sorry," he said.

"What have you got to be sorry for?"

He tightened his lips and shook his head. "I don't know. Sleeping on duty, maybe. I just feel sorry all the time."

"I didn't know you would be so shy," she said. "I read your beautiful poem on the F Train—'The Naked Truth?' Until this morning, I didn't know you were also a poet. A very romantic poet, at that! A little old-fashioned, but I like that. I like the old romantic poets much better than the Beats."

His eye-beams, through his horn-rims, rolled down to her open-toed pumps and back to her head, a crown of gold. He recalled Yeats's lines, "That only God, my dear, could love you for your self alone and not your yellow hair?"

His attraction for her was instantaneous, chemical, genetic, he might have said, as if they had been brought together from the ends of the universe by Mother Nature herself, as if she had always been there in his very marrow, though his body was much too small for such a woman to have got into. In short, it was love at first sight.

"I think you're just brilliant!" Amanda Quaint said. "Men with brains and sensitivity turn me on." Serge didn't like the phrase, "turn me on," but it sounded sweet coming from Amanda Quaint. When Bettina had said much the same thing, during the drive downtown, it had sounded ravishing, a vulture's voluptuous hunger.

Embarrassed, he blurted, "Benjamin Franklin said that a man's arm was just long enough to lift a glass of wine to his mouth," and drank off half the new glass of Champagne.

He was afraid to look in Amanda's eyes, for fear that they would not show responsiveness. "Quaint? Are you related to the Wiener King? I saw his balloon this morning."

"He's my grandfather," she said.

28

Serge looked up at the ceiling as if in search of the giant red advertising phallus. When he looked down, Amanda Quaint was gone.

Then he saw her being pulled off through the crowd by Bettina Battle. The angel of his desire was being kidnapped right out from under his wiener-focused nose.

Bettina had seized Amanda by the arm and dragged her off, kidnapped her from Serge, in order to offer Amanda double her current salary to join the staff of *Women's Omnibus*.

"We're looking for some new concepts," Bettina said, pulling Amanda away. "Sir Gay doesn't get it. He's a young fogey—never would have come up with an idea like your sky-mirrors."

"I think he's brilliant," said Amanda, "and cute, too."

"Don't get any ideas. That Nancy boy is my poodle. But, if you accept my offer—*entre nous*, I'm leaving to go into politics and the company is looking for a new editor—you might end up being his boss. Then he can be your poodle. But, listen, it's too noisy to talk in here. Come on outside to my limo. We can talk there. Bring your drink. Now what I want, darling, is for you to give two weeks notice to your present employer and join us at *Women's Omnibus* in a fortnit."

Bettina Battle had Amanda Quaint all to herself in her limo now. A signal from Bettina had set the wheels in motion.

"Wait!" cried Amanda. "I wanted to say good-night to Serge."

"Roll on!" Bettina ordered her chauffeur, and seized Amanda by the knee. "How would you like to replace me as editor of *Women's Omnibus* when I go on to bigger and better things? Eh, Sweetie, answer me that!"

Amanda lifted Bettina's hand from her knee.

"Bloody Hell!" cried Bettina. "If you don't learn a little flexibility, you'll never get anywhere."

29

"I'll take my chances," said Amanda. "And keep your hands off me, if you don't want this glass of Champagne ruining your makeup."

"Listen, lady, I have a Black Belt in Karate."

"Watch out someone doesn't hang you by it."

Bettina Battle looked ruefully at Amanda and roared again to her driver: "ROLL ON!"

Back at the meeting of the Lunar Society, Serge felt bereft by his loss of Amanda Quaint.

He felt like going home to his garret at the top of his family's house and having a good cry over a nice, romantic, melancholy poem—maybe something by Poe—say, "Annabel Lee."

But then he tried to look on the sunny side, as an old song encouraged. At least he had escaped being escorted home by the insatiable, black-belted "Battle of Britain." But having escaped "the Battle of Britain" meant that Serge was abandoned to the tender mercies of his mother and Auntie Janet Hoover.

2

By eight o'clock, they were walking the misty streets of Greenwich Village. His mother pinched his left ear. She was furious at something that he had inadvertently said at the Lunar Society. The tired tongue of his tired mind had tied the title "Mister" Freed to "Miz" Freed in his good-bye. Pulling on his ear was a nasty habit of hers. His ears were always red and sore from her gripping digits. From boyhood, he saw cauliflower in his future. And Auntie Hoover held his right hand with a rock-crushing grip. They lifted him over a puddle.

Auntie Hoover carried his scuffed Plutarch, at some point complaining about the state of the book's jacket and comparing it to the state of his London Fog, which, she reminded him, was her birthday gift to him.

She berated Serge for his carelessness, but he paid little attention, for he was used to being treated like a child by these two large and bullying women.

His mother agreed with his Auntie Hoover in her assessment of him. It made her furious, she asserted, *furious*, that he was still such an incompetent child. Fortunately, most of this washed right off his rumpled London Fog. He had heard it all before, and, anyway, nothing could erase the image, seen through his misty glasses, of Amanda Quaint's seven-inches-above-the-knee, mini-skirted form from his hormone-drenched brain, his post-pubescent, testosterone-soaked soul. Fecklessly, he tugged for freedom, but they were too powerful.

Serge had grown up in the Village, had lived in the same five-story brownstone on Bethune Street all his life. The house had been passed down from his grandparents to his mother and four aunts. The family had made its money in brassieres. "Uplift by Updike." The slogan alone had made them a fortune in the Forties. Serge did not fail to see the irony in this, since his mother was famous for bra-burning.

Serge came to recognize a number of ironies and oddities about his family as he grew up. His Auntie Janet Updike had married a man named Hoover, who had run away from their honeymoon, so it was said, the only residue of this vanishing act being Auntie Janet's last name. The other three sisters, Charlotte, Emily, and Annie, were ink-stained spinsters who ran Boadicea Press out of the ground floor of the five-story brownstone. Serge heard it bruited about that they had once tried their hand at show business, as a trio, but were no match for Motown, and surrendered quietly to a non-vocal lifestyle. Occasionally, while they worked, they harmonized such tunes as "There's No Business Like Show

Business," but when noticing that Serge was with them, fell into silence.

He would have described them as taciturn, if asked. Like many other failed artists, they had turned to politics. Their purpose was not money but a passion for causes, activism, anarchism, and general intellectual mayhem. They were as clever at stirring the pot as the three Shakespearean witches. Boadicea Press turned out what they referred to as "edification for the masses."

Even his friends, most of whom were themselves from artistic, bohemian, or eccentrically rich backgrounds, teased him about the oddness of his family, and made common comment about the women being so big and him being so small, so undersized and frail, wondering to his face, often enough, as to whether he was adopted.

And then, by her maternalism toward him, some might have thought him to be the son of their Puerto Rican housekeeper and cook, had they not known that that was impossible. Because his young friends were almost sure that the crazy Hispanic drag queen who tended him with such devotion, could not have given birth. Or could he?

Even the family's living arrangements seemed odd to those visitors who ventured into the upper regions of the house. His mother and Auntie Hoover had rooms on the third floor, the three Boadicea aunties had rooms on the fourth, and Serge shared the fifth floor servants' quarters with Juanna Donna Lorca, the transgender who ambulated about the house in high heels and flamboyant female costumes and dominated their domestic life.

It was as if the sisters were trying to put the thought of a male—boy or young man—as far from their minds as possible, even if compelled to admit his existence. Sometimes he felt like Mr. Rochester's closeted first wife in Jane Eyre.

But now, as he traversed the rain-gleaming streets of Greenwich Village, his American Paris, on wobbly knobbly

32

legs, he yearned for that hot little garret where he could at last be alone with his dreams of romantic love. Was Amanda Quaint to be La Belle Dame Sans Merci? Or was she as generous and open-hearted as he hoped, as her wide violet eyes would suggest?

As they approached the house, they saw that Juanna Donna Lorca and her twin brother Hector Alonzo de la Lorca were arguing on the sidewalk where a little group of neighbors and passers-by had gathered to watch, including his Boadicea aunties. The rubbernecking was understandable, even forgivable, considering the show the Spanglish twins were putting on.

Juanna Donna screamed like an excited cockatoo and Hector growled like an angry bear. The front door of the house stood open, suggesting that Juanna Donna had pushed Hector out of it and down the front steps, suggesting it because Juanna Donna was still pushing Hector away from the house, backing both of her straight arms with her considerable bulk. Everyone thought of Juanna Donna as "her," not "him."

Hector raised his fist and dropped it and raised it again and dropped it again, sorely tempted. "I don't wanna hit you, so stop pushing me," he said. "How would it look, me hitting a woman, because that's what you look like?"

"But it don't bother you to come here and ask a woman for money; it don't bother you that I've been saving all my life to have my dong removed."

"You are a disgrace to all us Spanish males!" cried Hector, who, except for his mustache and masculine garb, looked just like Juanna Donna, with his square, handsome face and short husky body. But there was another difference between them. Juanna Donna had had a nose job, giving hers a ski-slope tilt, while Hector's nose was straight and a bit flat, like a handsome boxer.

33

"It reflects on me!" Hector shouted. He looked imploringly at the onlookers. "This thing is my brother. Would you believe it? My *twin* brother!"

"But I will be your sister as soon as I save enough money! No longer will I be Juanna Donna, half man, half woman. Then I will be Doña Juannadonna, a true lady. But you will never be Don Hector because you are no gentleman, no hidalgo, no true caballero!"

"You drag queen!" shouted Hector. "The shame! The disgrace!"

"The shame of a man who only comes to his sister for money to pay gambling debts!"

The fortyish twins squared off and circled each other like boxers. Hector's cuff links glittered, as did Juanna Donna's innumerable bracelets. The ruffled train of her black and purple Bata de Cola flamenco gown swept the sidewalk, becoming a damp rag. Her mantilla, caught on one large earring, flew like a cape, and her pumps clicked on the sidewalk as she circled Hector. "Punch my knobs and I break you neck!" cried Juanna Donna, who had been taking hormones for years.

Hector paused to straighten his powder-blue tie, dropping his hands to do so, and Juanna Donna released a straight right to his chin.

"Son-of-a-bitch," he cried. "I didn't think you'd hit me. Look, everybody, I want you to know this is a man I am fighting with—a drag queen maybe, but a man just the same—and I have every right to hit back." And he did—right on the tip of Juanna Donna's ski-slope, Bob Hope nose.

"Now you've gone too far," shouted Auntie Hoover, stepping into the fray and walloping Hector left and right with Serge's Plutarch, a heavy if tattered tome.

While Juanna Donna and Hector were evenly matched, being twins, after all, Hector was no match for Auntie Hoover, who came at him like some kind of war machine, backing him up and finally causing him to turn and run from her onslaught, much to the amusement of the crowd, who hooted, cheered, and applauded. "Female assertiveness—" she said, looking after him, "macho men are no match for empowered women."

As if to emphasize what she said, the defective alarm of Schloch's Delicatessen down the street went off, sounding like a screeching banshee, and one could see from Hector's body language that it terrified him. He may have believed himself pursued by Auntie Hoover, a tank with a siren. He ducked into the sanctuary of the first bar in sight, Rocky's Rendezvous.

Juanna Donna felt satisfaction in her knowledge that Hector had entered a gay bar. The last laugh was on him. Schloch's alarm stopped screaming with a final gurgle, and peace was reinstated on Bethune Street.

In the house, in the kitchen, holding a hanky to her bloody nose, Juanna Donna said, "I hopes you no expect no food from me. I'm nobody's Sancho Panza. You Quixotes get yourselves some queki de limón, if you wants."

After checking Juanna Donna's nose and seeing that there was no real harm done, Serge's mother and four aunties busied themselves at the unfamiliar domestic task of making tea and serving themselves cake. They sat at the long kitchen table, like a group of irritated firemen just in from a chemical burnout.

"Put your head down between your legs," Dagmar advised Juanna Donna. "Isn't that a good cure for a nose bleed?" she asked Auntie Hoover.

Auntie Hoover said, "Boxers put their heads back." Auntie Hoover was a boxing aficionado. The three Boadicea Aunties devoured their lemon cake, making masticating sounds of supreme satisfaction.

No help from that direction.

Juanna Donna's eyes flashed at them. She pulled a bloody paper towel away from her nose and said, "Ain't any of you got normal female nursing instincts like Juanna Donna, whose brain has been marinated in estrogen? O.K." she added, "you're all testosterone titties, but then you could at least be gentlemen. A gentleman would help me. ¿Ya no hay nobles hidalgos ni bravos caballeros, who can protect us females? They have all left it to your Auntie Hoover to act like a real he-man, out on the street at least. But not in here!"

She watched in disgust as Auntie Hoover heeded nothing but cake. "You'll see," she cried, "I won't cook nothing 'round here for a week, and you all starve and see if I care. Some gentlemen, some true caballeros! Bad pipples, I say." She looked at Serge with disgust in her burning eyes.

"Bad pipples! I got to take care of my nose," she told him, as she staunched the flow of blood with a new handful of paper towels. "Oh, my God!" she shouted, "there's blood on my beautiful mantilla. I have wiped my nose with it. I have to soak it, queek." She headed for the upper regions of the house.

"I have an idea for a story about a brave caballero," Serge told her, following in her wake, "a real *macho* man. I've been thinking about it for some time and I'm going to call him Resurgius."

"What kind of name is that?" she asked, turning to him on the staircase.

"Dog Latin for a resurgent Serge, a comeback kid."

"Comeback from where?" she asked, still holding a wad of paper towels to her nose.

"From being pecked raw, Juanna Donna, that's where. Can I have a few of those peppy-steppy pills you're always popping when you clean? I'm going straight to my room and get started, and I need some pep. I've had a long, exhausting day, but, boring as it sometimes was, aggravating as it sometimes was, it was also inspiring, because . . . I fell in love

36

today—love at first sight—and so, at last, I've got the heroine of my book to further my inspiration—someone to put on a pedestal and look up to; and I need my energy tonight; while it's all hot in my brain. Energy! I'm determined to get started right away. Right now! Tonight!"

Juanna Donna reached in her skirt pocket and filled Serge's palm with little red pills. "You can hop all night on these little red diablos," she said. "Once I stay up for a week. Remember that time when I cleaned the whole house and everybody get mad at me because I threw everything out? It was them diablos."

"But I'm afraid, Juanna Donna. I'm afraid I won't have the will or the energy to come home every night and work on this book. Writing a novel is a marathon. I'm just not sure I can maintain the discipline required. That's why I want you to do something special for me. I want you to promise me that you won't let me weaken, that you'll make me write every night, until I'm done, that no matter how tired I say I am, or how tired you think I am, you will help me to complete my task. Swear it!"

"Suppose I have to box your ears or throw a bucket of cold water in your face?"

"No matter what you have to do, just don't let me weaken."

"These I swear to, cross my heart and hopes to die. See, nothing crossed 'cept my toes stuffed in these pumps, but I can't help that. I will be your second will, I swear before God and Puerto Rico. Now, get busy! Hit those keys!"

Serge took the pills and went into his room. Soon the little red diablos made him feel as if he had a rocket in his brain. He was lifting off.

He stripped to his polka-dot boxer shorts and sat down at his desk.

37

Outside his open window, before which sat his broken air-conditioner, there was a God-like roll of thunder, and rain swished down from above in silver streaks like swords.

A breeze wafted in and his brain was alive, inspired. He wanted to bang out the title of his proposed opus in caps so large that the world could not fail to read them. But, disappointed at the size of the typed caps of his title, he took up a marking pencil and furiously printed across the top of the page and underlined—

RESURGIUS

3

"You look kinda droopy," said Bettina Battle. "I hope you've been burning the midnight oil on that UNIVAC article. How's it coming?"

"Oh, coming right along," said Serge, looking at her through bleary eyes and blurry glasses. She was barring the entrance to his cubicle and he imagined how a caged guinea pig must feel. She didn't even provide him with a nowhere wheel to run on. Bettina loomed over him like Wonder Woman about to lasso an evildoer. Her incredulity was tangible. She waited, threateningly, with the patience of a cat playing with a mouse, and Serge said, "Really, Bettina, it's going fine."

"It had better be," she warned, turning to scan the enormous room full of workers like a sniper seeking a target, beading in on one here and one there with telescopic and predatory phthalo-green eyes. Serge knew that further reference would be made. She turned back to Serge. "Have you given any more thought to my offer?"

"I thought about it most of the night. It kept me awake. I only had two hours sleep, so, if I look droopy, it's your fault."

"Come back to my office later if you need some Scotch in your coffee." As if in the throes of a drug-induced hallucination, Serge saw the mask of her face morph from iron warning to lascivious rubber invitation. He blinked in an effort to focus, then saw her toss him a wink as she went on to her next harassment, the object of which might be male, female, or potted plant.

He wanted to do as Juanna Donna had ordered and call Amanda Quaint, but he was very much afraid that she would reject him. Bettina Battle, attractive as she was, simply turned him off. Her subdermal coldness and raptor-like aggressiveness made her seem anything but a beautiful woman. Rather more a bird of prey.

He wasn't often pursued by beautiful women. He wasn't often pursued by women at all—except for his mother and aunties, whose pursuit of him was like that of a riot squad. He remembered a love-struck stick-figure of a girl in grade school, and didn't a young woman once wink at him on the subway? Or had she caught a bit of dust in her eye? He had always preferred to think that she had winked. But it was a strange fix he found himself in, being pursued by a beauty who gave him the sinking sense of a green-eyed monster.

Now on the other hand, Amanda Quaint was easily as beautiful as Bettina Battle but radiated a tolerant kindness, "a glad kindness," as Yeats had put it in a poem, that, strangely enough, made him even more afraid of her than of Bettina Battle. Just what was this fear he felt? Well, he knew, didn't he? It was the fear of rejection. Why should such a lovely and decent young woman want a little skinny sack of bones like him? Bettina Battle would devour whatever was put before her, but Amanda Quaint was a woman of taste and discrimination—she liked his poetry—and so would fastidiously pick and choose.

He trembled at the thought of making the phone call that Juanna Donna had ordered him to make on pain of a spanking. How could he muster the courage? He must play the man, the he-man, the hero. He must be Resurgius! Fearlessly, Resurgius would pick up the phone and call.

Serge dialed for an outside line. He dialed the number of Amanda Quaint's office. When a voice came on the line, he said in his own cracked voice, "Amanda Quaint, please."

"Whom shall I say is calling?" said a quick New York accent.

"*Re-sur-gi-us,*" he said, his voice cracking like a four-teen-year-old's. "No, no, no—I'm sorry, I got confused—tell her it's Serge Bering-Strait." And by this act of derring-do was actual magic in the form of electrical sparks produced on the line and the voice of Amanda Quaint poured like honey into his right ear, "Hello, Serge! I've been hoping you'd call me."

Oh, the wizardry of Edison! Faraday and Electricity! It was the voice of his beloved!

> *Mary had a little lamb*
> *Whose fleece was white as snow*
> *And everywhere that Mary went*
> *The lamb was sure to go!*

Was it the telephone or the Victrola? It was Edison, wasn't it? Serge was rattled.

"Is that you, Serge? Where are you?"

"_____"

Serge, for a hair-raising instant, could not speak. Then, his wild reddish hair settling on his head as after a bout with one of Tesla's electric arcs, he squeaked—

"Yes, yes, I'm here." And now so were the words—"I was wondering would you—could you—do you think we might—what I mean is—"

"I'd be delighted to meet you after work. Would you come over to Rockefeller Plaza and meet me? I'll be behind the statue of Prometheus. Shall we say sixish?"

"Abso . . . abso . . ."

"Absolutely," said Amanda Quaint. "I'll be waiting."

And true to her trueness, just as Serge Bering-Strait had known her nature to be honorable and trustworthy, there she was waiting behind the glistening, fountain-wet buns of the golden statue of Prometheus. Yes, Prometheus had brought fire and there she was, the flame in his heart, looking even more beautiful than he could remember, her blonde hair in a golden French twist, a white lace blouse tenting her ample bosom, her Mary Quant mini valancing unimpeachable legs, her pink-peeping open-toed pumps heeled five up, and, most striking of all, her violet eyes seeking him in the crowd that seemed to be sucking up all the air around him. How was he to speak to her without air with which to waft his words?

"Serge! I'm so happy to see you! Why do you look at me like that?" she asked, looking down at him. "Are you hungry?"

Hungry for the lips of my desire, Serge might have answered with Ernest Dowson's words but didn't.

"I'm famished," said Amanda, taking his arm and leading him hastily around to the front of the al fresco restaurant and down its steps. They were seated at a table from which vantage they could see Manship's bronze, gold-leafed statue of Prometheus stealing fire from the gods as a gift for humankind in all its full frontal glory. To Serge, it was the very vision of Resurgius, his hero. Behind Prometheus, the seventy-story RCA Building towered up and into cloud-piercing invisibility, the late sun peeling the skyscraper's façade, huge shadows wavering up its vanishing height.

41

The polyphonic chatter of countless voices, accompanied by the flappings of the flags of all nations, did not make their own words indistinct, for Serge and Amanda were focused on each other. Serge said excitedly, "I started a novel. Well, maybe it's just a novella—maybe it's going to be kind of short, I'm not sure. I guess it all depends on what happens next. It's going very fast," he rushed on, "now that I'm on to it."

"What's it called? What's it about?"

"The hero is named Resurgius, and he looks like that Prometheus, all golden muscles, not like me at all, and it isn't autobiographical like so many first novels. No, it's a work of the imagination. It's futuristic. But it's a love story, for sure. Resurgius is the kind of guy who never has to say he's sorry."

"But he'll say it if he should, won't he?"

"Sure, he's not afraid."

"Can I read it when you're done?"

"You'll be the first, Amanda, because I trust your judgment."

"Really? It's so sweet of you to say so."

The waiter brought them their drinks—a Whiskey Sour for Serge and a Screwdriver for Amanda.

"Cheers!" said Amanda. She put her drink down. "How exciting that you've begun a novel. I'm facile enough for articles, but I could never dream of writing a novel. But you—you being a poet—I bet the words just cascade from you."

"Well, sometimes they just dribble. But don't underrate yourself," said Serge. "Your article on sky-mirrors is one of the things that inspired my novel."

"Really? How thrilling! But you know, I was assigned to write that article and, in truth, thought the whole idea was crazy. I, for one, like to sleep at night. It's plain nutty! Just another way of getting more work out of us poor peons."

"Gee," said Serge, "I thought there was something romantic about it."

"That's what I mean about you," Amanda picked up enthusiastically, "like all real poets you see romance in everything. You have a romantic heart. That's what I love about your poetry—

> The night's an Arab's sheet
> Of swirling blue and black.
> The earth is at his feet,
> The stars are at his back.

Oh, it gives me goosebumps! Did anybody ever tell you that you look like a skinny Dylan Thomas? All that wild red hair, and that cute little bulbous nose. If only it were red, too, then you'd look just like him, but I don't suppose you drink enough."

"I had three Whiskey Sours in a row one night!"

"*Did* you? Well, I really wouldn't want to be friends with a boy who drank too much, even if he was a poet."

"I'm only going to have one—now."

"After we eat, shall we take a walk?"

"Where to?"

"Oh—uptown—maybe up to Central Park. It's such a beautiful early autumn evening. I love autumn, don't you?"

"Oh yes," Serge said. He would have loved anything that she loved. For he loved her more each instant that they were together.

"Tell me about yourself," Amanda said later, as they joined the flow up Fifth Avenue, toward Tiffany's and on up to the Plaza Hotel and Central Park. He had to reach up to hold her arm, his thin fingers gripping a solid bicep. The power of her beautiful body thrilled him.

"I'm twenty-three years old," he said, "and a graduate of N.Y.U. School of Journalism."

"What's your family like?"

43

"Women."

"What?"

"All women. I have a mother and four aunties."

"Oh, yes, I know who your mother is, and I know your Auntie Janet Hoover. They're famous in lib circles. You say you have three other aunts?"

"Yes. Charlotte, Emily, and Annie. They run Boadicea Press."

"Oh, we all know Boadicea Press. I read a number of their books when I was taking Women's Studies at Harvard. Let me see . . . there was *The Tyrannical Male, Football Wives,* and *Beaten Down and Beaten Up.* Those are a few of the titles I remember. Personally, I think they're a little extreme. I have a grandfather, a father, and three brothers who are almost as sweet as you are. I don't think we have to defame the whole male sex just because of the misbehavior of a few."

"That's my point," said Serge enthusiastically. He was almost swinging by her arm and tap-dancing as he tried to turn and look up at her. She took such long strides. Strident, that was her walk, strident—but she was so sweet.

"That's my point exactly," Serge repeated, "that you don't defame a whole sex just because you've got a mad on at a few members of it. Men say derogatory things about women, too, but they're doing the same thing. They're stereotyping. They're not trying to understand. I try to be fair-minded."

"As do I."

"I can tell. A lot of women don't, though, don't try. A lot of women just think men are no good, especially nowadays, with the Women's Movement in full swing. Wow, I grew up seeing the whole thing from the female point of view. The only masculine point of view I got at home was from Juanna Donna, who is more of a woman than a man, at least nowadays. On the other hand, I hardly knew my mother—

44

hardly *know* her. My real mother, the mother who raised me—well, I know it sounds crazy—has been a transexual man who was much more maternal than my birth mother."

"My goodness! Tell me about it."

"Well, Juanna Donna's our housekeeper. She even taught me Spanish, or, what you might call, Spanglish, a mixture of Spanish and English. Juanna Donna came from Puerto Rico just about the time I was born and got a job as our housekeeper and really became my nanny, although in those days he called himself Juan de la Lorca, or so I've been told. He calls himself Juanna Donna, nowadays, and, to tell you the truth, I've always called him—or her—that, and I'm not a bit sure what his real name is, really. I'm pretty sure her last name is Lorca, though, like the poet."

"Garcia Lorca?"

"Right. But she'll always be Juanna Donna to me. I think I named her that when I was a kid and everybody started calling her that. But Juanna Donna's no poet." He put a hand on his heart. "Poet or not, male or female, she's like a mother to me. Sometimes I think the male can have more maternal instincts than the female, at least that's been my experience— and bigger boobs!"

"There's truth in what you say," said Amanda. "I bet you'd make a wonderful father. Even now, I'm writing an article on the more extreme forms of feminism, which I call— the article, I mean—'Have Some Feminists Gone Too Far?' It poses the question whether a small group of libbers—and remember, I consider myself a serious libber—want social equality—equal pay, for instance, for equal work, or actually want superiority; whether we want—or should I say *they* want—loving relationships with men or no men at all. At times it seems as if the latter is the truth of the matter.

"Take the case of Valerie Solanas, the founder and only member of S.C.U.M., the Society for Cutting Up Men. I've read something she wrote and it's absolutely insane. She sent me a manuscript, hoping, I guess, that I had some pull and could get it published in one of the magazines. I was free-lancing at the time. Poor thing! She's bound to wind up doing herself or someone else some harm. We libbers are not all like her! I don't like the idea of some women speaking for other women. We're independent thinkers, each and every one of us, or should be."

"How wonderful!" cried Serge, bouncing along beside her, enthralled by her words, only vaguely aware that they were approaching Fifty-Ninth Street and Central Park South, walking just to be walking and talking—"Because my novel is a spoof on the very extremists of whom you speak. I try to keep it amusing, but thinking of them can still hurt a fellow."

"That's because you're a poet and are highly sensitive," said Amanda, "but you mustn't become bitter. There's so much sweetness in life and you must try to focus on it."

"Oh, it's O.K.. I haven't the strength for much bitter-ness."

"But you must keep your spirit up. You must not slump."

"I stand erect when I'm with you."

"That's quite a compliment. Look," Amanda cried, "we've walked all the way up to the Hotel Plaza. Look," she cried again, excitedly, "the Hansom cabs are waiting across the way. Shall we go for a ride through the Park?"

"Amanda, my dear, they are not Hansom cabs, no matter what they tell the tourists. A Hansom cab has two wheels, seats two people, and the driver rides in back. You must have seen them in a Sherlock Holmes movie. These are four wheeled carriages and the driver drives from the front. See that fellow?"

"Yes, I see what you mean." She laughed, "You cer-tainly have a didactic streak in you."

"I'm sorry," he said, "I'm always trying to get things straight in my own mind. But that fellow!" He pointed to the

46

first carriage driver in a queue of carriages. "That carriage driver is Juanna Donna's brother, Hector."

"How interesting," said Amanda.

"That's Juanna Donna's *twin* brother."

"That's her twin? He doesn't look a bit feminine to me."

"Juanna Donna has had her nose done and has been taking hormones for years. She has boobies and wears dresses, the fancier the better. I guess you could say she's left her twinship. This was probably how she looked when I first knew her but I can't remember that far back."

"He looks very macho . . . except for the love beads."

"Yes," said Serge, "that's something different."

They had approached within a few steps of Hector's carriage and Hector had recognized Serge and called out, "Sergey, qué passe? Are you come up here to take the beautiful lady for a ride through the park?"

Hector jumped down from the carriage. He was wearing a top hat and carried a buggy whip. "Please meet my wonderful old horsy, Hidalgo, a true gentleman." Hearing his name, Hidalgo turned his grey head toward them, fixed his big brown eyes on them, and whinnied. He looked old and tired and patient.

"What a sweet animal," said Amanda.

"Allow me to introduce myself, Señorita—Hector de la Lorca, at your service," at which he bowed to Amanda.

"This is Señorita Amanda Quaint," said Serge.

"Enchanté," said Hector, bowing again. He said, "It's best in French."

"Enchanté," Amanda responded.

"You are taking the señorita for a carriage ride through the park, are you not?"

"Oh, let's do," said Amanda. "It's so romantic."

The lights in the buildings all around them were coming on, one at a time and then in clusters. It was almost musical, the way they would run vertically or horizontally or then in a

47

whole block of fifty or more windows, like the tentative beginnings and then the first full riffs of a symphony. Da-Da, Da, Da, Da, Da! And the tiny twinkles of the night lights in the darkening park could be seen across the way like lightning bugs.

"Will there be a moon out tonight?" Amanda asked Hector.

"When you get in the park the moon will be clear as a golden bell in the sky." He took her arm and helped her into the carriage. "If the señorita would not mind waiting for a moment while I speak to young Serge." And he turned to Serge, took his arm, and led him a few feet off from the carriage.

"Serge, my young friend, true son of my sister Juanna Donna Lorca, it has occurred to me that you might take pity on someone who is, after all, almost a member of your family, by blood, which is thicker than water, that you might consider helping me in my time of great distress."

"Well," said Serge, surprised by such a turn, "what can I do for you, Hector?"

"I have a gambling debt, so I borrow money from some people down on the docks who say my carriage and Hidalgo will be collateral for the loan. But the interest on the loan goes up so fast that the carriage and Hidalgo will not cover it. I ask them then what would happen if this should come to pass, and they say that I have knees, don't I? By which I think they mean I will be harmed. If I could get them the money before the interest goes too far, this would save me bodily injury. Enough money would save my poor old Hidalgo and the carriage. As you know, I went to see Juanna Donna to ask her for help, but you saw what happened. She hit me."

"But, Hector," said Serge, "she is saving all her money for the big operation. You know what I mean. You know how important that is to her."

48

"To become a woman," said Hector sadly. "I know. But I am thinking when I see you, maybe out of your deep and abiding love for who is really like you mother you will help you uncle to set himself free of this terrible trap he is in."

"How big is this trap?"

"Fifteen Hundred Yankee Dollars would free Hector from a terrible fate."

"Fifteen Hundred Dollars! That's a lot of money, Hector."

"But you make good money, no? Is not so much for you, eh?"

"They really mean to hurt you?"

"They really mean to hurt me!"

"I have some savings," said Serge. He took out his checkbook and wrote Hector a check for what he needed to get himself out of trouble. He handed it to Hector. "You must promise me, Hector—no more gambling!"

"No more gambling, Señor! But you must promise me, please, please do not tell our Juanna Donna that you have lent me this money. She would be very angry. Now," said Hector, his voice lightening with relief, "I shall take you for the best, most romantic moonlight ride through Central Park that anyone has ever taken, with my compliments and Hidalgo's, at which Hidalgo turned his old gray head toward them and said something indecipherable and, no doubt, in equine Spanglish.

Hector kept Amanda and Serge in the park for hours (over two hundred dollar's worth of ride, gratis), a great, stretch-marked moon overhead, pointing out places of inter-est like the Wollman Rink, the Sheep Meadow, the Pond, the Zoo, and the Carousel, and considerately falling silent and almost invisible when they came to dark stretches under cover of the leafy trees, the short dark tunnels, and the glowing high-arched bridges where he expected they needed privacy for petting and for the suction-cup snap-release of kisses, which he could hear between the clops of Hidalgo's echoing hooves.

They emerged from the park after midnight, drawing up before the splendiferous doors of the Plaza Hotel. Parting is such sweet sorrow, the Bard had told them both, and so, with one last kiss and reaching arms they said farewell. Amanda hailed a cab. Serge found a subway. Each dreamed of the other on the way home. At the stable on Tenth Avenue, Hector gave Hidalgo a cube of sugar and kissed him goodnight.

At home, Juanna Donna had waited up for Serge.

"What is the idea of coming in so late? How you gonna write tonight?"

"Oh, but I really want to write tonight! I have so much to say. My heart is full! Give me some of those little red diablos and dame una café, por favor—con leche! I'll write all night and believe me, Juanna Donna, I'll work all day tomorrow and feel like a new man, sans sleep, sans everything! I am inspired because I'm in love!" After changing into pajamas, bathrobe, and slippers, he sat down at his Olympia and began to conduct his symphony.

Coming up the stairs with a tray of coffee and a demitasse of little red diablos, Juanna Donna could hear the typewriter in action, like a syncopated clock.

4

39 Whitehall Street. So long as the Viet Nam war raged on, that infamous address struck terror into the heart of every young pacifist who was registered for the draft in the New York City area, and Serge Bering-Strait was no exception. A vaccine could prevent polio, but there was no way of being vaccinated against the draft, an epidemic that led to the crippling horrors of boot camp and perhaps even to death. And now Serge had been struck down in the very blossom of

50

life.   He dropped the brown government envelope and wobbled down the hall from his room to Juanna Donna's room on afflicted legs. Thought was beyond him. Emotions, like a thousand stampeding cows, crushed reason under hoof. Instinct alone sent him to Juanna Donna, a terrified child to his mother, to his Madre/Padre, to be taken to her ample, estrogenized bosom and held in hirsute safety.

"There, there," said Juanna Donna, "you mustn't be afraid, leetle Serge," and she rocked his tearful being in her arms. "I saw that nasty envelope when I took in the mail this morning and I knew right away what it was. Maybe I should have called you at work. But I was thinking maybe he wants to be macho about this, maybe he wants to act like that superhero he's writing about . . . what you call him?"

"Resurgius," he sobbed.

"Si, Resurgius!   But I know that a writer is different from a hero"—she patted his hair, pushed it back out of his eyes—"and Juanna Donna Lorca, she cry too. She cry all morning, but then she get the idea how to get you out of this if you want to get out of it."

Serge stepped back and looked at Juanna Donna, his tearful blue eyes flashing with hope. "How? Quick, how? Tell me before my knees buckle!"

"I know you are my proud leetle nooky man, but you must pretend to like other boys. You must pretend, my leetle macho niño, to be almost as gay as Juanna Donna," and she flourished her fan, cling-clanging her bracelets. "I know lots of gays who want to get in and they pretend to be straight, so you don't want to get in, you pretend to be gay. Simple, eh? You know me all your life. If I had started my hormones when you were leetle, I would have suckled you. Just act like me and say what I would say. I show you how."

The brown induction envelope with the voice of authority emanating from it ordered that Serge bring toothbrush and toilet articles to the Armed Forces Induction Center at 39

Whitehall Street on a Friday at 5:30 A.M. Early September had been unusually warm, summery, but now autumn had set in and a cool breeze flowed into the car from the open window on the passenger side. Juanna Donna drove, chattering away to keep Serge's mind off where they were going.

Bettina Battle had been informed that he might not appear at work that day—or, for that matter, a long time into the future. Serge had called Amanda Quaint as well. She had assented to write to him as soon as he could send his address—just in case anything went wrong. No "Dear Serge" letters, she promised. His mother and aunties had decided on protest and had left the house at three A.M. bound for Peter Minuit Plaza where a number of celebrities were expected to gather, placards and megaphones in hand. Old Beats, young Hippies, and Flower Children were out in full pacifistic force, carrying "Make Love, Not War" signs and chanting "Hell no, we won't go!"

Juanna Donna, wearing a long, multi-colored serape, jangling earrings, and made-up to look like a Ma Jode who had struck it rich, came prepared to join the protest. She found a place to park, some distance from the Induction Center, and they walked the rest of the way, soon finding themselves in the midst of protesters and mounted policemen. Among the protesters, in the twilight morning, Serge saw Doctor Spock of baby book fame, several actors whose names he couldn't place, and the bearded Beatnik poet Allen Ginsburg, who wore an orange batik shawl, a huge flowered tie, a rosary, and a Buddhist amulet. There were cymbals on his fingers, of the sort affected by Egyptian belly-dancers.

"I'm gonna get me some of those," said Juanna Donna, pointing at Ginsburg. "Now you remember what I tell you," she said, letting go of his hand like a mother sending her child off to kindergarten on the first day. He waved to his own mother and aunties, but they were too involved in their chant of "Hell no, Serge won't go!" to notice him as he entered the

52

faded nine-story red brick building of 1886 construction with barricades like vampire's teeth at its mouthing Moloch-like entrance.

He was no longer Serge Bering-Strait, but one of many, as he stepped through an elevator door that bore the slogan "The Security of World Peace Starts Here." Soon he was stripped for his physical, during which brutal military medicos subjected him to a number of dehumanizing indignities, such as having him bend over while they stuck their rubberized fingers up his ass and felt around. It was horrible, but why hadn't he had those medical fingers up his ass when he needed them to make the required weight, which he failed to make by about a finger's worth—they had him stuff down a banana and that qualified him—and yet it put him in the mood for Room 604, the psychiatrist's office.

Now he did as Juanna Donna had told him to do. He tried to behave like Juanna Donna, queen of high camp. He rolled a thin, feminine shoulder at the shrink, flirtatiously, and said, in an unnaturally high-pitched voice, "Hi, Big Boy," the very words Juanna Donna had told him to use. It wasn't easy, and it turned him red in the face, but still he said it, mortified, desperation being his king—or his QUEEN—at this most embarrassing moment. It was a question of do or die, so he did.

But what most injured his pride was that the shrink showed no doubt. "Gay," he said, with complete indifference. "Take this paper and go," and he stamped something on the paper. Serge felt as if the shrink had stamped "Gay" on his forehead.

When he left 39 Whitehall Street, a free woman—he meant MAN—relieved, happy, and ashamed, he saw his family being hauled off in a police van. Oh, well, it wasn't the first time that they had been hauled off in a Black Maria. But he had no one to tell that he had escaped the clutches of the military, death in Viet Nam, the end of Resurgius, the end of Amanda Quaint. Juanna Donna had been taken away as well and he had no way to get home because he could not drive, and, if he could, had no keys to the car anyway and so he must walk through the streets of lower Manhattan, the fingernail tip of the island, where no bar was open yet, and find a subway station. But where to go? It was still too early to go to work at *Women's Omnibus* in the American Rubber Climax Building—he shivered at the thought of rubber fingers adroitly invading his sanctum sanctorum and squeezed his pained self shut at the bottom—up tight though he may seem—and there was no one at home, his family by now, no doubt, behind bars, almost certainly singing, "We shall overcome."

The day grew light as he wandered, and, as he wandered, he wondered if he had done the right thing. He was distracted from his ruminations when he looked up at the early morning sky and saw the huge, familiar, still lighted wiener hovering overhead. The lights blinked on and off, reciting the mantra QUAINT WIENERS—*QUAINT!*—Oh, Amanda!—in many colors and in a fabulous syncopation. He only wished for Amanda's sake that he could be more like his hero, Resurgius, but, as Juanna Donna had said, a hero is one thing and a writer is another, seldom the same.

In Battery Park, he sat down on a dewy bench to give himself some horizon therapy, but the Statue of Liberty loomed before him and, like all women, fixed his attention. Now she was a proper mate for Resurgius, he thought, big, beautiful, and stalwart, leading the way with her torch, book in hand. Yo, Mama!

He could see Resurgius following her in adoration, as he would follow Amanda Quaint. This was Friday and, on Monday, Amanda might start work at *Women's Omnibus*. He would see her all day every day from then on. O joy! And O joy, too, because he was free of the government! It did irritate him that the minions of government so readily believed him

54

when he told them that he was gay. Then he wondered if they knew what they were doing—if they saw in him something that he didn't know was there. He was an aesthetic type of person, even a bit prim perhaps, yes, rather pale and prim and thin and proper; but no, he was mad for Amanda Quaint, so he couldn't be gay. What it was, was that Juanna Donna had so well instructed him as to how to act, and Juanna Donna was an expert on both sexes. Well, enough of that! It was the government that was crazy, calling him gay, not Juanna Donna.

The phone rang and rang. Standing in his cubicle, holding the receiver, Serge realized there was no one at home yet. Probably all still at the police station. He was anxious to let them know that he had escaped the military, especially Juanna Donna, who would be a happy little mother to hear it—a mamacita.

"New concepts!" cried Bettina Battle, her lower lip waving a spittle-stuck Virginia Slim cigarette like a baton. Serge could see and hear her vividly from across the enormous office which faded around her. He was no more than seated at his Selectric when she was upon him.

"Where's my UNIVAC III piece? I could have written the damn thing myself by now. HOW UNIVAC WILL CHANGE WOMEN'S LIVES. Statistics Prove Women Superior to Men Any Old Day of the Week. Roll out the stats! What's the matter with you, Bering-Strait? You little twerp, you great twit! By the way, you're late! What's the meaning of dragging your skinny bum in here at Nine-fifteen?"

"I was almost drafted," he said. "Don't you remember? I told you I had to report for induction this morning."

"Well, when are they taking you?"

"They don't want me," he said, actual tears welling up in his eyes.

"Why not? Is there more than appears the matter with you?"

"I have a physical problem."

"What? Can't get it up? No balls? No dick? You certainly keep it zippered up!" She shouted so that the whole office could hear.

"Flat feet," he said, mortified.

"Flat head, more likely. New concepts come out of heads shaped like rockets," she shouted. "New concepts are ejaculations from erected heads. New concepts come like cum! Let me hear those fingers make music on that Selectric. I want to hear Mozart's Third Divertimento for the UNIVAC emanating from within your cubicle in five minutes."

She tugged the stuck Virginia Slim from her lower lip, waving a little spot of blood that dribbled down her chin vampirishly. "Hit those keys!" she cried, spraying tiny blood spots on his shirt. In a second he could hear her some distance away using the lash of her tongue on somebody else. He could hear the poor victim screaming inside his or her head, another lashed oarsman on the great pulsing trireme called *Women's Omnibus*.

Before he could write "Statistics show . . ." he was summoned to Bettina Battle's corner office. She leaned back in her pink padded swivel chair, another Virginia Slim stuck to her lip, her long legs and spiked heels up on her desk, and gave him a girlish smile as he entered. He closed the glass door behind him.

"Got anything on that . . . what is it you're working on?"

"UNIVAC. Statistics. Women are superior . . ."

"Got anything on that yet?" Her voice was soft and oleaginous.

"You just left me two minutes ago. I've hardly had time to get the paper in the machine."

"Sit down, Bering-Strait—Gay! Was I a bit harsh on you? I mustn't let anyone in the office see that I have favor-

56

ites. You can understand that, can't you? You're not still crying, are you?"

"That wasn't about you. Just nerves from the Induction Center."

"Oh, that's right. You were drafted or something—or was it that you were not drafted? Wait a minute. Let me sort it out. I know—you were not drafted because you have flat feet, right? But there's nothing else wrong with you, is there?"

"No, I'm fine."

"A little slow, maybe, eh?"

"I have an I.Q. of 168."

"But that's in male terms. That would only be about 68 in a woman. Still, you're a cute little fellow, and I've decided to take you to a play tonight. What do you think of that, hah?"

"I'm awfully tired already. I had to get up at three o'clock this morning to go in for induction."

"Say, isn't there some way we can use that as an advertising concept? Write something up and show it to me. MEN DRAFTED BY REASON OF INFERIOR INTELLECT. Something on that order. Now, about this play—it's called 'Oh! Calcutta!' and the actors take off their clothes in it. Wobbling breasts and dangling dongs all over the stage. Definitely a new concept. Eliminate the story and give us the naked truth. That's all people want anyway. They really want to go about sniffing at each other's rear ends like dogs, so let's get to it. This should put an end to all that old fashioned talkie trash that Tennessee Williams and Eugene O'Neil write—and Shakespeare, my own countryman, he's the worst. Don't you agree?"

"I like Shakespeare," said Serge tentatively.

"Yes—but naked! To be naked, or not to be naked. That is the question. Sometimes costumes help, I admit, though. As your poem puts it, 'The naked truth will lie. The night's an Arab's sheet,' and all that shit. But a good looking bum is always a turn-on. What's a sycophant, Serge?"

"An ass-kisser."

"Even better, a brown-noser. That's what I mean about new concepts, Serge. New concepts! The world will never get anywhere without new concepts. I'll pick you up in my limo outside the building at closing time. Do you agree? I warn you, put a sock in your cake hole." She slammed a hand on her desk.

"Well that's settled. But remember, if you stand me up, I'm going to be very hurt. It's likely to bring out the bloody wrath in me." She winked, but Serge knew she meant business, and he couldn't afford to be fired just when Amanda Quaint was coming to work there.

"Of course I'm only ragging you, Serge. You know that, don't you, my little poodle? What, do I see more tears? Stop thinking about that nasty old Induction Center, will you? You're a free man now, no more Royal Marines. I've slept with all of them. Not a real man in the lot. O.K., buzz off and get me those stats! Oh, and that other thing—what was it?"

"An advertising concept from the Induction Center."

"Right! Find a product—food-on-a-stick for instance—and have all those naked inductees eating it while the doctors stick their rubberized fingers up their bum holes. You see that—I can come up with a new concept just like that," and she snapped her fingers, then pointed at the door. "Out, out, brief candle," she commanded, "I'm feeling conceptual."

While he worked, Serge constantly reminded himself that Disraeli had said that there were three kinds of lies; white, black, and statistical. He tried to shape UNIVAC's results to suit Bettina Battle's concepts, nodding off occasionally into the land of Resurgius where he was king. Once he ripped a cigarette from Bettina Battle's lower lip and she bled to death, but something happened and he ended up saving her by

58

pressing his shirt tail to her lip like a pressure bandage. She opened her eyes and kissed him in gratitude; but no, it was not a sweet or grateful kiss, it was a lascivious kiss, filled with a viper-like tongue, and he tasted blood and venom. He pulled away and Bettina screamed, "You swallowed my Virginia Slim!"

That woke him. There they were again, the statistics; but thankfully the wall clock, based on Greenwich mean time, told him it was time to go home—oh, no, not home! He had to meet her outside and go to see "Oh! Calcutta!" Well, at least the Eden Theatre, where it was playing, was in the East Village, close to home. He picked up the phone and dialed home once more. Juanna Donna's breathless question whistled in his ear.

"Did it work? I knew it would! We was all released right away. You hurry home now. We waiting for you. We celebrate your freedom, yo! Land of free, home of bravo!"

Serge told Juanna Donna he had an assignment. Bettina would not take no for an answer. But he'd be there as soon as the play was over. He promised.

Bettina was in a kittenish mood when he got in her limo. She held out a Martini to him—there was a bar in the car—and he took it from her and sipped it until she plunged her long red fingernails into it—God knows where they had been—to retrieve the olive. Then he could no longer touch it. She snuggled close to him and he fell asleep and then she shook him and he woke up. They were outside the theatre. She took his hand and led him into the theatre, led him to their seats, sat him down beside her and seized his arm in both of hers, cuddling it. "Poor little dickey-bird," she whispered, "you must be exhausted."

He nodded, his eyes closed beneath his office stickum spectacles. She said, "I want you to pay attention to this play.

59

I want you to review it." He opened his eyes to a group of naked actors and actresses prancing about on stage.

"I want you to review their bodies—do a John Simon on them, every crack and dimple—every stretch mark and wimple. If you look closely," Bettina went on, "you can see that every one of them has different colored pubic hair. I want you to match the color of the pubic hair to the particular actor or actress. It's a concept I thought of coming down in the car. Brilliant, isn't it?"

If the Martini was soporific the revue was even more so. Sophomoric and soporific, like wordless naked Shakespeare without the desperately needed poison to put an end to the whole show.

"What are you going to say about it?" Bettina wanted to know, leading him back to the car.

"It's definitely a new concept, a kind of nudist camp version of a Mickey Rooney movie where he shouts, 'Let's put on a show.'"

"That's not the kind of thing I want," said Bettina, frowning. "What's the matter with you, Bering-Strait, don't naked bodies turn you on? Aren't you normal? I expected to finally get a little action out of you. Didn't the naked bums of those actresses turn you on?" In the limo she grabbed his crotch. "Isn't anything going on down there? Here, feel this," and she put his hand on her breast. "What about that, hah? I get more erection out of my nipples than you do out of your willy. Doesn't that dickey-bird ever spread his wings?"

"I don't have flat feet," Serge said, inspired.

"What are you talking about?"

"Prepare yourself for a new concept," he said, pulling his hand away, "the shrink at the Induction Center said I was gay."

"Gay? A Nancy boy?"

"Gay!"

"You're not!"

60

"I am!"

"Well, Sir Gay, Lord Doily Carte," she said, lighting a Virginia Slim, "no wonder I can't do anything with you. Why didn't you tell me that before? Here I was thinking that I was unattractive to you. How could you let me think such a thing? Everybody wants to get into *my* knickers."

"And I would too, if it weren't for the fact that I'm gay."

"Well, now I understand—and I needn't be hurt, need I? Sex and the Single Girl, and all that."

"Not at all," said Serge. "It has nothing to do with you."

"But didn't I see you eyeing Amanda Quaint at the Lunar Society shindig?"

Serge saw that he must be very careful here. What's a sycophant to do? Of course he realized that he was betraying everything Resurgius stood for, but he had already been certified not only gay, but a coward by the government. Why not make use of it? He could still feel the psychiatrist's stamp upon his forehead. "You saw an exchange of—ideas—of concepts."

"Concepts! Of course! You were having an exchange of concepts."

"You hit the nail on the head, Bettina."

"Don't I always, Bering-Strait. I've got big hair up here and I've got big hair down there, and everybody knows it."

"You said it."

"Of course I did, and I'll say it again."

Serge had been looking straight ahead; now he peeked sideways so that he could see what he knew he would see, the Virginia Slim rowing the air as Bettina Battle repeated, "I've got big hair up here and I've got big hair down there. Now, did you match up the pubic hair with the actors?"

"You bet I did," he said. "I wouldn't let a concept like that pass me by."

"You gay guys are so good at such things, so sensitive," Bettina said, satisfied as a cat who has just ingested a goldfish. Something was going on in the cartoon balloon above Bettina Battle's head, an inspiration, a change of plans. She told the driver, "Take us to Studio 69."

Even Serge had heard of Studio 69. It was famous for famous people, for drugs, Roman orgies, and costumed lunacy. It was reported that the psychedelic lighting—swooping, parti-colored Strobes—and ear-splitting decibels were enough to make one drunk as a dancing bear. People who hadn't had a drink or taken a drug staggered out of the place to their limos.

"My sweet little Sir Gay, I forgive you for your coldness, now that I know you're gay," said Bettina Battle, "and I'm going to take you to a place I know you'll enjoy."

"But I have to go home and work on that article about the UNIVAC machines, and I'm already exhausted. I had to get up very early this morning to be at the Induction Center at five-thirty. I shouldn't even have gone to the play tonight. You're running me ragged."

"Nonsense! You're only a snot-nosed kid. Look at me. I'm thirty . . . I'm almost thirty. Besides, I can get you something at Studio 69 that'll keep you awake all night and all day tomorrow, too, better than a rubber thumb up your arse—if you thought that was exciting. How do you think I do it? Where do you think I get my energy?"

"Red diablos?"

"You mean those little candy coated Benzedrine pills? Kid stuff, Bering-Strait! I'm talking about speed or coke. How do you think I keep my figure? I haven't eaten since Whitsun."

"What's Whitsun?"

"It's fifty days before the Late Spring Bank Holiday."

"I thought it was religious—something to do with Easter."

"Not any more. It's a new concept."

She told the driver to let them out at the entrance to Studio 69 and drive around the block until they reappeared. She stepped to the front of a queue that vanished in the perspective of the street lights. A zoo of angry voices jeered them as they were allowed immediate entrance. Bettina had juice.

Temporal aliasing was immediate. The flashing, particolored Strobes made Serge's stomach feel like a backward-moving wagon wheel in a classic Western. In addition, the concussive, gut-punching music made his heart flutter. He could see—then he couldn't—then he could. When he could see, it was like seeing stars, exploding stars, exploding in an aurora borealis of colors, and ink-black night befell his every other augenblick. It was hallucinatory. Bettina said, "Isn't this heavenly?"

Serge thought it was like being in hell. "It's the pits!" he said.

"Yes," Bettina cried over the musical blast, "it is wonderful."

The ability to hear came and went like the ability to see. She dragged him through the crowd. Familiar faces, famous faces, appeared suddenly before him, then vanished in the ubiquitous chaos of the place. He saw a former First Lady, a movie star, a Wheaties-box athlete, a famously gay writer, and the great, high-cutting unisex designer, Hevonshe. Everyone seemed to be squirming, like worms dancing on their tails, like snakes in their mating ritual. Some wore masks, some wore capes, some were stark naked, and some looked like they were nine days in the pot. Mysterious hands grabbed at parts of his body. Naughty parts and imitation naughty parts, hot and cold, seemed afloat in the air; if you could call the alien-smelling atmosphere, which, if it had a color, would be dark green, air. Serge realized, now, that he was staggering, falling into people, distastefully touching

63

naked flesh and apologizing for it, while at the same time realizing that in Studio 69 no apology was necessary. That's what they were all here for, grab-ass.

In a flash, he saw Bettina, completely naked, handing him a shimmering drink of God-knew-what. "Find yourself a boyfriend," she cried, "you little fairy. This place isn't called Studio 69 for nothing."

And, in another flash, she was gone. But he had spotted something interesting, something recognizable, something that seemed to be alone in a distant corner. With strenuous effort, he achieved the distance between himself and the object of his interest. After all, he told himself, I am a journalist. Curiosity is my bag. He got up close and tried to see what he had seen from a distance. The strobes made it difficult, so he found their rhythm and tried to blink along with them, putting together an image in time, a monument.

Yes, it was he—it! What he had read referred to once as "the white mole of Studio 69." The famous artist of multiple images, the former First Lady back there in the crowd being one of them. Yes, there was the old crazy white mop on top, wild and dry as if it had been hung over a clothesline in the sun. It stared out from behind not dark but black glasses. Could it see or did it care to see? Did it need to see? The white mole of Studio 69 sat at a table on a raised platform, so Serge thought that it must be looking out at the crowd. Serge climbed the steps to the platform and stood behind it. Nobody seemed to notice or to care. Oh, said Serge to himself, this is too good to be true. The white mole of Studio 69 was eating from a bowl of Campbell's Alphabet Soup. Serge leaned down and put his mouth close to the white mop and said, "Why Campbell's soup?"

The artist's head did not turn. The artist showed no surprise. The artist seemed scarcely alive. But a soft voice came in answer to Serge's question:

"Because it's cheap. Now buzz off."

Someone took Serge's arm and led him down from the platform. He looked back to catch another glimpse of the famous artist, but, as in a magic trick, the artist had vanished.

Advised by glaze-eyed guides, Serge went hunting for Bettina through the labyrinthine upper regions of Studio 69. He listened for her British accent as he walked dark halls and light and peeked into large rooms and small. The sweet burning, woody smell of marijuana permeated the air and gave him a giggling contact high, lending to the unreality of the hallways. Other odors assailed his nostrils, animal and chemical, and every light in the place, even the merest hallway bulb, blinked on and off in a heartbeat rhythm, causing his eyes to roll in his head and cross behind his spectacles.

Finally, he found Bettina Battle engaged in a very peculiar activity with a man with devil's horns and a woman with a swishing, camelopard's tail. He waited, half blinded, half drugged, respectfully outside the door, until Bettina's final scream suggested satiation, then stepped in and told her that, if he were to write tonight, he must leave, must go home and go to work, as he was already thoroughly exhausted. How much of what he said registered with her, he couldn't tell—the lights, the darknesses, the concussive music, the man with the horns and the woman with the tail, who knew if his words reached what was left of Bettina's mind? But apparently she had heard something of what he'd said, or understood his body language; and somehow got the message. She gave him a packet of white powder, a silver straw, and told him to snort it up his nose, "Make five lines of it and snort it up your nose," she said.

"You'll be able to work all night and feel fresh in the morning. Time it," she yelled, above the ear-splitting boombox of the place. "Spread it out." And she waved him away, returning the valves of her attention to the horny-headed man and the tail-snapping woman. He pushed the package back at her and she finally received it, shaking her head in disgust at

65

him, but the lights flashed out, and he could not see what happened next.

Outside, cabs, as well as dark limos, patrolled the real world.

At home, Old Glory flew upside down at the top of the mast, figuratively speaking, because they had beaten the draft and raised hell at the Induction Center. There was the sense of a crowd forming for a triumphal march. Government had been bested and, in Serge's case, humiliated. Dagmar Bering-Strait was, for once, not furious; she was, in fact, ecstatic; but she had been furious earlier in the day, as she hastened to tell Serge.

"I tried to bite a cop's ear off, but all I got was a mouthful of blue fuzz from his uniform. Disgusting stuff with the distinct flavor of authority."

Auntie Hoover said, "She had to rinse her mouth out and I still had to pick pieces of government shoddy from her tongue. They were going to charge her with assault—"

"I was furious!"

"—when it was clearly we who were assaulted."

"Don't you ladies want to know how Serge got away?" asked Juanna Donna. "You did what I told you to do, didn't you, niño? You came on strong and feminine like Juanna Donna herself would have done."

"Arms akimbo," said Serge.

"And they just let you go?" asked his mother.

"No fuss—they just let me go. They didn't want me. Gays are undesirables in this man's army."

"We're all so proud of you," said Auntie Hoover.

The three aunties of Boadicea Press applauded.

After a ceremonial burning of his draft card, Juanna Donna led an exhausted Serge up to his bedroom.

"I'm pooped," said Serge, and threw himself on his cot in a short Moog heave of compressing springs. "Thank God tomorrow's Saturday and I can sleep late!" he said.

"Juanna Donna has thought you would be like this, but now is time for work. You don't use it, you loose it! You got to get this story out of your system, or you will be one miserable niño tomorrow. I know you. Now get up and hit those keys. I give you a few diablos to get you going."

As she spoke, Juanna Donna busied herself. She sat Serge up on the edge of his cot, rolled his Olympia over his knees, and pushed several pillows behind his back.

"I can't, Juanna Donna dear, I'm exhausted. Give me a break." But he didn't want to disappoint her hopes and said, a little weakly, "All right. Get me some coffee and get me some of those little red diablos. Wake me up! Get me going! It's wonderful to have such a great coach who always has my best interest at heart. You are my true mama-papa. Nobody else cares if I fulfill my destiny."

Juanna Donna dumped a pitcher of ice water on his head. "You make me promise, remember?"

"Did you have to do that? I wasn't asleep!"

"No, but you was trying. Now go get in cold shower and come back and start again."

After a shower and two red diablos, not only did he feel as though he had had a night's sleep, but he felt as if he had more energy than anyone in the world. He felt like Resurgius himself. He could feel the little debilitated straps of his muscles swelling and rippling. Another diablo and he felt mighty, more powerful than a locomotive, faster than a speeding bullet, able to leap tall buildings at a single bound.

"Up, up and away," he cried, sitting down. Wow! He was ready! He had so much to say! A veritable logorrhea was welling up in him, like a pleasant and bottomless regurgitation.

"I feel . . . like Resurgius himself," he cried. "This must be the way he feels all the time. Like a dynamo! I can do it, Juanna Donna!"

"Of course you can, Mighty Mouse. Now hit those keys!" cried Juanna Donna. "Start the next part—go, go, go!"

Pecked raw from before he was a fledgling, and plucked many times thereafter, Serge still had the strength of a raptor whose talons, and even beak, ripped, rat-a-tat, at the torn keys of his Olympia. Oh, he spread his wings wide and soared like a condor over the high Andes of his mind, his telescopic vision seeking out, through his blurred horn-rims, any quiver of the Zorro of justice. In short, his new chapters, imminent and beyond, would even the score.

5

Serge had been up since three the previous morning. The Induction Center seemed like a nightmare from his youth of decades ago, his day at the office a long twilight sleep, "Oh! Calcutta!" was a crazy dream, Studio 69 a walk through hell to get to heaven, his sexual struggle with Bettina Battle—oh my God, he hadn't really married her, had he?—no, that was another part of this multiple act play in which he was starring as a split personality—and his all night wrestling match with his novel—what part of what was that? His head plunked against the Olympia, and Juanna Donna Lorca, like the ministering angel that she was, appeared at his door. She decided that it was time to put him to bed.

"You will finish this Sunday," she said, "and I no mean maybe!" and she tucked him in, kissing his bruised forehead. "What a macho leetle poet," she said, proudly.

He woke at five o'clock on Saturday afternoon with strong feelings of misgiving, but, when he saw the manuscript of *Resurgius* sitting next to his Olympia, he realized that his misgivings were uncalled for—he had not married Bettina

68

Battle, a.k.a Miz Bet, in his novel; he had not made love to Amanda Quaint, a.k.a. Miz Amandalay. What a drooping sadness befell him at that realization! In fact, he had never made love to anyone in his life. Juanna Donna Lorca had once made him a Christmas present of an inflatable rubber lady, but he had never gone near her, because he found her boxed, unfolded personality incompatible with his own, although she did come with a blonde wig, his favorite hair color. Even now she was under his cot, her cellophaned box collecting dust. Yes, as sleep fell away, he recognized himself to be free and virginal, a ripe apple on a branch of the tree of life, an unplucked grape, an . . . oh . . . ripeness is all!

He stepped into the shower and let the water wash the last of his fatigue away, the final dust of that terrible yesterday which he had endured and ultimately triumphed over. For once, he was one up on his hero, Resurgius, who, as he recalled now, had made a botch of things. Serge Bering-Strait had made no botch. Now, as he dried himself, his mind was seized by the image of one person, the beauteous Amanda Quaint. He dressed, knowing that he must see her, that he must see her because . . . because he must tell her, that, when he first saw her, he knew . . . he knew . . . but what was it that he knew? He knew that he loved her, that—it was LOVE AT FIRST SIGHT!

Dressed now, he gathered together the carbon copy of his manuscript and stuffed it into an envelope. He had to share what he had done thus far with Amanda. His compulsion to see her was so powerful that it wasn't until he got off the subway in Brooklyn that he thought of calling her. The whole mindless trip down to Brooklyn to see Amanda was like the tropism of the moth to the flame; but "I can't just pop in," he realized, dropping a dime in a public telephone slot, his heart pounding so loudly that he feared not hearing the dial tone. Oh magic! It was the voice of an angel, his special angel, but what to say?

"_____"

"I hear you breathing," she said.

"It is I," he burst out. "It is I, Serge Bering-Strait."

"How wonderful! Well, this is the strangest thing. I've been sitting here, curled up on my couch, reading your poetry—

> Now what kind of moon is it, darling,
> that, so blandly turning blue,
> overhangs us here in greenly summer Brooklyn
> while the astronauts go round
> and the sea at Coney rises,
> all its little lucky ripples
> wiping off the darkened sand?

'O Popular Moon!' Oh, I just love it! You have a truly romantic soul and should never be required to write articles for silly women's magazines. I wish you were right here with me now."

"Well, I am . . . almost . . . right there with you. I mean, I'm down at the corner telephone booth."

"Well, come on up here right away. I'm all by myself and there's no one I'd rather see. No one! No, wait! Let me finish reciting 'O Popular Moon!'

> Now what kind of moon *is* this,
> questing for the old romance?
> Acknowledging our loneliness,
> we know better than to ask,
> returning from the Goldman Band
> and kinder songs of long ago.
>
> Your pearl, your blue, your golden loneliness
> bring in our need,
> which we acknowledge, seeing you

sailing light, O, all unburdened.
Burdened by my loneliness,
I hold her gentle hand in Prospect Park,
walking from the Goldman Band
and the dismantling of the instruments.

"And the dismantling of the instruments! You mean the scientific dismantling of romance, don't you? You mean that the symbolic-romantic moon is being taken away from us— the populace—and with it the kinder songs of long ago; but you also mean what you wrote in that poem in the subway, 'The Naked Truth,' that even love is true, if we should make it so. In other words," she rushed on, "it's up to us, what kind of world we live in, whether we listen to 'Lady Be Good,' which I am playing right now, or acid rock—am I right?"

"I guess so," said Serge. "I don't really think about it that much. I wish I had thought to bring you flowers," he added.

"But I have your flowers," she said. "Your poems! A whole book of them. After I read 'The Naked Truth' in the subway, I went right out and bought a copy of *The Last Romantic: Poems by S. Bering-Strait,* published by Boadicea Press."

"My aunties published it as a birthday present to me when I was eighteen. I don't think they liked the book much, though. They're not very romantic."

Amanda Quaint's residence was an ancient Brooklyn Heights mansion on Columbia Heights that overlooked the harbor. The Esplanade was at her back door, where an evening promenade of lovers and loners walked to see the early evening Manhattan lights go on like tuneful notes. Neither could they fail to see the giant hot dog in the sky that refused, night and day, to let them forget, for an instant, QUAINT WIENERS. To some it was becoming an annoyance, to others something like a Christmas tree. The sky over

71

New York was prettier for it, or the sky over New York was becoming junky, it depended upon the subjective aesthetic values of those who looked at it.

Amanda's mansion on Columbia Heights was an inheritance, its twenty-odd rooms too much and too many for one person to feel cozy in. Amanda had set up an apartment on the first floor and left the rest of the house to webbing mites and spiders. She also owned a beach house in Easthampton. Her family's main abode was a five-story brownstone in the East 80's.

She was from a very wealthy family. Her grandfather, Manny Quaint, a billionaire, was known as the Wiener King and had taught her a strong work ethic, along with other old-fashioned values. Now she busied herself, preparing for her visitor—her "gentleman caller," as she quaintly allowed herself to think of him. She loved *The Glass Menagerie*. She put on a pink silk hostess robe and brushed her hair out. She could have been a model, but preferred being a writer. She loved writing and writers and, for her, the best writers were poets. And here she had one buzzing at her door!

He was unprepossessing, a small young man with a baby face and pale red hair, but it was not his physical attributes that interested her. It was the soul of a poet inside of him that drew her to him. She took his wrinkled London Fog and seated him on her couch.

"I'm so sorry just to pop in on you like this," he said. "Lady Be Good" was playing in the background somewhere, Sinatra imploring.

Oh sweet and lovely,
Lady be good,
Oh lady be good to me.

"It's hard to explain," said Serge. "I dreamed about you all night and when I woke up, I had an uncontrollable desire to let you see the manuscript; even though I haven't finished it. I know I told you I'd show it to you when it was done, but

72

I couldn't wait. I had to know what you'd think of it. Maybe you can give me some advice about the ending."

He pushed the envelope containing the manuscript into her hands. "There's a character in it that I think was subconsciously inspired by you—a very beautiful, a very wonderful girl, I assure you—and I was up all night writing about her, and I slept all day, and dreamt about you, and, when I woke up, I felt that I just had to see you. I was on the subway before I knew what was happening. Then I realized that I should call you . . . and why would I think a person like you would be home and free on a Saturday night? I don't know what I was thinking!"

"*A person like me*—what kind of person do you think I am?" She put a silver ice bucket with a bottle of Dom Pêrignon in it on the coffee table, two stemmed glasses, and said, "Will you do the honors? Exactly six and a half twists will do the trick."

"I know," said Serge, struggling to open the bottle, "I watch the French Chef, too."

"Of course you do," said Amanda, tousling his hair. "I love curly hair. You look just the way a poet should look." Amanda Quaint lit a long cigarette and watched as Serge popped the cork and poured them each a glass of Champagne.

"To your story," she toasted. "I can't tell you how delighted I am to see you," she said, fairly bubbling.

I am so awf'lly misunderstood,
So lady be good, to me.

"Do you like 'Lady Be Good'? I thought you would. It's one of those *kinder songs of long ago* that you write about in 'O Popular Moon!'."

"I sort of . . ." he began, hesitantly—"at the party at Hettie Freed's, the first time we met, I . . . I felt, instinctively, you might say, that you were different . . ."

"Different?" She held her glass at eye-level and gave him a quizzical look.

73

"I know you're one of them—"

"One of what?" She was frowning now, a slight darkening.

"Well, you have to be . . ."

"Be what?" There was a touch of annoyance in her voice this time.

"Well," he said, "you're a writer, an editor. You have to be . . . aggressive!"

Oh, please have some pity.
I'm all alone in this big city.

"As a modern woman, I have to be . . . assertive. But that doesn't mean that every fiber in me isn't female."

"Bettina Battle is female," he blurted, "but you're not like her."

"She's a horrid woman," said Amanda Quaint. "This book you're writing—is Bettina Battle in it? I mean, a character based on her? It's about time somebody did a job on that virago!"

"Well—it's sort of inspired by Plutarch's *Parallel Lives*. It's also sort of a science fiction story, I suppose. Sort of a combination of both. In my life, you see, genres and genders are all mixed up."

"What did you say it was called?"

"Resurgius. I made that up to sound Latin. He's the hero. He's sort of me with muscles."

"You wouldn't be the same with muscles. I'm not attracted to muscle men. I'm attracted to soulful men. Am I really in it?"

"You're the heroine."

"Really! I'm so honored."

"At the end, you and Resurgius get married and live happily ever after. At least, I think that's the way it's going to end. That's the way I'd like it to end."

"I think I'd like it to end that way, too."

74

The envelope containing *Resurgius* sat on the coffee table.

"Now let me read what you've written so far," she said, assuming an editorial air. "I'm going to take it to my room. You wait here. I'll be back in no time. Play some records. Drink some more Champagne." And off she went, envelope in hand.

In her room, she threw herself on the bed, and began to read.

CHAPTER ONE
THE UPRISING OF THE DONGS

Miz Mandalay, a magnificent Amazon in her early twenties with splendidly developed anti-sex objects, held a dominatrix degree from the University of Xantippe, where she had written an eyebrow-raising thesis in which she had attempted to show that certain ancient Dongs, despite their sexual swinishness, had manifested indications of emerging mental capacity, and had even been capable—this is what had shocked the Univacual Council—of a kind of tenderness. Her thesis was later published on Say-screen. Had the times not become more liberal, this thesis might have consigned Miz Mandalay to the lower levels of government.

But these were turbulent times. Dongs were cracking the information barrier, seeking a newer world, protesting the mandate of Shame-school, speaking boldly out from their hiding places, demanding Dong suffrage and all sorts of outrageous rights. Perhaps the most threatening of these revolutionary Dongs was a Spartacus-like character called Resurgius, known for his Tarzan-like physique, poetic speech, and flirtatious nature. Lately, he had been in the news several times for acts of rebellion that had landed him in Remedial Shame-school, and no one knew what new outrage this caped crusader with the big R shield on his powerful pectorals would commit next.

Whereas, after the Great Succession, Dongs were content to be allowed to walk in the gutters, with their heads hanging, and manifesting upon demand every sign of shame, from reddening cheeks to the squeezing of the legs together, today some dared to go about right on the sidewalks. Some even mingled with the Mize—one infamous Dong reportedly was having a lap-dog affair with a superdoopermodelmiz. This, despite the fact that Dongs were not generally allowed to get close enough to Mize to play at lap-doggie, with their tails wagging.

Of late, small, radical groups of Dongs had been making open protest; as has been said, some had gone so far as to ask for suffrage! (Not that the vote meant anything, even to the Mize; but the idea!)

To liberals of Miz Mandalay's persuasion, these indications of unrest among the once shamefaced Dong population were healthy signs, showing that today's was a healthy, vital society. Some radicals, like Miz Mandalay herself, would give the Dongs a half-vote. She, being a Univacual Council member, knew that the vote was merely symbolic, but also knew that that was precisely what made it important. She would liken it to a valve from which to release the steam of frustration from the pressure-cooker of society.

"After all," she told herself, "the Dongs are human beings, even if they are—*well, Dongs."*

Ah," sighed Amanda, her heart filled with compassion, and read on. And Serge sat on in terror, waiting, waiting, taking tiny sips of Champagne to wet his dry lips, replaying, over and over, "Lady be Good."

Oh sweet and lovely lady be good . . .

And then Amanda appeared. Her eyes were happy-damp and shined in the soft light of the room. Now she wore a pink

76

negligee that Serge could almost see through to a body that rivaled, if not exceeded, the body of his own literary dream-girl Miz Mandalay. He gulped.

"It's wonderful," she said softly.

"Wonderful? What's wonderful?" Serge said, trans-fixed.

"*Resurgius*! Your novel," she said with emphasis, see-ing that his mind was absent. "I mean, as far as you've gone with it. I really want to know where it's going to go next. Will Resurgius and Miz Mandalay get together?"

Serge had risen to his feet at her entrance. Now she pulled him down beside her on the couch. She put her hand on his neck and felt his fear in the throb of the vein there. Experience told her that he was a virgin and must be treated gently. After all, he was a poet and extremely sensitive. It would be so easy to hurt him and she wanted him so badly now. She must gently, ever so gently, absorb him.

Amanda Quaint leaned over to Serge, framing her face for a kiss. "Well?" she said, widening her violet eyes, and he kissed her, right on her soft red lips. She moved a few inches back, keeping her eyes fixed on his. Her hand was in his lap. "What's that?" she asked.

"Resurgius," he said, flushing.

> *I tell you I'm just a lonesome*
> *babe in the wood,*
> *So lady be good . . . to me . . .*

She drew him to herself and—absorbed him.

In all his twenty-three years nothing so miraculous had ever happened to him. He felt himself enveloped by love, while little estrogens, like microscopic lady-bugs leaping from her, tickled his palm, his chest, his thighs, in a way he might have described in *Resurgius* as heavenly. Oh, oh, oh, this was love. Amanda would have agreed. At last she pos-sessed her beautiful poet, body and soul.

Later, they took a walk on the Esplanade. It was a lovely cool September evening, and many mildly bundled lovers strolled along with them, casting their eyes across the water at Manhattan's blaze of light. They stopped and stared across the harbor, true lovers now, and Serge could not resist reciting a poem he had written at another time when he stood on the Esplanade and looked across the harbor, but that time at the morning lights of Manhattan going dark, a time when he had stood, alone and loveless, and dreamed of having a companion like Amanda beside him to recite it to—

"Across the bay, where East and Hudson meet,
Manhattan forms Prometheus from themes
of stone and steel. I walk the Esplanade
and watch the morning remnant of the moon
pale overhead, slow-swinging scimitar!

I've walked all night, anticipating light.
But more than having light, I want to be
one for whom light adventures into change
and gives me place to say in certain praise
—O light, allow me several such days!"

"Oh, yes, 'From Brooklyn Heights One Morning!' I read it. It's in *The Last Romantic.* Naturally, I just loved it! I've gone out many times in the morning to see the lights of Manhattan go out like that from here, but, naturally, I could never write it like that. It's just wonderful!"

Serge turned to Amanda. "Are you my girl now?"

She studied his magnified, intensified eyes through his spectacles. "Serge, I am. I love you."

"I love you too, Amanda."

Amanda's face grew serious. "I've been wanting to tell you all evening—tell you something—and I'm not sure how

78

you're going to like it. I hope it won't make you angry or hurt or anything . . ."

"Nothing you could ever say would make me angry or hurt or anything."

"Well, here goes . . . you may have heard . . . I'm going to be your new boss. Bettina called me this morning to tell me to come in Monday prepared to take charge. She said you were too inexperienced, and told me quite frankly that she didn't want me either but was overruled upstairs. She's lost her influence with the board." She studied Serge. "You won't mind having me for a boss, will you? Of course, that's only at work, you know. Away from work, you shall be Resurgius. I'll see to that."

"I'd heard you were going to be the new editor of *Women's Omnibus.*"

"Bettina Battle is no more. I start Monday. I know you were hoping for the job."

"Bettina's been teasing me with it. But, to tell you the truth, I'm relieved to know that I don't have to give my all for the cause. I could never see myself as the editor of a magazine anyway. As you say, I'm a poet. But maybe I can be of help to you on the job."

"I know you'll be a big help to me, at first; but, eventually, I'm going to let you write whatever and whenever you feel like writing. You have the soul of a poet and you should do nothing all day but write poetry, and I'll see to it that your little cubicle is undisturbed by mundane matters like food-on-a-stick or UNIVAC III or whatever. You're going to transcend, or I'll know the reason why. I don't even want you to know how I wrested the job from Bettina. Such lovely little ears as yours should be spared the details of the blood sport that is magazine editing. Suffice it to say, blackmail was involved."

"Blackmail?"

"A tape of Bettina being naughty reached the board, I have no idea how."

"Where's Bettina going?"

"She's going to fail upward into politics."

"Oh, thank you, my Jumbly Girl!"

Amanda took his arm and snuggled close, leaned down and kissed the top of his curly head. "My Jumbly Boy," she cooed.

She walked him to the subway, for he had to get home so that he could get up the next morning, Sunday, and work on *Resurgius*. He felt that he was nearing the end, but who knew?

6

Champagne always made Serge hungry and now he discovered that lovemaking with a real woman had the same effect. He was famished, but it was after nine and he didn't want to bother Juanna Donna with his needs. He knew that he need only mention his hunger and Juanna Donna would go to the kitchen and prepare him a hot meal. It would be selfish of him to allow her to do it. So he decided to stop at Schlock's Delicatessen and pick up a chicken salad sandwich and a container of chocolate milk—he was fearless now when it came to chocolate-induced acne; for, after tonight, he must think of himself as a veritable Resurgius, impervious to the minor threats of life. He could almost feel himself turning into bronze.

Now, Schlock's bag in hand, he crossed the street toward Rocky's Rendezvous, peeked in, and saw something shocking. Juanna Donna sat at the bar near the window, in plain view. He had almost passed Rocky's Rendezvous when he realized what he had seen. But Juanna Donna, with a bandage on her nose and a cigar in her mouth, and a bottle of cerveza on the bar before her—she would drink nothing from a bottle, only an appropriate glass—it was impossible!

He took several backward steps to get a second look. What could have happened to her nose that she would need a bandage of such dimensions? She had had only a tiny red spot on her nose, hardly anything at all. Had it become infected? Had she needed the emergency ward at St. Vincent's? Smoking a cigar? Impossible! He entered the bar and stepped up to—*Hector!*

"Hector! What happened to your nose? Why are you wearing women's clothes? Why on earth do you look just like Juanna Donna?"

Hector put a finger to his lips. "Ssshhh," he shushed. "I can get arrested for dressing like this. Sit down and I'll tell you about it."

Serge listened as Hector explained the situation. He told Serge that he had had a nose job with the money Serge had given him. Yes, he knew that Serge meant for him to pay his debt to the loan sharks with that money, but it was not enough, as he soon discovered when he tried to pay an intermediary. The interest rate was so high that he would never be able to pay his debt, over Ten Thousand and going up by the minute. He said he decided that the only thing to do was to become another person—to become Juanna Donna. Well, not really Juanna Donna.

"My new name is Lola Fabiola. The plastic surgeon showed me noses and told me that the one that was best for me was one that looked just like Juanna Donna's because I had the same nose to start with that she had before her operation. What could I do? Then I thought to myself that I should go ahead and make a complete transformation. And here I am, Lola Fabiola, twin sister of Juanna Donna Lorca. We are twins again, thanks to you. And I am safe from the loan sharks. But now I need a job. I can't go back to driving a carriage through Central Park. Not like this. I was thinking

81

of becoming a housekeeper like Juanna Donna. What do you think?"

"I don't know. Wow! You look just like her—except for the cigar. She'd never smoke a cigar, or drink beer out of a bottle. She's too much of a lady."

"Bartender," called Hector Lola Fabiola Lorca, "bring me a glass."

From up the street came the caterwaul of Schlock's untamable burglar alarm, and in the door came a raiding party of badge-waving policemen. In seconds, Serge was lined up with the others along the bar and searched. Fortunately, he had his wallet and identification on him and so was told to leave and warned not to come back to Rocky's Rendezvous. He waited outside to see what became of Hector, a.k.a. Lola Fabiola. Stealthily, the police brought a Black Maria to bear on Rocky's Rendezvous, and, in a few minutes, a half-stripped Lola was being put aboard.

"Get in there, you fag!" cried a cop, and pushed poor Lola roughly through the iron doors.

"What have I ever done to you?" he, she, cried. "Some day we'll fight back," yelled Hector, finally coming out of his closet, becoming the true twin of his sister once again. It was hormone time for Hector—for Lola Fabiola, proud sister of Juanna Donna Lorca.

As the Black Maria pulled away with its sad load of gay citizens, Serge could think of nothing more effective to do than to throw his bag with its chicken salad sandwich and chocolate milk at the retreating vehicle. What would my Resurgius have done, he wondered. Suppose those poor prisoners of love in the Black Maria had been Resurgius' fellow sufferers? How would the great Resurgius have saved them? Serge felt his bronze melting back into weak flesh. He must run and tell Juanna Donna what had happened. She would know what to do. Serge sneaked into the house and crept up to Juanna Donna's room.

Amazed as she was at the story of Hector's transformation and arrest, which Serge blurted every which way he could, like a child telling his mother about his encounter with bullies, Juanna Donna had the presence of mind to call a lawyer.

"Your Auntie Hoover, she una abogada—whats chew say?—she a shyster! Mouthpiece? A *lawyer*, that's it, but I no like to ask her for to help. She likes to get her big nose into everybody's privates. Anyway, she in politics nowadays. Worse than before! And I don't like to use Mr. William Kuntsler, you family lawyer, because everything gets back to them. I'll call Acey Doocy. He understands this kind of problems."

Serge stood by, filled with concern, as she called Counselor Doocy at home and explained the situation to him. Apparently satisfied, she hung up the phone and said to Serge, "Now you no worry 'bout Hector or 'bout me or anything. Everything be fine. Just no breathe no word of this to your mama or your aunties. What they don't knows won't hurt them. Them bodies too busy already."

She handed Serge his manuscript. "I took this from your room cause your Auntie Hoover searches it tonight. She and your mama were furious when they found the inflatable señorita. They take it, but they wasn't half as mad as they be if they read your book."

"Did you read it?"

"Just enough to see what you been up to, you leetle macho, and I know they would not like it, not one leetle bit."

"Why not? What's it got to do with them?"

"Why, it's all about them. And I got to tell you, you make them look pretty funny."

"It's not about them," said Serge, wide-eyed, puzzled, and Juanna Donna could see that he honestly, truly, hadn't realized what he was writing.

"Sergio, you stupido! Anybody can see that it's about them."

"That's not the way a writer works," Serge objected, haughtily. "Sure, I've used a little bit of them, I guess, but each and every character in the story is an amalgam of many people I've met and known over the years."

"Now Serge, how many pipples have you met and know? Except for work, you hardly never go nowhere. You hardly ever *been* anywhere. You stay lock up in your room all the time, like that Boy in the Iron Mask. I'm just warn you, Serge, they ain't gonna like how you show them. The only thing you change is that you made them more real than they are! And, my leetle Negrito, they no see themselves like that."

"Really?" Serge hadn't thought that he was writing realistically but more in the manner of science fiction and fantasy. It occurred to him, not without a certain satisfaction, that he might be more of a Balzac than a Bradbury. It occurred to him that he might be possessed of a strange genius for realism, one of which he was heretofore unaware. A new gravitas weighed upon him, like Earth on the shoulders of Atlas at Rockefeller Center.

"It's past your bedtime," said Juanna Donna. "I mean, if you gonna to write tomorrow and finish that story. Remember, it's Sunday all day tomorrow."

After a night's sleep, Serge woke on Sunday morning, a virgin no more, rolled up his pajama sleeves, and began to write what he thought of as, maybe, the penultimate chapter—in any case, he felt that he was near the end of the story—of his great Balzacian novel *Resurgius,* the first, as he now saw it, of at least fifty of its kind. It was said that Honoré de Balzac, greatest of all French novelists, drank a hundred cups of coffee a day. When Juanna Donna came bustling in with a pot of coffee, he told her, "Keep it coming!"

Serge put the last period to his chapter called "The Eternal Triangle," sat back in his chair, and was considering his work, when Juanna Donna swooshed in, wearing a polka-dot babushka, her pale blue raincoat, and straw-topped platform shoes that displayed her beautiful crimson-painted toenails, and carrying a wet pink parasol.

"I'm sorry I no keep up with the coffee," she said, breathlessly. "I go to Mass and then I meet Hector and Acey Doocy, the lawyer. I tell you about it later. I know is a bad thing to interrupt you when you write, but they wants you downstairs right now. You mama and the aunties have that box with the inflatable señorita in it and I think they pretty peesed-off 'bout it. Look like they have a family council. Bettina Battle down there, too. You better hurry. Here, put on your robe."

"Is it pouring outside?" asked Serge, still in the last scene of his story with Resurgius and his beautiful Miz Amandalay making love.

"It drizzle out, but pour poison down in livingroom. You go down, you walk into hurricane. Be brave, mi poco bravo!" Serge was so involved with his story that he was having a hard time understanding the reality of the habeas corpus or what was required of him. Juanna Donna got him into his bathrobe and pushed him out the door. "Don't tell them I gave you that bustious inflatable señorita, or this Spanglish housekeeping he-she will never hear the end of it."

Pushed out the door, Serge wondered what a "bustious" inflatable señorita was and how he could possibly be involved with one; but, downstairs, he saw, sitting in the middle of the dining room table, the dusty box with Li'l Abner's naked Daisy Mae on it, gleaming, where angry fingers had clawed the heavy dust away, *bustiously*, through unopened cellophane, and remembered it, of course, his heart sinking, his blood-pressure rising, and his poor, hen-pecked nerves pulsating like Broadway neon.

His mother, Auntie Hoover, Bettina Battle, and Aunties Charlotte, Emily, and Annie, sat at the dining room table and looked up at him as he entered the room as if he were a despicable felon, a disgusting fellow, or maybe they saw him as a mutant—he tried to interpret their gaze. He remembered now that Bettina Battle had become employed as speech writer for his Auntie Hoover in her quest to get Mayor Dimwiddy elected governor; otherwise, he could not account for her presence. Her expression was a bit different from the others, more of a smirk.

"You sent for me?" he asked.

"Don't be too hard on him," said Bettina Battle to Auntie Hoover. "He looks so cute in his little blue robe, like a baby taking his first steps."

"If you please, Bettina," said Auntie Hoover, in the strained, strangling voice of Eleanor Roosevelt, "stay out of this. Now then, as chair, I call this table to order. Is the whole cabinet present? Is the board all here? What is at issue here is the possession of this female-demeaning sex toy. Why was it found in the dark dust-bunnied recesses under your cot? Speak up, Serge!"

"I'M FURIOUS ABOUT THIS!" cried his mother.

His mind only half present—half, back in the brassiere factory hideout of his novel with Resurgius, Serge couldn't help himself: he giggled.

"Do you find this amusing, young man?" asked Auntie Hoover, at first as though from a great distance, but then catching up with reality. Now Serge was here, in the dining room, the box on the table, where he did not wish to be, and no longer snuggling in fiction with Miz Amandalay doing what comes naturally.

"I see nothing whatever a bit amusing about it," cried Auntie Hoover.

The MacGuffin, the dingus, the box, was on the table.

"The Boadicea Press finds nothing amusing about it, either!"

His aunties sounded like the singing group they once had tried to become. Uncanny harmonics! A clangy madrigal!

"It's not a Greek tragedy," said Serge. "I'd forgotten all about it. Somebody gave it to me and I just stuck it back there. I've never touched it. You can see the package is unopened and you can see the dust on it. I should have thrown it away. I just forgot about it."

"I know why you never went near it," piped Bettina Battle, in an allusion to her belief that he was gay.

"I won't have such a filthy thing in my house," said his mother. "I don't know what to do with you. You're too old to be spanked."

"Oh no he's not," objected Auntie Hoover. "I'd take the backside of a hairbrush and welt his skinny ass."

His mother continued berating him. "When are you going to grow up? You're twenty-three years old and still living up in that garret, and doing God-knows-what up there. It's a disgrace!"

"I shudder to think," said Auntie Hoover, "what's going on up there while I sleep in my bed at night. I've suspected you of unspeakable acts. I remember hearing you making strange noises. Do you remember? I banged on your door and told you to stop."

"I was fourteen!"

"But did you ever stop?"

"It's the wrong kind of doll," Bettina said. "It ought to be Li'l Abner, not Daisy Mae."

"Shut up, Bettina!" cried Serge. "Nobody should worry about that doll when Bettina's around."

"What do you mean by that?" snapped Bettina.

"Yes, what do you mean by that?" snapped Auntie Hoover, but Serge's mother put an end to the inquisition by shouting that she was furious, ripping the package open, and shaking the inflatable Daisy Mae out.

"Look at this disgraceful thing!" She held the doll up by its creamy shoulders for all to see and, with a shocking suddenness, the doll inflated, first bustiously, then with an evil hissing sound, its legs lifted to the ceiling, catching the chandelier, and exploding, orgasmically, on a hot, phallic-shaped 60-watter. His mother was left holding an empty, torn rubber skin, and a mop-like blonde wig. Catching her breath, she said, "I want this wicked thing out of my house!"

Bettina Battle screamed with laughter. Auntie Hoover looked at her as if she were missing a cog. The six ink-stained hands of the Boadicea Press were frozen in a defensive position. Auntie Hoover shook her head. "Go to your room, Serge. But you haven't heard the end of this!"

"You aren't the boss of me," Serge said, under his breath, but he ran up to his room in immense relief, even though he knew, tragically, he would never hear the end of it.

Now there was a mad storm outside and long tears of rain streaked Serge's window. "They're all crazy," he told Juanna Donna, who was waiting in his room with a steaming pot of coffee and a box of Danish pastry.

"You no need tell me," said Juanna Donna. "Remember, I work for them before you was born. From the day I come to this house, I lay down the law to them. They run what they want but I run the house. I'm the head honcho, uh honcha, round here. I was only a few years older than you now. But I was out on my own too long already to let them treat me how they treat you. I was a servant, but I was *UNE HOMBRE*. Trouble is, they think you a snotty-nosed kid. They don't get it that you're a leetle big macho man. You got to assert yourself, leetle negrito."

"But I was never out on my own, like you."

"Me and Hector . . . I mean, Lola Fabiola, we been on our own since we was in short pants. We was on the streets, shining shoes. Tough guys. Plenty macho. Nobody could tell one of us from the other. It was neat. The cops didn't know which one to haul in. In those days, we even use each other's names. Hector would be Juan. I'd be Hector sometime. Then I came out of the closet. I became real me, Juanna Donna Lorca. You *know* twins can't be that different, but Hector, he play macho man, make himself chase muchachas, drinking and smoking like Juan Wayne. Walking around in a closet of his own. But truth catches up—how you say, will out—out of the steenking closet, as Alfonso Bedoya have said in 'The Treasure of Sierra Madre.' Caramba! What a man! Dios! What big white teeth!

"I met Lola Fabiola and our gay Mick counselor, Acey Doocy, down at Rocky's Rendezvous after Mass, and when I first see Hector I think I am looking in the mirror. And you're right, he look just like me again. We twins again! He's out of the macho wardrobe, wearing a very smart knockoff Uncle Milty drag gown, a magenta cloche hat with a gold horseshoe pin, turned up for luck, and a feathered boa, despite the trouble he got in last night. Our Mister Doocy is going to sue the City, Mayor Dimwiddy, and the police department for Rocky's and all the queens was arrested. We got a lot of angry gays down there. I not be surprised if they has a rebellion—a riot even, someday. They'll call it Rocky's Riot, when the queens gives it back to the cops. But, that's all, now. I don't wanna keep you from you writing."

"I don't know if I'm in the mood to write, now—after that brouhaha downstairs. Besides, love has me distracted, too. I'm in love, Juanna Donna."

"I know you are," said Juanna Donna, tears welling in her eyes. "I could tell from the book. It is good thing, to be in love. Tell all about it in your book. Write it all out. Explain it to yourself. I know what it's like. Juanna Donna has

89

been in love over a thousand times. I have exact number in my diary."

She sighed, fluttering her long dark damp lashes. "It's like you say in that poem of yours that's riding up and down in the subways, 'The Naked Truth'— And even love is true. if we should make it so."

"No, no!" cried Serge. "I was wrong. Love isn't willed. It's a happening. I didn't know it then, what they mean by 'falling in love.' You fall. It just happens. I think I got that other crap from *The World as Will and Representation.* Schopenhauer."

"Ain't he that Kraut philosopher you tell me 'bout? The one whose disgusted mama kick him down the stairs?"

Serge's eyes went dreamy. He said, "No, you can't will love. It just happens. You really do *fall* in love. You don't do it; it happens to you."

"My leetle niño is grow up," said Juanna Donna, looking at him with damp, proud eyes, full of motherly pride.

"But don't you let mama or the aunties see *Resurgius* or they might kick you down the stairs, you leetle Schopenhooser. You know your mama. She'll be you-know-what!"

"Furious!"

"You better believe it, niño!"

"Does that mean that you don't think Boadicea Press would publish *Resurgius*?"

"Get real, niño! What you think?"

"But, Juanna Donna, I can't believe that they would refuse to publish a first novel by their own flesh and blood. I just can't believe that."

"I no want to discourage you in any way, bebe. Maybe they not hard as I think they is. The important thing, for leetle Master Bering-Strait, is that he finish the book. We'll worry about the other later."

"I've got to believe they'll publish it."

"Of course you do, bebe. Don't worry 'bout that now. C'mon, hit those keys! I'll keep the coffee coming for you— just like—who's that Frog writer you been talking about so much lately?—Balls Sack?

"Bal-Zac," corrected Serge.

"Si. Balls Sack!"

8

At nine o'clock Monday morning, when Serge arrived at his cubicle, he found a memo from Amanda Quaint on his Selectric. The memo was a summons to her office, which had been Bettina Battle's. In fact, he could see through the glass walls of the editor's office that both women were there, Amanda's Ferragamo boots on the editor's desk, Bettina's ice pick heels chopping a circle around Amanda. It was clear, even at a distance, that they were in discord. Bettina's Virginia Slim was dancing between her lips as she spoke. Amanda's arms were up behind her head in a manner indicating glacial unconcern. Serge knocked at the door. Bettina strode over and pulled it open, her cigarette still fanning the air, making warlike smoke signals.

"What do *you* want, you great sexless little twit?" spat Bettina Battle.

"I sent for him, you abusive bitch, and don't talk to him like that," said Amanda Quaint, one eyebrow lifting like a feather on fire.

"Well," said Bettina Battle, "now that you're here, maybe you can help me talk some sense into this woman. I'm trying to turn over the helm to her, show her what to do and how to do it, and she won't listen to a word I say. She comes in here and puts her boots up on the desk and won't pay any attention to me."

"Oh, Bettina," said Amanda, not unamiably, "put a sock in it. Serge, I just wanted to tell you that I re-read your manuscript and I'm even more impressed. That's the project that I want you to devote yourself to all day today. Got it?"

"What is that?" asked Bettina. "What project? I already gave him his assignment. He's on UNIVAC III."

"This is something else," said Amanda. "Much more important." She put her index and thumb together and threw Serge a wink. "I didn't want you to sit all day wasting your valuable time on worthless nonsense, without telling you again how much I loved what you are working on, and that you should carry on with it today." She gently waved her hand in dismissal. "Off you go," she said. "I hope you'll have something very exciting to show me later."

Serge walked through the bustling office as if on clouds. Vindication was in the air. In his mind, the music of Amanda's voice blocked out the racket of the office machines and prattling voices that he heard on ordinary days, days before Amanda was in charge, days of the "Battle of Britain," the dark days of food-on-a-stick, sky-mirrors, and UNIVAC III. But suddenly those days came rushing back like a mountain flood.

Behind him, the door of the editor's office flew open, giant voices were heard, and Serge and everyone else in the office had their attention called as to a catastrophe.

Amanda Quaint and Bettina Battle struggled in the doorway of the editor's office, Bettina screaming like a banshee and Amanda roaring like a lion. Amanda got Bettina facing out toward what had become an audience, lifted a booted foot, and shoved Bettina out of the office and into the copy pool. Bettina's dangling Virginia Slim dropped to the floor, spreading brimstone cinders. Everyone waited, breathless. What would she do next? Serge's writer's mind, gleeful of disaster, was ashamed to think that this Donnybrook could make a great scene in *Resurgius*. Perhaps he could use it. Oh, the cold heart of the creator!

In high dudgeon for dignity's sake, Bettina looked out over the heads of her audience. Then she stomped on her cigarette, strode to the elevator—somehow, too fast for human eyes to see, she had gathered up her things—and plummeted sixty-nine floors, a fallen magazine goddess. As far as *Woman's Omnibus* was concerned, that was the ignominious end of Bettina Battle.

For Serge, and perhaps for some others, this incident was a joy to see; but he, at least, had probably not seen the end of Bettina. The dark thought occurred to him that she could still make trouble from her new post with Auntie Hoover and the Dimwiddy gubernatorial campaign. But, he told himself, *carpe diem*, seize the day and be happy. Two such gifts as his compliment on *Resurgius* from Amanda and the departure of Bettina do not often occur in one day. He was thrilled. From now on, when he looked up from his work and saw the glass tower of power of the editor's office, he would know a friend was there, and a friend in a tower of power is a friend indeed! And so he put himself to work for his friend, trying to grasp the next part of *Resurgius*, thinking, unaware, through his lunch hour.

It felt like some kind of delayed reaction shock. He began to twitch all over. He could feel his eyes rolling in his head; the madman, the lover, and the overwrought poet. He seized his Selectric and stamped out—CHAPTER . . .

He couldn't remember what chapter it should be; he typed on—THE BATTLE OF THE SEXES

He felt it! He was going to write prophesy. Yes, and it was inspired by Plutarch's *Parallel Lives* and Xenophon's *Anabasis* (thought of as an advance) and *Katabasis* (thought of as a retreat). The Mize, led by Jaye Edgahoover with Furius at her side, would advance and the Dongs, under the leadership of Resurgius the Great, would make them retreat.

In an earlier chapter, his Auntie Hoover had become Jaye Edgahoover, Boss of the Universe; his mother, Dagmar, had become her second in command, the frightening Furius. He had already written of them as these characters and now, inspired by the office battle between Amanda and Bettina, he saw a greater conflict—and a longer novel. All of this formed in his mind in a flying instant in time, a shooting star.

What he was about to write, what he was writing, this long war, would take up the whole middle of his great novel, *Resurgius*. The novel was going to be a full-third longer than he had originally planned. He was not near the end at all. He was just getting started. Where had his mind been? Of course there had to be the Battle of the Sexes. How not? Onward! Anabasis! Onward to katabasis, the humiliating defeat of Jaye Edgahoover and Furius, and the glorious triumph of Resurgius! He wrote on . . .

The Ovary Office of the Pink House was a-bustle with activity.

When word was brought back to the Emergency Session of the Univacual Council, that Miz Mandalay had been kidnapped by three Dongs disguised as superdupermodel- mize, and that she had been taken away in a golden condom- like balloon, resembling a giant wiener, the members of the Council chorus cried for revenge. This was very much to Jaye Edgahoova's taste, and she made good use of all this feline fury.

"Hear me, Mize," she roared, "the Dongs have stolen from amongst us the flower of our regime, the magnificent Miz Mandalay, whom we all know and love. Who knows if right now she is being tortured with Dong love by that mus- clebound scoundrel Resurgius? First it was our adored Miz Bet who vanished pneumatically down a tube. Now it's Miz Mandalay. Who will be next? This is war! And I declare it right now on the Dongs!"

"Yea! Yea! Yea!" came the waves of approval. Vox populi, vox dei!

"Long live liberty!"
"Crush the Dongs underfoot!"
"Stab them with your stiletto heels!"
"Put their donkey eyes out!"
"Hang them by their willies!"
"Freedom now!"

"Then let us withdraw, at this moment of crisis, my Atalantamize, my beloved Amazonian angels, to contemplate the grave implications of our actions and to make detailed plans of attack."

A crescendo of approval!

"It has been your decision," cried Jaye Edgahoova, flushed with success, "I am only your servant." With which she withdrew. The trembling, quaking, expanding Universe was waiting to see what little ole she would do next. Sturm und Drang on the march.

In the Ovary Office, she called for her chief of Shrike Police, one Furius, a flame-haired ex-barmiz from Hoboken, who was notorious for having bitten off the ears of at least twenty Dongs—it was a dastardly lie that she had bitten off anything else or more than she could chew.

"Furius," said Edgahoova, "you are now looking at the absolute Boss of the Universe. The Dongs have played right into my hands. I can wage open war upon them and get rid of Miz Mandalay at the same time. Get me a Pink Dongly. I'm thirsty."

She took out a cigar, a Dongatella, bit off the tip, and began to puff illegally in a no-puffing zone. Authority says yes to itself and no to everyone else.

Other employees went out to lunch or ate at their desks. Visitors came and went, murmuring approval of the new editor as they passed his cubicle. But Serge was heedless of the advancing day until his phone rang and he heard the meek voice of one of his Boadicea aunties on the line—Annie, the

95

one who had always been most sympathetic to Serge but, as he believed, was too afraid of the others to show it.

"Yes, Auntie Annie?"

"Serge, dear, you must come home now, immediately. We're having a family conference about your book."

"What? How did you get my book?"

"Your Auntie Hoover was looking through your room and came upon her name, or a name that was *like* her own, on a page in your wastepaper basket. Then she did a really thorough search in your room to find the manuscript it came from and could not. However, it occurred to her that it might be in Juanna Donna's room, and she searched there, and found it, among Juanna Donna's flounces. This was just after you left for work. We've all been reading it ever since."

"Did you like it? Did you think it was funny? Did you think it was realistic?"

"Well, Serge, dear, I, personally, thought it was rather amusing, but I'm not so sure your mother and your Auntie Hoover share my opinion."

"Juanna Donna told me that they might not like it, but I've always been absolutely confident that you and Boadicea Press would want to publish it. Am I right? Is that what the meeting is about? Do you want me to come all the way home just to tell me that you are going to publish my book? Can't you tell me now?"

"Well, Serge, it's not my place to tell you what's going on here," she said in a retreating voice. "You'll just have to come home. It's *that* important."

"You always said that a good editor could tell a good book by the first sentence, Auntie."

"That's true! I would have thrown *Moby Dick* right in the fire after reading 'Call me Ishmael!' But that's beside the point. Suffice it to say, Serge, you must come home right away." And she clicked off.

High hopes! They're probably throwing me a surprise party, thought Serge. They must have loved *Resurgius.* After all, Amanda did. Now they want to show me their appreciation of my genius. Only one thing concerned him though—now everyone who counted had read his book, but it, as yet, had no ending, no end to its arc, no climax, no denouement. And his deep, considering mind had been working out this problem as he went about his quotidian business or slept. But he must get more black on white as another practical writer, like himself, Guy de Maupassant, had put it, and now, with this interruption, this distraction, how was he to finish? The gossamer structure of his novel's ending, so carefully being constructed in his mind, was being blown apart. He felt a soft vibration of his exquisitely sensitive nervous system as he contemplated this problem—so he set it aside and returned to first and happier thoughts.

Yes, so far, so good. He had written a blockbuster. "From high to low, doth dissolution climb," as Wordsworth, another bookworm, had put it.

He pulled on his London Fog and went back to Amanda's office. "They want me to come home," he told her. "I'm pretty sure they'll publish my book."

"How wonderful!" cried Amanda. "You go ahead home, but you've got to be back here for my inauguration party at five. There'll be Champagne and the works. You wouldn't miss that, would you?"

"Not for a million dollars," he said.

"Off you go then."

It was a hat trick, the third, and final, great gift of the day! Boadicea Press was going to publish *Resurgius.* He had always been sure that Juanna Donna was wrong, that his mother and aunties would love *Resurgius,* once they had gotten over any superficial likeness to themselves—that parallel lives thing—and they would see the humor in it, for they were big-hearted people, not so petty as Juanna Donna believed them to be. They were his family, after all, his nearest and dearest. Blood was thicker than ink, or something like that. They would recognize his Balzacian, Bradbury-like genius—how could they fail to?—and Boadicea Press would be his. He could see a lovely hardbound volume with Boadicea's trademark of the great woman warrior herself on the cover and his name and that of his great hero—*Resurgius*. O joy!

Dashed!

Inside the front door stood Juanna Donna's shopping cart, filled to the brim with groceries. Something was amiss.

Serge walked into a battlefield that was in the throes of an earthquake. It was as if several strong women stood face to face at God's Great Judgment Seat. Cripes! His mother was furious, Auntie Hoover was roaring, and Juanna Donna was a whirling Dervish. The Aunties of Boadicea Press cowered in a group hug.

"I have warn you," cried Juanna Donna, stabbing the air like Zorro with the épée of a long magenta fingernail, her twenty elaborate bracelets clinking, "since I come here twenty-five years ago, that if you ever, ever went into my room snooping, I would leave this house. But I never caught you before," and her voice rose an octave, "but you go into my room to find that manuthing, and Juanna Donna, she never will not *not* keep her word when she say something, so she is leaving this house, and you lazy-assed intellectuals can just learn to cook and clean by yourselves like everybody else. Soon you pipples is be up to you ankles in pig shit!"

"You wouldn't leave me," Serge said, horrified, terrified, mystified, a giant tear rolling down each pale cheek. But no one was listening to him.

"Listen here, Juanna Donna," said Auntie Hoover, waving a finger, "I had every right to find out what Serge was writing about me—about all of us. I'm the boss around here."

"*I'm* in charge around here," cried Serge's mother, furiously. "This is *my* house."

"Of course I meant *you*, dear," said Auntie Hoover. "I'm speaking for you."

"Listen ups! This here is Juanna Donna speaking, and, when she say something, she mean what she say. Juanna Donna keeps her sacred word. I am leaving this bughouse. I send for my things," and her hand drew dismissal into the air. "Hasta la vista!"

"Where will you go?" said Serge's mother, placatingly.

"I stay with my sister Hector until I get my own place. I going to retire and live like human being instead of prisoner. I have set aside a bundle. Juanna Donna, she no need this aggravation. She only stay for Serge, and now he grown up and got to learn to be un hombre and stand on his own leetle feet. Youse beeches keep him being like a teeny-weenie niño." She showed them how small Serge was by rubbing her thumb and index together.

"I don't like being bullied by a servant. I *never* liked being bullied by a servant!" cried Auntie Hoover. "*I'm* the boss around here!" she added, jabbing a thumb into her chest. Her face was crimson.

"Juanna Donna is always Capitaine of her ship. And Juanna Donna she is not going to lie to you no more. I gotta new ship just waiting for me if I wants to be Capitaine there; a bigger and better ship than this barge!"

The Boadicea aunties were crying. No one in the house could cook. Would they ever eat again?

"You're the cause of all this," said Auntie Hoover turning to Serge. "Go to your room."

"Yes," said Juanna Donna to Serge, "go to your room! I left you something there, something very important to your future. You can reach me at Hector's." Suddenly, she was gone. Suddenly, impossibly, Juanna Donna was gone.

Serge didn't know which way to turn. Now he was stupefied. "What happened?" he implored of the giant in the sky, his hands up.

Serge's mother said, "Juanna Donna came home from shopping and found us reading your novel."

Auntie Annie said, "She knew immediately that Auntie Hoover had found it in her room and blew up. It was awful. I'm sure she doesn't mean it."

"She'll be back with her tail between her legs," growled Auntie Hoover.

"I don't think so," said Auntie Annie, shaking her head in sadness.

"Why is it all my fault?" begged Serge.

"Because you wrote that disgraceful libel called *Resurgius*," cried Auntie Hoover, "hereinafter," she went on legalistically, "to be known as Exhibit A, or the traitorous Resurgius Papers, insulting every member of this family, making us look like idiots or worse."

Serge turned to Auntie Annie. "Does this mean you're not going to publish my book?" He leaned over the table and, with great stealth, gathered up his dog-eared manuscript.

"I told you to go to your room!" cried Auntie Hoover. "We'll talk about that piece of trash later. Publish it? We'll burn it! Go to your room, I said, you over-aged adolescent!"

"You've made us all furious," said his mother. "Go to your room!"

"Better go," said Aunt Annie.

"Better go," chorused Charlotte and Emily.

Dizzy with confusion, Serge climbed the stairs up to the top of the house. He had never felt so alone in his life. He was ostracized, defeated. But then—a warm greeting, a hint of hope. On his cot lay his overnight bag, fully packed, along with his trusty Olympia in its closed case. And there was a note in Juanna Donna's scrawl.

Dear Niño,

100

I have watch you grow up, but I have watch that these womans don't let you grow up. I packed your bag. There's everything you need. This is your chance to make a man of yourself. Follow Juanna Donna into the big world. Take these things and go! You never regret. Call me at Hector's.
  All my love and hopes for you,
    Juanna Donna

The roar of argument followed Serge as he left the house, unnoticed, his overnight bag, containing his precious novel, in one hand and his Olympia in the other. He felt just like Thomas Wolfe leaving Asheville. "You can't go home again," he said, sadly quoting the great Tar Heel. He knew now that he had overstayed his welcome by five years. "*De trop, de trop,* wherever I go," he muttered, rags and quotes always at hand. He should have left home when he graduated from NYU, but it had been so easy not to. Perhaps he *was* an emotionally retarded adolescent, as Auntie Hoover had suggested. Perhaps it was time for him to be a real hero, like Resurgius.

The changeover party at *Women's Omnibus* had already begun when he arrived back at the office. There were balloons and streamers, and over the editor's door was a banner that read, THE QUEEN IS DEAD—LONG LIVE THE QUEEN! AMANDA RULES! Out of the crowd, Amanda materialized. "Come with me," she said, leading him back to the privacy of her office.

"I've left home," he said in a quavering voice, following her, unwinding like a spring. "I'm going to the YMCA. My mother and my aunties hated *Resurgius*. They said it was about them—it isn't of course; I just used bits of them, I admit it—and that it made them look ridiculous. Of course, I had no such intention. They have misinterpreted everything. And, for the first time in my life I've come to realize that they have nothing but contempt for me. *And* Juanna Donna has left us. I'm alone in the world and I'm losing the structure of

101

my novel. I can't remember what to do. It's horrible!" Withheld tears puffed his face.

"Life is like a minefield," he said, unoriginally, lugubriously, "you almost make it across and then something blows up." And he dropped his overnight bag and Olympia on the floor of her office, in desperate emphasis.

"There, there," Amanda said, pushing back a cowlick of his rusty hair. "Calm down."

"Oh, Amanda," he cried, "you're so STRONG!"

"Stuff and nonsense!" Amanda told him that she knew all about it. When he asked how, she told him that Juanna Donna had called her, that in fact, she and Juanna Donna had been in communication for some time.

"She waited down at the corner to see if you would leave and called me immediately to tell me that you had. We are both very proud of you. We know that it was a very brave thing on your part to leave that house. Let me say quickly, my darling poet, that *I* was touched by your lovely portrait of me in the book. You made me a bit ditzy at first, but of course, I understand that the story required it, and I find it incomprehensible that your mother and your aunties can't understand the requirements of fiction. The story is perfectly innocent fun."

"But it has its serious side," Serge put in, puffing up a bit.

"But of course! What's important now is that you write the end of it. Juanna Donna and I have a plan. You are going to live with me and Juanna Donna is going to become our housekeeper. She is waiting, even how, at the house. On the front stoop. So don't keep her waiting. Here, take my keys. As Christopher Marlowe wrote, *Come, live with me and be my love and we will all the pleasures prove.*"

"Oh, Amanda," Serge cried, swooningly. "How wonderful!"

"I have to work late tonight," she added, "after the party. The house is huge and empty and I need somebody to clean it up and to take care of us—especially you, and, more especially, until you have fully given birth to *Resurgius*. I know that Juanna Donna always keeps the coffee coming. Now I want you to take a few days off and finish your novel— which I think is hilarious."

"Hilarious? But don't you think it has a lot of . . . mmm, *gravitas*?"

"Oh yes, Sweetheart, at times it's very heavy."

"Auntie Hoover—who, as you no doubt know, my love, is a lawyer—says its libelous."

"Oh, phooey! She's just worried about any impact it might have on Mayor Dimwiddy's gubernatorial campaign. We'll have the legal department check it out. Your Auntie Hoover won't be able to do a thing. Now, off you go!"

"But Auntie Hoover is dangerous. She's a . . . *Desperada*!"

"Nonsense! In fact, I might as well tell you this now: I'm thinking of serializing *Resurgius* as a spoof in *Women's Omnibus* with my article 'Have Some Feminists Gone Too Far?' as a sort of introduction to it. It'll show the world that there's a new editor in charge, one with new ideas, new concepts. How do you like them apples, my darling?"

"AMANDA RULES!" cried Serge.

9

It was almost midnight when Amanda sat down at the kitchen table in her Brooklyn Heights mansion, weary from her long and difficult first day in command of *Women's Omnibus*, but buoyed and full of hope for the new order of things, the life she would share with Serge and Juanna Donna.

"So, I will be Capitaine of this big casa," said Juanna Donna, serving them tea.

"Yes," said Amanda, "you will be Captain at home and I will be Captain at work. We'll have the third floor fitted out for a complete apartment for you, just as we talked about. I would have had it done already, but of course I couldn't know just when you would make up your mind to put our plan into action and I've been so preoccupied with work. Serge and I will take the second floor. We'll leave the upper floors locked up and we'll all enjoy the parlor floor, where we'll party. You'll cook and keep house. And we'll have the whole place cleaned up, painted, etc., so you can have a fresh start. Of course, I wouldn't expect you to try to fix this big place up by yourself. It's too much. I'll get you some help. I've been very neglectful. Just sat around and let it all go to pot."

"Why you not care? You are reech and important and very beautiful, so why you not care?"

"Why don't I have an active social life? Is that what you mean? I work hard and I don't need men. Most of the men I meet I don't care for. My Sergie, of course, is quite different. He's not a man, he's a poet. I am not afraid to say I love him because I am not afraid of anything."

"I worship you, Amanda," said Serge. "You are the Queen of my heart."

Amanda took Serge's hand across the table, squeezed it, and continued. "It's exactly what I told you," said Amanda, speaking to Juanna Donna, "the other day when we met for lunch. The world is a difficult place and poets lift us above it. I promised myself when I was a little girl, that I would never fall in love with anyone but a poet. Oh, maybe a composer . . . but no, I like poets better. And I think Serge is a great poet."

"Juanna Donna is so very happy that a woman like you know what a good boy and high brow her Serge is."

Pride goeth before a fall, Serge cautioned himself. Listening to the two of them, he was becoming embarrassed. Who would have thought this situation could come to be?

Only a few hours ago, his back was to the wall, so to speak. When he had arrived at the office, he had no idea what he was going to do next; and then, quite suddenly, everything changed for the better.

He understood now that these two sitting with him had been like guardian angels all along, watching over him, helping him to do his work, planning this very situation. What wonders they were! But he had to go to the bathroom and he could not sit and listen anymore to himself being celebrated. How could he ever live up to such—he hoped they weren't misplaced—high hopes in him? How all this came to be, he wasn't certain; but it was a miracle, wasn't it? And a further miracle was that the whole ending of *Resurgius* suddenly constructed itself in his mind, like a golden castle appearing out of nowhere. He saw again how he had planned it to go. It was there, and then he entered a tunnel and it was gone and now he had emerged from the tunnel and it was there again. The mind is an enchanted thing, as Marianne Moore, who herself had once lived in Brooklyn Heights, put it, an enchanted and enchanting thing!

Serge got up and went to the bathroom, his ears burning. He lifted the seat and stood over the commode in frustration. He had to go but nothing came. He struggled. He strained. Still, he could not pee standing up. He felt the disconnect between his body and his mind. Finally, he surrendered to necessity, lowered the seat, took down his pants, and sat down, disappointed.

"I know he loves you like a mother," Amanda said to Juanna Donna. "And I know you'll take good care of him when I'm not here. I'm going to be very busy with the magazine, especially here at the beginning. He needs you to watch over him."

"I start right away. I want to get Serge back to work on *Resurgius*. I promise him I see him through and Juanna Donna always keep her promises."

"So do I, Juanna Donna," Amanda said, taking Juanna Donna by the hands in a kind of unspoken vow of close friendship. "I mean, I want him to finish *Resurgius* as much as you do."

"Because, you see, Miss Amanda," Juanna Donna rolled on, "I was glad when Serge start to write this book. The reason is, to me, that I believe from the beginning that this book would be like—how you say?—*therapy*. I no smarty-pants, Miss Amanda, far from it, but I understands pipple, and I believe he explaining how he feel deep down to himself. They not so bad, those women, his mama, his aunties, they're just all about themselves. They never pay any attention to my leetle Serge when he grow up. I see they keep him like a leetle bird in their big red hands and no let him fly. As he grow, they crush his leetle wings. They don't mean to, I don't think. Just—they don't *see* him. And I know that it must be that you *see* him. You know he is a poet—a special person—and a poet is like a bird that must fly."

"Juanna Donna," said Amanda, "you are a true romantic. I think we're going to get along wonderfully."

"My toothsayer told me that we would. She told me what you would be like to leeve with and I even knew what you would look like before we met, from *Resurgius*. I knew you would be beautiful like Meez Amandalay in his book or like Daisy Mae in the box."

"You mean soothsayer, don't you?"

"No, Miss Amanda, I mean *tooth*sayer. She tells fortune by reading your teeth."

"Oh."

Bells were ringing. Serge woke hugging a pillow that a dream told him was Amanda; but she had deserted him and the bed several hours earlier, before light broke. The telephone was ringing. He went into the livingroom to answer it and discovered that Juanna Donna, who had slept on

106

the couch—Amanda had only used one floor of the house as an apartment—was gone as well. He wondered how a cup of coffee would materialize and thought of the kitchen, where it had always seemed to come from. The telephone rang again. He picked it up, but whoever had been there was gone. He called Amanda at work who told him that she had not called him. She was busy.

"Don't answer the phone," she said. "I don't want you distracted from your thoughts on *Resurgius.*" She hung up, but it was good to hear her sweet voice.

He went to the kitchen. There was a jar of instant coffee on the table with a note, compliments of Amanda, telling him to boil water, pour it in a cup, and put the coffee in it. Stir it, the note informed him. Apparently, Amanda thoroughly understood his domestic incompetence. Next, he underwent a terrible brain-strain that ultimately resulted in a cup of coffee, took the steaming cup to the windows, which were French doors, and looked out, considering, as he slowly came to full consciousness, what a lonely soul he was.

He went out onto the patio. A breath of autumn, winding between his skin and the inside of his striped pajamas, chilled him and rose goose-bumps. Directly below him was the long back yard, beyond that the Esplanade, beyond the Esplanade the blown and choppy waters of the harbor, where the Hudson and East Rivers met, and beyond that the towering Manhattan skyline. He went back inside, made himself a second cup of coffee, and toured the apartment with coffee in hand, wondering where and when and how he was to finish *Resurgius.*

The phone rang again and he picked it up to hear his Auntie Hoover's voice say, "Serge?"

"Don't call me here. I will not answer." He banged the receiver on its cradle.

Juanna Donna had left him a note on the coffee table in front of the couch. She had gone to Bethune Street to get some of her things, and would shop on the way back. Her trip would take a couple of hours. Back to work tomorrow, Juanna Donna told him in the note. She promised that the first thing she would do would be to set up a place for him to write. He would miss no more than a day away from *Resurgius*. It was nearly noon. Sun and shadows crossed the kitchen floor. The universe, if not himself, was on the move.

The doorbell rang. It rang again. He felt a sense of urgency. The bell was impatient. It rang again. Serge went on a quick search of the bedroom for a bathrobe—oh, if only he had Resurgius' costume with the big blue cape he could wrap around himself—could not find his bathrobe, hurried toward the door in his striped pajamas, and pulled it open a crack. Cool air and bright sun bedazzled him. Autumnal leaves. Then he saw a long red limousine with a mustard colored streak along its top parked in front of the house. The red limo was impressive and he saw it before he saw the man standing in front of him. He saw the man's straw skimmer before he saw the man. The man's clear blue eyes looked straight into his.

"I'm Quaint, the Wiener King. Got any beer?" The man wore a mustard-colored suit, a red hot bow-tie, and tan rattan-like shoes. He was about Serge's height and weight. Those were the only resemblances. He had a pleasant but bulldog-like face and there was a huge, ginger, walrus mustache under his sharp nose. His voice sounded as if he were chewing gravel. He must have been eighty years old.

"I say, are you altogether there, son? I repeat, I'm Quaint, Amanda's granddaddy. I stopped by to see her at the office and she told me to come down and take a look at you. She said she's gonna marry you. This was my house before I gave it to Amanda," he added, pushing Serge aside, establishing his authority, and heading for the kitchen.

Serge followed him, leaving the door wide open behind him. "Here's a box of wieners," said the Wiener King,

"Quaint Wieners," and he walked into the kitchen and dumped the box on the kitchen table. "Now how about those beers?"

The Wiener King sat down at the table and looked up at Serge. "Son," he said, "one look at you at the front door and I knew something. I'm Quaint and I'm quick. You've got something missing. What do you suppose it is?"

Serge stood looking at the Wiener King, fully aware now of who he was dealing with, but dumbstruck.

"What you're missing, son, is a mustache! A good thick beaver mustache would make a man of you. Look at me! Everybody does! And they do what I damn well tell 'em to do because I've got a voice like a bear and a mustache like a beaver pelt. You need hair on your face. You're smooth as a boy. Hell, you're as smooth as a girl. But I don't hold that against you. I didn't realize what a gruff voice and a big mustache could do until I was nearly thirty. It was just about then that I went into the wiener business, and the bigger my mustache got, the bigger my wieners got. I drink nothing but beer and eat nothing but wieners. This diet has made me disgustingly rich, and kept me slim and healthy. I'm almost ninety years old, you know," he yelled. "I know that's hard for you to believe. Wieners bring optimism and optimism brings optimal health. Now where's that beer that you keep promising me?"

"I don't know if we have any," Serge finally got out.

"Hellfire and brimstone! How can you live without beer? It's the staff of life in a bottle. Wieners are the staff of life themselves, so beer is like a wiener in a bottle." He gave Serge the once-over. "Why is a young man your age still in his pajamas at this hour of the day? Oh, never mind! Did I tell you, I stopped by to see Amanda at her office and she told me to come down and take a look at you. She wants to marry you. You look O.K. to me. Hell, you must be or she wouldn't want you."

"Marry me?"

"Why, yes, of course! What do you think you're doing here? She told me you're some kind of poet. But that's O.K. You won't need money in this family. She makes a lot and I have the rest. The main thing is that you're a good decent chap. But I still say that that baby face needs some hair on it, poet or not."

There was a racket in the hall and five workmen in paint-splashed coveralls walked into the kitchen. One of them said, "We're the painters. You left the door open so we came in. Where do we go? What do we do?"

"Hello boys, I'm the Wiener King," said the Wiener King. "You boys got any beer? When I was a house painter, which I was when I was young, we always brought beer along with us, and nowadays they got those cooler things to keep it chilled. We didn't have them. We had to drink warm beer. I repeat, boys, where's the beer? If you've got the beer, I've got the wieners, as you can see. Had any lunch?"

In ten minutes, five workmen, Serge, and the Wiener King sat around the table, drinking beer and talking, while the aroma of grilled wieners filled the kitchen, the Wiener King regaling the painters with tales of ancient days when he himself had been a house painter in the Bronx.

"Now let me tell you something REALLY interesting," the old man shouted, clearly feeling his beer; but he was stopped by the cling-clang entrance of Juanna Donna and Lola Fabiola, a.k.a. Hector.

"Now let me tell *you* something really interesting," said Juanna Donna. "This party is over! You painter men get upstairs and get busy. Third floor. You know what to do. And make room for movers. They be bring up my things. Serge, you been drinking beer?"

"No, no, Juanna Donna," said Serge, shaking his head, "only coffee." Serge answered the elaborately costumed person who asked him the question because he assumed that

110

only Juanna Donna would ask such a question; but, in all truth, he wasn't sure whether he was speaking to Juanna Donna or Hector, so alike were the twins now. They had become doppelgängers again.

When he first knew them, as a little boy, they were identical; then Juan turned into Juanna Donna, gradually, but before his eyes, and now Hector had turned into Juanna Donna, or Lola Fabiola, and he could hardly tell them apart but for what they said. After a moment or two of sharp contemplation, Serge stretched out an arm and indicated the person he thought was Juanna Donna.

"Mister Quaint, I would like you to meet our house-keeper, Señorita Juanna Donna Lorca, and her bro—eh, sis-ter—Señorita Lola Fabiola." He scratched his head. Did he get it right?

"Manny Quaint here, Amanda's granddaddy," yelled the Wiener King. He got to his feet and gave the twins a courtly bow. "I may wonder how many beers I've had, for I'm seeing double. How amazingly charming it is to meet two such attractive señoritas. Nature might have been satisfied with one. Mother nature might have thought that she had pressed her powers to the limit in creating one such beauty, but *two*—two perfect specimens of womanhood—well, it simply takes my breath away. If I had the stamina that I had in youth—say, at seventy—I wouldn't know which one of you to pursue first. But one question might clear my mind. Which one of you likes wieners?"

"Both of us like wieners," said Juanna Donna, taking two from the table and handing one to Lola Fabiola.

"Alas," cried the Wiener King, "I am confounded. If only I were a polygamist and could marry you both, my Spanish beauties."

"Then we would be very rich?" asked Lola Fabiola.

"You would indeed, ladies," yelled the Wiener King, "but there's a law against what I have in mind, even though

111

with enough beer and wieners aboard, it's a fact that I can run in two directions at once. In other words," he said, "I can defy nature itself," and he winked and donned his skimmer. "Serge," he said, "I feel a bit wobbly. See me to the front door, will you?"

Two of Juanna Donna's movers carrying a heavy chest of drawers toward the staircase passed them in the hall.

At the front door, Serge had the wit to ask, "Do I meet with your approval, sir?"

"Oh, you already had my approval when I came. Whatever Amanda wants—well, Amanda always does the right thing, so I know you're the right thing for her. I just wanted to get a look at you, see what it is that she likes about you, that she loves about you, and I think I can see it. I think I see a good heart and a sweet nature. Don't hide your light under a bushel, son. If Amanda loves you, you have a right to be proud. There's a durnblasted good reason for that love. But you need some hair on your face. Grow that mustache!" The Wiener King's chauffeur came up the steps and took him by the arm.

Serge hadn't thought so far as parental approval. "Do you think Amanda's parents—"

"Don't worry about Amanda's parents. I'm the one you have to impress. What I say goes. They're rich from having me; I'm rich from having money. I'm the *law*. *I'M* THE WIENER KING!"

The patient chauffeur helped the Wiener King down to his limo, where the W.K. turned around and yelled, "Later!" And, with one last wave of his skimmer, he was off in his Wienermobile.

The after-image of the Wienermobile had not yet cleared from Serge's mind when Bettina Battle appeared at the foot of the steps as if materialized by a Roddenberry beam. She looked up at Serge. "Who was that?" she called. "Wasn't that the Wiener King?"

112

"Bettina! What are you doing here?"

"I'm a reluctant emissary from your family. They've had a change of heart. Your Auntie Annie talked to your mother and your mother talked to Auntie Hoover and Auntie Hoover sent me to get you. Why won't you answer the phone? You could have saved me the trip. I had no desire to come down here to Brooklyn. I don't particularly want to see you, after the way you've treated me, and I certainly don't want to run into Amanda. But I am under orders from your Auntie Hoover to bring you home for your mother's sake. She's not furious any more—*au contraire*. Aren't you going to invite me in?"

"All right," said Serge, stepping aside, "if you must; but this is a very busy house today."

A large white van pulled up and parked where the Wienermobile had been. A number of bustling men appeared from its recesses and in seconds were carrying pink bathroom fixtures up the steps, forcing Serge back. Serge heard Juanna Donna directing them up to her apartment. The men brought in a bath and shower unit, a sink, and, following behind the bobbing commode, Bettina Battle entered.

"I've been here before," she said, seizing Serge's hand and pulling him into the kitchen behind her.

The house rang with the hammering of construction, and the workmen who passed through the kitchen did double-takes, seeing Bettina, statuesque and pulchritudinous in her mini-skirt and five-inch heels. Serge saw their eyes pop and knew that their mouths were watering. "Fix me a nice cup of tea," she said, sitting down at the table.

"I get it," said Lola Fabiola through seven veils, innocent of Serge's desire to get Bettina out of the house.

Bettina lit a Virginia Slim and let it dangle from her crimson lips while she talked. "I've been ordered to bring you home," she said, "dead or alive. I just have to get you there and then you can do whatever you want after you've seen them. My job is at stake. Your Auntie Hoover doesn't take no for an answer. I'll lay my cards on the table. How much do you want?"

"Much what?" asked Serge, not getting her drift.

"Money, of course. I'll give you five hundred to come to Bethune Street with me. This is the first important job your Auntie Hoover has given me as her assistant and I've got to get it right. Five hundred bucks isn't bad for a trip to the Village, is it? Look, the money's about two-to-one, so I'll make it five hundred pounds. What do you think?" She took a sip of tea from the cup Lola Fabiola had set before her and blew a tornado of smoke at Serge.

"I wouldn't go back with you if you gave me the Exchequer and threw in Fort Knox. I wouldn't go anywhere with you anyway. I know what you get up to in that damn limousine of yours. And Amanda wouldn't like it either."

"Amanda! Amanda! Do you know what that bitch girlfriend of yours did to me? She blackmailed me! She taped me when she was in my car with me and gave it to the board of directors of *Omnibus*."

"Magazine editing, I've heard, is a blood sport," said Serge. "Amanda told me so."

"Aren't you shocked, Mister Goody Two-Shoes?"

"A woman's got to do what a woman's got to do," said Juanna Donna, appearing in the doorway. Bettina looked at her, whirled about in her chair, and looked at Lola Fabiola.

"My God!" she cried. "There're two of you. I thought the one who got me the tea was Juanna Donna. Who's the other dervish?"

"That is my bro—" started Juanna Donna—"my sister Lola Fabiola. Maybe when you come to Bethune Street you saw my brother Hector. Well, he is my sister, and once again he is my twin. I am glad there are two of us but I am sorry there is even one of you, Mzzzzzz Battle. Why you let her in, Serge?"

114

"Just one minute here," said Bettina Battle, pulling herself up to face an enemy attack. "Who do you think you're talking to?"

"Juanna Donna know who she is talking to, who is not who she pretend to be. Juanna Donna, she hate a fake, a big tall fake in a mini-skirt." She went around the table and lifted Bettina to her feet, stood her on her towering heels.

"You big bony stack of stink," she cried. "Juanna Donna has dream of giving you heave-ho lots of time from Bethune Street but now in Amanda's house, I can do it, because I am Capitaine here."

"Unhand me," cried Bettina, "you walking stack of carnival tents!"

"I unhand you O.K., because I no like to touch you, you phony phooey! I catch you stand up to pee at Bethune Street. You are what Serge call a Dong." She looked at Serge and Lola Fabiola and pointed at Bettina.

"This is no woman! This is like me and you, Lola, but too phony to be what she is. She got a string on her crotch that she tuck back up. *He* got a string, the beech!"

Now she lifted Bettina Battle and carried her kicking to the front door, Serge and Lola following. "You go back to Auntie Hoover with your tail between your legs and she take care of the rest of you."

"Serge," cried Bettina, "for God's sake, help me!"

Juanna Donna set her—eh, *him*—down on the stoop and closed the door after her—eh, him. A couplet from Edgar Allan Poe popped into Serge's mind—

Is all that I see or seem
But a dream within a dream?

Serge went to Amanda's bedroom, found his clothes, and got dressed. No one noticed as he left the house. It was good to be out and away from all that hammering and yammering. He spent the afternoon contemplating the sliding slate of the harbor from the Esplanade, watching people promenade, putting the parts of the end of *Resurgius* together in his mind, and watching the sun slide down into the west. And then, not soon enough, it was time for his angel to come home, and he returned to the house. What a relief! The workmen were gone. Hector—Lola Fabiola—had gone back to Bethune Street. Juanna Donna was making *arroz con pollo*. The house was quiet. Later, after dinner, alone, he told Amanda what had happened with Bettina. "How could I have missed such a thing?" he asked Amanda. She saw that he was in a state of consternation.

"So far as I know," said Amanda, "only Juanna Donna and I knew about it. Look at her. No one else could possibly tell." Amanda told him that Bettina Battle was out of their lives forever. She told him that she had talked to Juanna Donna about what had happened, and that he should not concern himself with it, but concentrate his attention on finishing *Resurgius*.

There was no question that Amanda knew best, that she was the Captain of him, so he listened to her advice, dreamily snuggled his head into her more than ample bosom, and went to sleep while watching Resurgius, broadsword in hand, slaying a dragon that looked rather a lot like Auntie Hoover.

Waking, alone again, Serge, sandy-eyed, found his way to the bathroom. He stared at himself in the mirror. He needed a shave. He decided not to touch the area under his nose and above his upper lip. Staring hard at his reflection, he thought he could detect the beginning of a bushy red mustache, something that might one day resemble the Wiener King's. But perhaps it was only morning shadow enhanced by his hopeful imagination. He sat down on the john to pee, realized what he was doing, and jumped up. He turned around and lifted the toilet seat and filled the bowl the way Gargantua had filled the Seine, the way Resurgius had filled

116

the River Slime. O joy! O gratification! *Viva machismo!* Hooray for John Wayne!

"Good day, Pilgrim," he said to his willy, shaking the last drops from it, "and thanks."

Serge found a pot of coffee waiting for him in the kitchen, and a note directing him to the second floor, where everything had been prepared for his task of finishing *Resurgius*. He had slept late again, and Juanna Donna had to shop; but she would be right back, her note informed him. Walking about in his P.J.s., Serge began to read his penultimate chapter: "A Byzantine Betrayal."

"O, betrayal!" Resurgius cried, "O, treachery!"

"Alas," said Miz Amandalay, climbing in next to him, "she loved you not too well, but, rather, too wiseguyly."

Wiseguyly! It was as if he had intuited Amanda's knowledge of Bettina's secret. He began to put things together. When Bettina kidnapped—well, commandeered—Amanda from the Lunar Society party, something must have happened. Amanda must have discovered Bettina's secret—and the tape!—she must have recorded everything Bettina said—and he had enough experience with Bettina to imagine what that might have been—and later sent the tape to the board. *Blackmail!* Now he understood clearly. Oh, what a mighty woman was his Amanda Quaint! If only she could share her strength and empower *him*!

Everything had been arranged for him—chair, table, typewriter, and paper. He sat down at his Olympia, and—DA-DOT, DA-DA!—began—CHAPTER . . .

Again, he couldn't remember what chapter it was. He was never any good at numbers.

Losing shame and gaining pride with every advance, the Dongs had fought their way to the Pink House. It was over for the Evil Mize. The rest of the female population sent

117

emissaries to the Dongs to inform them that they, too, were happy to be out from under the oppressive thumbs of the dictatorial Mize. The war was over.

Handy Mandy, as Resurgius sometimes called Miz Mandalay, because she had been so helpful to him during the war, asked Resurgius what he thought should be done now that they were in power.

"The New Order should not be one in which either sex is in a superior position, nor should it be one of equality— male and female are obviously not the same. They are two halves of a whole. In other words, they are complementary." He studied the beautiful woman before him. "Ah, but you are my better half."

He went on: "This revolution business is too much for me," he said, pushing his hornrimmed glasses up through his lush locks to the top of his extra large and scholarly head. "I just wish I could go off to some distant paradise and lead a quiet, meditative life, reading the rest of the Western canon, re-reading all the wisdom books, and studying Eastern philosophy."

You're just tired," Miz Mandalay soothed. "You've been through hell."

"To hell and back," Resurgius said stoically.

"My hero," Miz Mandalay commented, squeezing his powerful thigh.

"Mandalay?"

"Yes, dear?"

"Would you consider giving up all this—the political life, I mean—and running off with me to a desert planet, where it would just be you and me and the drifting meteorites?"

"Well, dear, I do so hate to see you give up all that you've fought so hard for; but, naturally, my love, whither thou goest, I will go. In the face of love, the life of politics seems but pale mundane trash. After all, as Jaye Edgahoova

118

might say, politics is nothing but the profound entertainment of the people. I am no longer that interested in entertaining the people. I am in love, and therefore selfish; and perhaps that is the best way to be. At least, if I'm minding my own business, I won't be doing them any harm, poor devils. Pity poor people, they have no sense. I often wonder why they do what we tell them to."

"Because they're afraid to think for themselves. Because they mix us up with their ideals, their hopes and dreams. They're the lemmings and we are the force of the ocean, drawing them to us. That's all."

"It's really quite sad."

"Then you'll go with me?"

"Anywhere, anytime."

"Tomorrow morning, to the moon. From there we can get the shuttle on to Mars."

"It'll be like an old-fashioned honeymoon."

"Let's start tonight. The honeymoon part, I mean."

"Oh, you!"

But it was only a dream, and in dreams begin responsibilities, as the ancient Irish were wont to say. They knew that people, all people, needed them as they represented, as a power couple, the true balancing and partnership of the sexes.

Next day, Resurgius brought charges against Miz Bet and banished her to the dark side of the moon, where rumor had it that she joined Edgahoova.

The disposition of Furius was another matter. The woman was half mad, and so in good conscience could not be punished. Resurgius, after much deliberation with Handy Mandy, decided to have her institutionalized in one of those charming new Neptunese padded cellular houses in Washington Square in Greenwich Village.

Resurgius and Handy Mandy were married. Both died in office, Resurgius first—of a heart attack from carrying

119

Handy Mandy's luggage—and Handy Mandy, in her sleep, twenty years later. Both were beloved by the populace.

10

"That last chapter is wonderful," said Juanna Donna. "I so glad for you that you have done it and so proud of you, my little Mighty Mouse. No, no, Juanna Donna has said wrong. You not my little Mighty Mouse. You my mighty macho man, Resurgius himself! I never call you anything but my mighty macho man again, 'cause look what you have done!"

"And Juanna Donna, I have more big news for you. You know my problem . . . "

"You mean the way you has to go to the bathroom?"

"I do it like John Wayne now. I could stand up and do it right against a tree."

"Is a miracle! And you know what do that to you? Is because you wrote this book. And what is that I see beneath your nose? Don't turn away. You don't fool Juanna Donna. Is a leetle red mustache coming out there? Very macho!"

"And I owe it all to you, Juanna Donna. To Amanda, and to you and those little red diablos that kept me going when I was so exhausted at night."

"Phooey! There is no such thing as little red diablo. I have been giving you Doctor Spinoza's Red Regulators. They for constipation, sluggishness, and change of life— which both of us is going through. See? You stand up at the toilet. They make me sit down. You no think I would give my bambino bad drugs, do you? I would never do that!"

"But why did they work? I mean, how did they keep me up to work?"

"They didn't! Is all a state of mind, niño—I mean, Resurgio—all a state of mind. The coffee must have helped, but mostly it was just being encouraged. Encouragement what inspired you."

"Well," said Amanda, late that evening, as she and Serge sat together in bed, "I love it!   But, as your editor, I think you're going to have to re-write that whole last chapter.

"No! What's wrong with it? Juanna Donna said it was wonderful."

"Why just everything! Why should you die and I live twenty years more?"

"That's what the actuarial charts tell us. On the average, women live twenty years longer than men. Besides, Miz Amandalay isn't you and Resurgius isn't me.   They are rounded, compound characters, each made from several people."

"Nonsense," said Amanda. "It's plain as day who they are. I don't like Handy Mandy. That's an awful name."

"But remember, in an earlier chapter, Miz Mandalay tells Resurgius to call her that. She says, 'From now on, I want you to call me Handy Mandy. Miz Mandalay is my old Univacual name'."

"And another thing," said Amanda, ignoring him, "all of these names have to be changed. I can identify everybody in this story. And what's more, I want a more romantic ending."

"Are we having our first argument?"

"Now, don't pout, Serge! Say, what's that under your nose? Are you growing a mustache?"

"Well—"

"Don't worry. I like it. It gives you a certain—*savoir faire*." She took off her reading glasses, put them and the manuscript on the bedside table, and slid an arm around his neck. "Come on, Sweetie Pie, come close."

Next morning, Juanna Donna woke them. "I has a message for you," she said, nodding at Serge. "Mama call and wants you come to Bethune Street."

Well, it was here—the moment he had dreaded. He must confront his family and tell them that he was not going to return to them; that he had a new life. But now that *Resurgius* was done, and with his new red mustache on his prow, he felt that he could do it.

On his way to the subway, Serge spotted the Quaint Wiener airship sailing off in the distance over Brooklyn, a red wiener hovering in the blue morning sky. He told himself it was a talisman, that it indicated that his meeting with his mother and his Aunties would not go too badly.

At Bethune Street, the door was opened by—

"Hector!"

"No, no, no, señor Serge! I am proud to be Doña Lola Fabiola Lorca, the true queen of the Lorcas. My sister, Juanna Donna, is only pretender."

"It's amazing," said Serge. "I only just left her and I feel as if I'm seeing her again. It's as if she'd been transported in a time machine."

"Come on in, your mother and your aunties are waiting to see you. Be nice. I think they want to make up with you."

Serge's mother, his Auntie Hoover and the Boadicea triplets were gathered in the living room, as for a family conference. Serge felt as if he had entered a scene from a Victorian novel. Mother and aunties didn't seem to know quite what to say or how to say it.

"It's good to see you all looking well," Serge said. It seemed a bit formal, so he added, "Look, I'm sorry if I caused you any pain. But I'm out on my own now, and I'm going to stay out, and—"

"Oh," said Auntie Hoover, "we don't mind that you've left us . . ."

"No," said his mother, "we're glad to see that you're standing on your own two feet. We never meant to hurt you. After all, you're twenty-three years old and you should be out on your own. My God," she cried, "you've got a whispy whisk-broom under your nose!"

"And maybe," Auntie Hoover rolled on, "we lost track of how old you were because sometimes it seemed as if you were never going to go out on your own. We're not really mad because you left home. But did you have to make such fun of us, ridicule us that way, in that awful book? It was shocking to think that you hated us so much. After all, we're just women, and you were a boy, and maybe we made mistakes bringing you up, but we always loved you."

"We always loved you," echoed his mother.

"We always loved you," chorused the three Boadicea aunties.

"And you made us look like monsters," said Auntie Hoover.

"But the characters in that story weren't *you*," said Serge.

"Jaye Edgahoova?" Auntie Hoover wanted to believe Serge but looked doubtful.

"And anyway," said Serge, "I'm a poet who wrote a novel, not a novelist who writes poetry. I should stick to what I'm—well, I write better poetry than I do fiction."

"I should say," said his mother. "The novel made me furious, and I'm so relieved to hear that you really didn't have us in mind."

"We should say," chorused the three aunties. But Aunt Annie threw him a wink.

He couldn't help smiling, and suddenly everybody was smiling, even Lola Fabiola, standing in the doorway with a tray laden with coffee and croissants.

"When can we all meet your Amanda?" asked Auntie Hoover. "Is it true, that she's related to Manny Quaint, the Wiener King?"

"She's his granddaughter."

123

"I should have Bettina contact him about a campaign contribution," she said. "He's richer than a king."

"And a wonderful old guy," said Serge. "He's going to buy us a slam-bang wedding."

"When's it to be?" asked his mother, full of uncharacteristic, girlish excitement.

"This coming June, of course. Amanda wants to be a June bride."

A comedy—even a sex comedy—thought Serge—should end with a wedding. And in June there was a photograph on the cover of *Women's Omnibus* magazine of the wedding of the Wiener King's granddaughter, Amanda Quaint, and the young poet, Serge Bering-Strait.

The ceremony took place in Central Park, at the Tavern on the Green, where the Quaint Wiener airship had touched down on a day when the sky was blue as only a wedding day sky can be. The photo on the cover of *Women's Omnibus* showed the beautiful bride helping her dashingly mustachioed groom into the gondola of the famous Quaint Wiener airship.

Whatever secret location they sailed off to, the honeymoon would certainly be in paradise. Yes, Amanda had removed the ring from Serge's nose and put it on his finger, and Serge just knew that, like a prince in a fairy tale, a fairy tale with a beautiful princess, they would live happily ever after.

MONSIEUR ÉLAN

He insisted on life before death.
He went about waking people up,
refusing to let them sleep,
shouting "Rise and shine!"
He played a bugle call.
He was all for the sun.
Everyone began to hate him
and to shun him.
But he sought them out,
banging a tin drum,
commanding quick march.
He pursued them through life
like the spirit of life,
glad to be trouble.
Finally, finally, finally,
we attended his funeral
and went home to bed,
just dead.

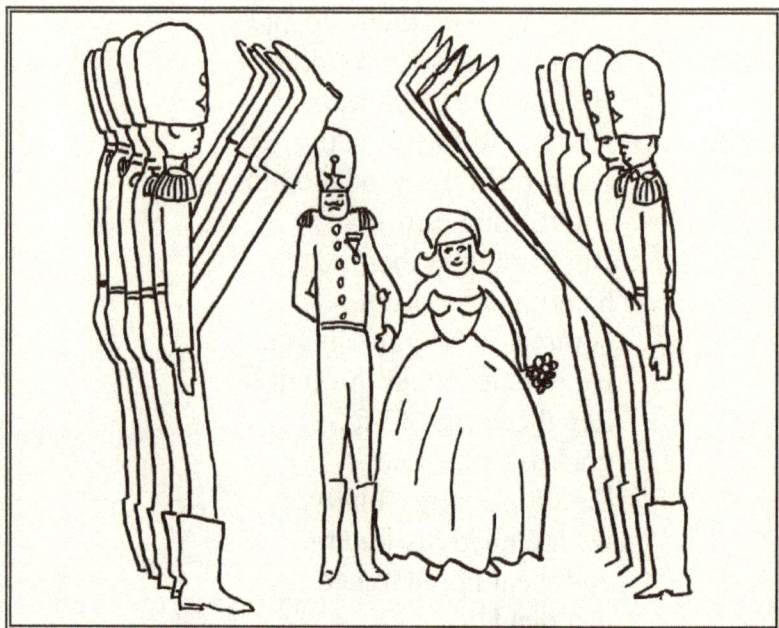

THE GIRL UPSTAIRS

West Seventy-first Street in Manhattan was a shabby, low-rent neighborhood in Nineteen Fifty-eight and they lived in the worst building on the block, a big, ancient brownstone warren. Vera had complained for months that the apartment was dark and dingy and Jimmy calculated that a coat of paint might just cozy the place up enough to make her feel more at home—to subliminally contribute to cooling her on the idea of striking out for Hollywood. Jimmy was a drama student and his mentor, a famous European dramatist, had pulled strings and had practically set up a very promising film gig for him. But Jimmy, an ex-Marine who was of a studious bent, was also attending N.Y.U. on the G.I. Bill, and had deep misgivings. He wanted an education. Something solid. Not the shimmering mirage of tinseltown.

Vera liked pink, so they went out and bought several gallons of pink paint. And one day when they were standing with rollers in their hands and the door open for air, the new young lady from upstairs, whom they had passed once or twice in the hall, stopped at their door, introducing herself as Lola Sherrill. She was eighteen, from Missouri, a singer, and was looking for work. Vera invited her down for supper. Lola said that she wouldn't dream of eating supper with them unless she could help them with the painting. Later Jimmy took a break and went into the kitchenette, a curtained, wall-debouched hall with a small bathroom to one side, to get a can of beer. He discovered that Vera was whipping up a big gourmet spread, to impress their new neighbor. "Paella," she said. "It's Spanish."

Jimmy drank his beer, listened to some jazz, thumbed through *War and Peace*, and after a while a knock came at the door. He opened the door, and there was Lola, in skin-tight, see-through leotards. "I've come to help you paint."

Vera called from the kitchenette: "Ask Lola to come in."

"Well, come on in, Lola," Jimmy said. He felt like an endangered species. He knew that, somehow, Vera would blame him for Lola's state of undress. He said, "I'll just break out more paint."

Vera popped out. She was hot and bedraggled from cooking, paint-smeared: had been hitting the bottle. And there was Lola, dipping her cello-bottom this way and that as she painted, her see-through tights displaying with perfect clarity the flexures of each ample adorable cheek. Vera stopped short in the doorway of the kitchenette, the curtain tangled over one shoulder, took Lola in with a deep inspiration, and looked at Jimmy as if he had pulled off Lola's knickers.

Jimmy stirred paint so fast that it spattered on his shirtless torso, turning his taut tummy pink.

Lola said, "I'm helping your husband."

Jimmy thought: "Either this is the dumbest dame I've ever met, or she has more chutzpa than a vacuum cleaner salesman in a marble hall."

Vera said, "Well, Lola, I think we should call it a day on the painting, now."

Jimmy thought it was about time for him to put his two-cents in. He said, "Maybe we can get this wall done before we quit. Why don't you just go ahead and concentrate on supper. It smells good." He meant it. They could use the help, and he didn't care what it wore, or didn't wear.

"Yes," piped Lola, "I'll help Jimmy get the painting done. I'm a good painter."

Vera went back to cooking. Pots and pans could be heard whizbanging in the kitchenette. Jimmy was having a good afternoon, even though Vera kept popping in and out; and every time she caught him looking at Lola, which he couldn't help doing, gave him one of her You'll-pay-for-this looks.

Vera came out, Merlot in hand, finally, to survey the job. She stood with Lola and admired the wall. Jimmy heard Lola say, "I'm glad I could be of help." Vera had the table set and told them to wash and come and eat.

At last, Lola's behind was out of sight, on a chair, and her legs were under the table.

"Oh, this Paella looks delicious," she said, and Jimmy felt her pink-nailed toes walking up his leg. No shoes, either, of course. He moved his leg away to see if the walk wasn't an accident.

"Yummy!" cried Lola. "You are a *wonderful* cook, Vera," and back came the tootsies.

"She sure is," said Jimmy in a disturbed voice. No doubt about anything now. Lola was pure brass.

It seemed to Jimmy that Lola certainly knew how Vera felt, maybe could tell that Vera wasn't too stable, and was actually trying to make her crack. He did not know how else to explain Lola, a stranger, sitting there wearing next to nothing, running her chubby little toes up and down his leg while his wife looked on! Vera didn't show it, but Jimmy thought that she must know what was going on under the table.

"Why doesn't she blow up?" he asked himself, and kept moving his legs away from Lola's groping toes; but he couldn't well dodge Lola and not be obvious about it. The table was too small. Then, through his alcoholic fog, he could see that Vera was on to Lola. He could also see that Lola knew that Vera knew, but didn't care what Vera thought.

They were all getting drunk. Vera slammed down her fork. "Whatever you're doing, Jimmy, I want you to stop it."

"Really, Vera, your Jimmy hasn't done anything to deserve the way you're treating him."

Jimmy got up and went to the bathroom. He took a long freedom-loving pee.

"Hell, no!" he said to himself, stepping out and zipping up.

"What have I done?" He was crocked, and not at all sure of what had taken place during the course of the evening.

"But if you feel that way," Jimmy heard Lola say, "I'll go up to my own place."

"Go ahead, you ungrateful little bitch!" said Vera, tears squirting from her eyes.

Lola said: "But not till we clear the air."

"You *want* him!" cried Vera. "You *desire* him!"

"I don't want your stupid husband," Lola shouted, then looked at Jimmy apologetically. "You're just crazy, that's all! Everybody in the building knows it. You're crazy. We *all* hear you!"

Jimmy went back to the kitchenette to fix himself a drink. Now Vera was crying, Lola consoling.

"Vera's about to be violent," he thought, remembering how she cried, like a bird of prey, before she swooped; and just then she flew by him, like a great mad bird, and locked herself in the bathroom. Lola pursued; pulled at the door knob.

"She's going to kill herself!" Lola cried. Jimmy told her not to worry. "She loves every ounce of herself. She's a performer."

Vera heard him—"I heard that!"—and flew out wielding her little pink Princess safety razor. She went straight for him. He fended her off, and she kept on going into the front room. Then swaths of pink paint came back, like watery cotton candy. *Swash! Swash!*

Lola had got more than she'd bargained for. She cowered behind the freshly pinked refrigerator. *Crash!* they heard the front window break. Vera had thrown an open can of paint through it.

130

Sirens sounded through the shattered glass.

Vera heard them. She was scared now. She had done something fairly serious this time and it panicked her. She charged back into the kitchenette and then locked herself in the bathroom again. "This time I really *am* going to kill myself," she shouted through the door.

Jimmy noticed that she still had the razor with her. Maybe she *was* going to do it this time. She had had enough to drink, meaning too much even for the survival instinct.

Lola put her arms around Jimmy's neck.

"What should we do?" she said, rolling big brown eyes.

He put a hand on the behind he had wanted to touch all evening, and said: "I don't know." He didn't.

Lola said, "Shall we break the door down?"

He told her that he couldn't; he had had occasion to try.

Vera screamed. It was the worst fit of many. Jimmy was more than a little scared himself. He put his drink down and put another hand on another cheek. What a behind!

The hall door was being pounded. "Open up, police!" He went to the door and opened it.

"What's going on here?"

He tried to explain the situation.

The building super, who was gay, stood behind the police. He liked Jimmy, disliked Vera. Jimmy could see that the super had been talking to the cops. They gave Lola the twice-over, but there was too much confusion. "Come on out of there," one of them called to Vera.

"I'm going to kill myself."

"Do you think she'd do it?" one of the cops asked.

"No," Jimmy said.

"Yes," said the super. "She crazy bitch. Oh, I sorry, mister, but I hear."

"I think she would," said Lola. Jimmy wondered if she wasn't hoping so.

"I will!" cried Vera.

"In that case," said a cop, "I'm calling Bellevue."

"No," Jimmy said. "Don't do that." He was weakening, as he often did, beginning to feel sorry for Vera. This was how he always lost his wars with Vera—pity.

"This is out of your hands now," said the cop. "Have you got a phone?"

"It's in here," said Lola.

The bathroom door flew open and there stood the wild woman herself. She had pink paint all over her, and looked pitiful.

"Don't let them take me to Bellevue," she cried. "Please don't let them."

"It's out of his hands," said a cop, grabbing her. "You're nuts, lady."

"They'll help you there, Vera," said Lola, nursily.

"You little. . ." fumed Vera, speech failing her, and *wham,* she threw her Princess safety razor at Lola. *Zing!* It missed. Both cops seized her arms.

Then the men in the white suits showed up. "We'll help you," they said.

Jimmy fixed himself a drink. He looked away while Vera was carried out in a straight jacket, screaming and kicking. He was not allowed to go with her. He went to the radio and turned it on. Music! Lola had assumed the role of hostess. She saw the whole menagerie out. Suddenly it was very quiet in the apartment.

Jimmy went to the window. Vera had cleared the glass out of it, but for a few jagged pieces. He leaned out and saw that there was a lovely long swath of pink paint down the front of the old brownstone. Below, there was a fracas. A small crowd watched as Vera was dragged, kicking and screaming, to the nut wagon. Lola came up behind him and put her arms around his waist.

"You poor man," she crooned.

A bitter little laugh caught in his throat. "She certainly brightened the old place up," he said. "Did they say when I can see her?"

"They said you could visit her tomorrow morning. Now you come over here and sit down. I'll fix you a fresh drink. Then, later, I'll sing you to sleep. I'm really a very good singer, you know. I'll be a star in no time."

The next morning Lola left him to find herself a singing job. She kissed him goodbye and promised more delights upon her return. Vera, however, was released to him at ten that morning. So there wasn't much chance for Lola to get at them again and Vera made it no chance at all. Jimmy was to accept that Hollywood offer immediately. After a few phonecalls, she insisted that they leave for the west coast that very afternoon.

After all, what could be better than La La Land?

TO A RAT

Rat, you frighten me,
though I understand perfectly well
that I as well frighten,
indeed frightened you,
coming around the corner
from the garbage bag,
your whiskers winking
on your corrugated snout
and your two little
beads of eyes glinting,
black beads
with some little mind
behind them
and a soul.

Ah yes, you have a soul:
I saw it with my own two
frightened eyes,
little rat.

I was alone
when you waddled
around the corner,
saw me and, for an instant,
flattened everything about yourself,
sniffing snout,
bead eyes,
long gray tail,
then scampered off,
terrified,
like the rat that you are,
you rat,
you dirty rat,

you poor little devil,
you sad little pilferer,
you filth, you pest,
you spreader of plague,
you biter of babies,
you rodent,
you cousin
of the bright-eyed squirrel,
you poor
relation, you scum,
you inelegant bum!

Now there's a trap
in the corner
with a cheese slice in it.
Don't make it snap.
Things are tough
enough
as they are.

COCKTAILS FOR TWO?

John Ciardi
liked Bacardi
but drank Chianti
with his Auntie.

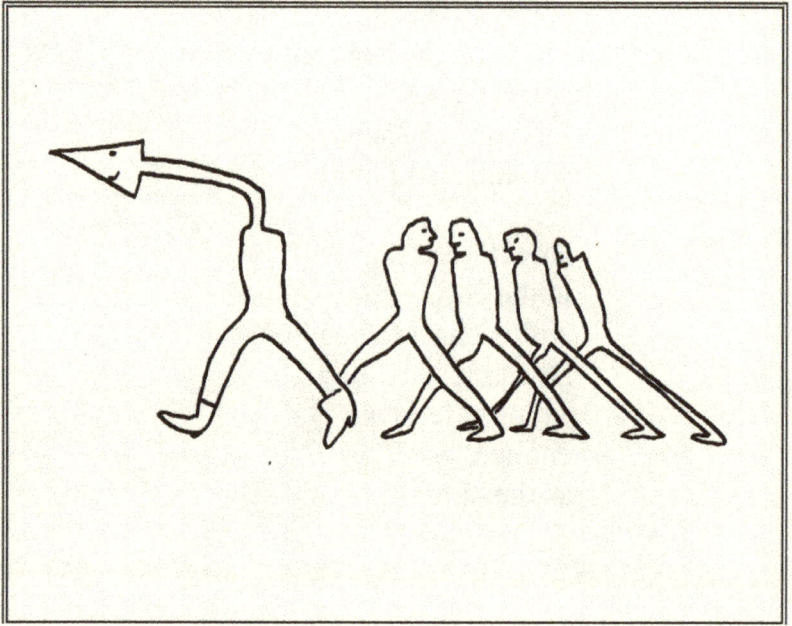

AN ACTOR PREPARES

The actor must use his imagination to be able to answer all questions. Make the make-believer existence more definite.

—Constantin Stanislavski

Jimmy Whistler, a struggling actor, and his widowed mother, Fay, superintended an upscale apartment building, named The Mondrian, in Greenwich Village.

His neurasthenic girlfriend, Phyllis, called Jimmy in the middle of August to tell him that her parents were coming East from Seattle for a visit—just a week-end—and she wanted him to go with her to show them around. In fact, she wanted Jimmy to play husband, which is what those two poor deluded people still thought him to be—their never-met son-in-law. The father, of course had been in and out of New York often, in the past few years, being, as he was, a pilot for a major airline, and having had, for a time, a regular run between New York and Seattle. About a year and a half ago, he had been switched to a run between Seattle and Tokyo, and that had saved Jimmy and Phyllis a great many headaches. Before that, when in New York, he'd tried to meet Jimmy several times, but Jimmy had always somehow avoided the encounter. Phyllis had met her father uptown several times, but had told him that her "husband" was called away, was sick, had to work, was drafted—any lie she could think up to save Jimmy the meeting and still not make her father suspicious. But this time her parents had written: "We are coming East to see a few shows, but more especially to meet Jim. We sincerely hope that nothing will happen to make that impossible."

"You've just got to meet them, Jimmy," Phyllis said. "I don't think they believe me when I tell them about you anymore. Please, just this once."

Jimmy couldn't find it in his heart to refuse her. But, on the other hand, he didn't like the idea of pulling off such an imposture. He was an actor, not a liar. He didn't want to lie to a couple of (probably) nice people, to make them think he was their son-in-law. Phyllis shouldn't have told them that they were married in the first place, but surely she should have told them that they weren't, by now.

The fact was that they were hardly even seeing each other nowadays. Jimmy had always considered Phyllis more of a friend than a lover, though that had been part of their relationship for a while, the result of Jimmy enjoying her intellectual companionship, and his affection for her, but she was not Jimmy's type when it came to amorous affairs.

Phyllis was careless in the extreme about her appearance—she'd let her teeth go badly, though her parents would have been delighted to send her to any of the best orthodonists; she did not eat well, and she experimented with some of the lesser drugs, so she was undernourished and sallow of complexion. She loved getting clothes at the Salvation Army and other thrift shops and often wore a hodgepodge of odd garments. Many things had conspired to cause Jimmy to want to keep his distance from dear little Phyl, for whom he otherwise felt a great warmth of genuine affection, perhaps even a touch of love. She had a wonderful witty quick mind and a charmingly skeptical view of life. She said it was "a bullshit world," and that she could prove it anytime she liked.

That was the situation. Well, that was the half of it. As if things weren't complicated enough, Jimmy's "in-laws" were coming to New York on the same weekend that Fay had invited her sister, Jimmy's Aunt Myrtle and her husband, Uncle O'Toole, as Jimmy had always called him, to visit. It was going to be a busy weekend.

138

Fay worked very hard on their super's basement apartment all week. She had polished the furniture, put up new curtains, waxed and rewaxed the rubber-tiled floor till it was gleaming—in short, she had prepared it for the inspection of her fastidious big sister, Aunt Myrtle, and for the enjoyment of her equally fastidious brother-in-law, Uncle Albert O'Toole. It was Fay's intention to show her lace-curtain Irish relatives how well she was doing—and, indeed, the apartment looked very pretty, entirely satisfactory for that purpose. By Friday afternoon, she had a roast pork in the oven, three pies baked, hors d'oeuvres on a platter on the table, drinks mixed, etc., and was in the process of getting herself dressed to receive her visitors.

Jimmy, too, was getting himself dressed in his best bib and tucker. He'd accumulated a few clothes in the past year, and was now able to make himself fairly presentable in a well-cut, good-fitting suit, a chocolate shirt, cream-colored tie, and a new pair of oxblood loafers. He was slimmer, now, than he'd been for quite a time, and he had a good tanning machine tan, and his hair, like the Washington Square grass of that summer, was bleached, with strands of bright gold running through it. He had gone to college on the G.I. Bill, majoring in drama, and was now appearing with an off-Broadway repertory company. Jimmy was dedicated to the art and craft of acting, and couldn't help but feel that this weekend presented him with a challenge, even if there was a lie involved. After all, acting was lying, of sorts, wasn't it? For now, his dilemma had no horns.

Fay and Jimmy had discussed the situation, and decided upon a plan of action. Since Fay had no intention of meeting Phyllis's parents and palming herself off as Phyllis's mother-in-law, Jimmy would tell Phyllis's parents that his Mother was away, visiting her sister in New Jersey, and that he had been unable to get in touch with her in time to have her back in New York to meet them. It was a frail story, but Jimmy thought he'd be able to bluff it through. Furthermore, he'd tell them that he'd volunteered to help keep the house that she superintended in good shape while she was away, and that would give him an excuse to spend some time with Fay and Aunt Myrtle and Uncle O'Toole. A lot would depend upon what Phyllis's parents wanted to do; and, of course, upon what Aunt Myrtle and Uncle O'Toole wanted to do.

First, Jimmy was to wait and meet and greet Aunt Myrtle and Uncle O'Toole when they arrived at five, then he'd make some excuse or other and leave and go over to pick up Phyllis, and, from there, go uptown to the hotel where Phyllis's parents were staying, and meet them.

At ten minutes after five the doorbell rang, Jimmy pushed the buzzer, asked who was there, over the speaker, and heard Uncle O'Toole, his voice full of static, say, "Jimmy? Is that you, Jimmy? Uncle O'Toole here. How do we find you?" They were in the lobby. Jimmy went upstairs and led them back down.

Nervous laughter.

Confusion.

Hugs and kisses.

"Say, this is a pretty fancy building," said Uncle O'Toole.

"What a lovely apartment!" said Aunt Myrtle.

"Do you mean you get this apartment free?" asked Uncle O'Toole. "Do you get tips, Jimmy? Well, let *me* give you a tip. Save your money. Ha-ha!"

"What lovely curtains!" said Aunt Myrtle.

"What smells so good?" asked Uncle O'Toole.

"Fay, you look lovely!" said Aunt Myrtle.

"You're lookin' good, Jimmy," said Uncle O'Toole. "Lost a little weight?"

"Do you get a salary here, too?" asked Aunt Myrtle.

"Quite a deal you've got here," said Uncle O'Toole.

They all sat down and had a couple of drinks together; then Jimmy excused himself, saying that he had to go over to the docks (his day job) to pick up his pay check, and that he'd be back as soon as possible.

He grabbed a taxi out on Seventh Avenue and scooted over to pick up Phyllis. When he got there, she was all aflutter. She was worried about how she looked, but Jimmy couldn't remember the last time he'd seen her looking so nice. She had her fine, pale hair in an upsweep, and was wearing a pretty teal suit. She wanted to know if she looked nice, and he told her that she did.

"Oh, this is such a lot of bullshit," she said nervously. "If only I didn't have to pretend with them."

Jimmy's sentiments exactly. Then she donned her tan raincoat and picked up her little native-American beaded pocketbook, and spoiled the whole thing.

"Haven't you got another purse to carry?"

"What's wrong with this one?"

"It looks like you picked it out of an ashcan somewhere in New Mexico," he said.

"Well, it's the only one I've got," she snapped angrily.

When they got out of the subway in the midtown area, Jimmy stepped into a store and bought a plain black pocketbook for her.

"But what'll I do with this one?"

"Put it inside the black one."

"Bullshit!" she said, as she did so.

Jimmy stopped her again, taking his handkerchief and wiping off some of the excess rouge from her face. He hadn't noticed it in the house, but out in the daylight she looked like she had a target on each cheek. Ordinarily, she never wore makeup, and, surprisingly, for a girl who could paint pictures, was considered by some to be a serious artist, she had developed no skill whatever in the use of makeup. Jimmy, on the other hand, had been taught to do theatrical makeup. He

141

stood, dabbing at her with his handkerchief, trying to tone her down a bit, while she cursed and complained, full of impatience.

"To hell with it!" she said. "Come on; let's go!"

"Well, you don't want to look like you're ready for a war dance, do you?"

"To hell with it! It's just a lot of bullshit."

The poor little thing. She was more nervous than he was, and he wasn't exactly calm.

Her parents were staying at a good hotel in the upper-midtown area. At the desk, Phyllis called their room. They were told to come right up.

Jimmy felt embarrassed getting into the elevator. The incongruity of their situation struck him. He disliked himself for feeling it, but Phyllis embarrassed him. She hadn't stood still for his treatment, and her makeup was smeared. The black pocketbook he'd bought her in such a hurry seemed far too large and awkward for her (still, it was an improvement over the beaded Indian one that was contained in it). And Jimmy could see, now, that her pretty teal suit had black cat hairs all over it; and her stockings hung loose and twisted on her thin legs. Some of the upsweep of her hair had come tumbling down, and despite the autumnal chill, she had beads of nervous sweat on her forehead, corrugating her face powder. Little Phyllis was not beautiful, but had she had the instinct for adornment of a primitive, she could have made herself appear quite attractive. But the instinct for adornment was completely missing from her personality. Makeup was missing from her makeup. Looking at her, Jimmy wondered what her parents would think. Here he was—tall, well-built, and, by most accounts, good-looking. Would they think he was some kind of fortune hunter, taking advantage of their little Phyllis? Some kind of rogue? How could they ever understand how it was that Phyllis and he had got together? How could they understand the tenderness he felt for her, his

142

admiration of her gutsyness and her artistry? How, perhaps, theirs was a case of friendship gone too far?

The elevator stopped: they got out and found the appropriate door and knocked.

"How do I look?" Phyllis asked.

"Fine," Jimmy said. "You look fine."

The door was opened by a round-faced, good-humored-looking man of medium height, wearing a grey pilot's uniform. He had a ruddy complexion, blue eyes, and close-cropped salt-and-pepper hair. He was holding a cocktail glass in his hand.

"Daddy," Phyllis said, and threw her arms around his neck. Then she pulled away and turned to Jimmy, saying:

"Daddy, I want you to meet my husband, Jimmy. Jimmy Whistler."

The pilot, smiling, extended a hand to Jimmy. Jimmy took it and shook it.

"So you're my son-in-law, are you?" he said; and Jimmy thought for an instant that he doubted it.

"Meet your mother-in-law, Jimmy." A slim, attractive woman stepped forward.

"Mummy!" Phyllis cried, and threw herself into her mother's arms as she had into her father's. When "Mummy" had disengaged herself, she came to Jimmy, put her arms around his neck, and planted a kiss on him.

"My, Phyl, but your husband is a handsome young man," she said, and then to Jimmy: "I want to welcome you into our family, Jimmy. Do you realize that you and Phyl have been married for over three years and this is the first time I've laid eyes on you. Well, I certainly like what I see."

Jimmy felt crummy. How could he have ever got himself into something like this?

"Have a drink, Jimmy?" asked the pilot.

"Yes," he said, "please."

"Canadian Club?"

"Fine."

"Soda?"

"Please."

"Ice?"

"Please."

"Well, Phyl. . ." said the mother, holding her daughter at arm's-length and looking at her, "you look just fine. Married life seems to agree with you."

"Yes," said the father, handing Jimmy a drink, "you look well, kitten. You know," he said, speaking to Jimmy, "Phyl was a sickly little girl. She had one thing after another. Not like her sister at all. Her sister was a regular little butterball. But Phyl looks like she's putting on some weight, now, too, dear," he said, addressing his wife, "doesn't she?"

"Yes, she looks wonderful."

"I bet," said the father, "that you make her eat; don't you, Jimmy?"

"Yes, I try." It was true; but Phyllis was anorexic.

"Oh, I can see it," said the mother.

"Why don't we eat now?" said the father. "Let's go down to the restaurant and we'll all have a nice dinner. How's that sound?"

They went down to the hotel dining room and ate. The mother had fried shrimp, and Phyllis and the father and Jimmy had Lobster Newburgh. Jimmy was so nervous during the meal that he choked. All he could think of was getting away from these good people before he tipped his hand. They weren't unusually inquisitive, but naturally they had a great many questions to ask of the young man whom they thought to be their son-in-law. That was what they took him for, it seemed. And they seemed to like him, too. Jimmy wondered how Phyllis was going to explain this away in years to come. She'd probably tell them that they'd got a divorce on the grounds of mental cruelty and Jimmy's stock with them

144

would hit bottom. Even now, that future time troubled him. Being an actor, he liked to be liked.

Phyllis was ecstatically happy. Jimmy could see that she was very proud of having got herself married, in their eyes. Probably she never thought the day would come when a young man whom she could claim as her husband would sit at a table with herself and her parents and please them so. For her sake, Jimmy was very attentive to her, and tried to show the parents that he loved her, which, in fact, he did. But he felt that the whole thing was not only preposterous, but sad. He knew in his heart that he wouldn't be with Phyl much longer, and this seemed an awful crime to commit near the end of their time together.

They left her parents that night with the understanding that they would meet at ten the next morning and that they'd take a tour of New York together, and, later, Saturday evening, they'd all go to a play, and afterwards have a few drinks and a snack somewhere.

Phyllis knew that Aunt Myrtle and Uncle O'Toole were at The Mondrian, so she didn't object to Jimmy taking a different train and going straight there. When he kissed her goodbye on the subway platform, she thanked him for going to meet her parents, and said: "Wasn't it really nice? I mean, they're real squares, but aren't they nice? Do you like them, Jimmy?"

Jimmy said that it was and that they were and that he did.

"Oh, Jimmy, why can't we be really married?" she asked wistfully.

He felt like a criminal.

When he got to The Mondrian, there was a party in full swing. Fay was dancing with Uncle O'Toole, and Aunt Myrtle was engaged in a monologue about her grandchildren. They were three sozzled sheets in the wind. Jimmy sat down, nervously exhausted, but relieved to be at home, and let Aunt Myrtle chatter at him while he drank a good stiff drink.

Aunt Myrtle was only about two years older than Fay; but Fay, who'd kept her figure, looked about twenty years younger. Uncle O'Toole, who referred to himself as "a tough guy from Joisey," was a lean, dapper man in his late sixties. He did not have the same settled appearance as his wife. He was a wiry, energetic man, full of fun.

"Let's go out somewhere," he said. "This is Greenwich Village, ain't it? Let's go out and get a look at some characters, whatdaya say?"

"Now, O'Toole," Aunt Myrtle put in, "we can't afford to spend—"

"What the hell, Myrt!" said Uncle O'Toole. "You only live once, right Jimmy? Whatdaya say, Fay? Shouldn't we go out and see the characters?"

Uncle O'Toole won the day, or the evening. Jimmy took them out to a place on Seventh Avenue where beer was served in pitchers and a banjo-band played Gay Nineties music. They loved it. They sang with the band and drank the beer until none of them could talk or walk normally, and then Jimmy took them home in a cab. Fay gave them her bed and she took Jimmy's and Jimmy left them all there, puffing and snoring, and went over to Phyllis's to sleep. He set the alarm, and next morning, bright and early, he was there when they came to.

Uncle O'Toole leaped out of bed as full of energy as he'd been early the day before. Aunt Myrtle seemed groggier, but came around fast after an eye-opener. Fay had a hangover, and felt sick. She spent some time in the bathroom, throwing up. Jimmy felt like he was sleep-walking.

Aunt Myrtle wanted to know if there was much of that "mess-sin-ation" around Greenwich Village.

Jimmy gathered that she meant the mixing of the races.

"About as much as anywhere," he told her, never having thought much about it.

Uncle O'Toole said:

"I don't approve of that; do you, Jimmy?"

Jimmy told him that he had nothing against it. "I wouldn't go out of my way to marry a black woman," he said, treading where the ice was thin, "but if I fell in love with a black woman, and we wanted to marry each other, I'd marry her."

"You *would*!" exclaimed Uncle O'Toole, shocked. "But suppose you had a daughter," he said, explaining the problem succinctly, "you wouldn't want your daughter to marry one, would you?"

"Well," Jimmy said, "it looks like if I had already married one, and I had a daughter, I couldn't offer much of an objection to my daughter marrying one, too, could I?"

"Mmmm," said Uncle O'Toole, thoughtfully. "I see your point."

"You're not going to marry one, are you?" asked Aunt Myrtle, genuinely frightened.

"I haven't been asked."

"My God, Fay," cried Aunt Myrtle, "Jimmy isn't thinking of marrying a colored girl, is he?"

"He's only teasing you," Fay said.

"Oh," said Uncle O'Toole, "I get it," and laughed.

Aunt Myrtle said:

"Well, for a minute there, I thought my poor sister was going to become the grandmother of a pickaninny. And me the great-aunt of one. You mustn't do that to her, Jimmy. I know you've got some weird ideas, but she's had a hard enough life as it was, with your father." The thought inspired her. "Oh, what a strange man your father was! I wouldn't have put it past *him* to marry a colored girl."

"Now let's leave him out of this," said Fay. "He's gone to his rest. Let's not talk about him when he's not here to defend himself."

"Well, I was thinking of the life he led you. My dear Albert has never treated me in such a way. He's worked hard all his life. He always supported his wife and children; didn't you, dear?"

"Yeah," said Uncle O'Toole devilishly, "but sometimes I think maybe old Elliot had the right idea."

"Oh," said Aunt Myrtle, turning red, "to say such a thing!"

Jimmy left them there to hash that out, while he went uptown with Phyllis to meet her parents. When he got back from taking a scenic cruise around Manhattan Island, from looking at the "ant-like" people from atop the Empire State Building, and from climbing into the Statue of Liberty's head, the same discussion was still underway back at The Mondrian.

"Why did that man wear his hair like that?" asked Aunt Myrtle.

"He looked like a girl," Uncle O'Toole said.

"Why do you live over here?" Aunt Myrtle wanted to know.

"Was he queer?" asked Uncle O'Toole.

"I'd like to see a lesbian," said Aunt Myrtle.

Next thing Jimmy knew, he was coming out of a theatre on Forty-sixth Street, having just slept through a Rogers & Hammerstein revival. Years before, his coach, Dr. Zolauf had introduced him to them at Carnegie Hall. "You've got to be carefully taught," came to mind.

Phyllis and he walked hand in hand, ahead of her parents. Phyllis said:

"They really love you, Jimmy."

He'd been turning on the charm. Once, in drama school, he played the Hairy Ape, and he felt suddenly swept with nostalgia for the part.

Then he was at The Mondrian again, sitting at the table, and Aunt Myrtle, now thoroughly sloshed, was saying:

"Let's go out and see if we can find a lesbian bar."

"Let's go out, Jimmy," said Uncle O'Toole. I want to see some Bohemians."

Jimmy took them to the White Horse Tavern.

"This is where Dylan Thomas drank himself to death," he said.

But it cut no ice with Aunt Myrtle. Far as she could see, it was just a dump. And who was this Dylan Thomas and where did he get such a funny name?

"He was a famous Welsh poet," said Jimmy.

"Famous for getting drunk and not supporting his wife and children," Uncle O'Toole said, showing a dumbfounding knowledge of modern literature. "I heard all about the bum." This turned several poetic faces in the crowd. The White Horse was a shrine to the Welsh poet.

"Your Uncle O'Toole knows just about everything," said Aunt Myrtle with pride and conviction. "Go ahead, ask him about something."

Jimmy sat, dazed, smiling, his head nodding approval, his mouth in a frozen smiling rictus.

Phyllis's parents left on Sunday afternoon. "We are so glad to have you in the family, Jimmy," her mother said. And to Phyllis: "You take good care of our son-in-law, Phylly, do you hear?"

Aunt Myrtle and Uncle O'Toole left on Sunday evening.

"See you all of a sudden," Uncle O'Toole said waggishly.

"We've had a wonderful time," Aunt Myrtle said, "even if I didn't get to see any lesbians."

149

Exhausted, embarrassed, and ashamed, but having completed the greatest performance of his life, and one that he vowed would have no encores, Jimmy collapsed on his bed at the Mondrian. It had been an epiphany. Now he thought he knew the difference between acting and lying. He hoped he did.

EDUCATION

Because he never went to college,
my father sold the Book of Knowledge.
Myself, I never went to school,
but did devote myself to pool.
Both of us ended on the rocks,
graduates of old Hard Knocks,
alums of Loving Kindness, yet
ignorant on how to get
along in life without degrees,
no forests for us, only trees,
yet publishing our poetry
in *Yale* and *Southern* and *Sewanee*.
Sometimes the editors write back,
Dear Professor, you're no hack,
we wish to publish "Ode on Birds"
in which we find such lovely words.
And I write back and say to them
I'm no professor, all the same.
I never even went to college,
but daddy sold the Book of Knowledge,
and I read it, growing up,
when he and I would share a cup
of sherry over Heraclitus
knowing nothing'd ever right us,
knowing nothing quite stands still,
that only changing always will
keep you up with changing things,
like that river on time's wings
that you can't step into twice
even if you'd pay the price.

Now that dear old daddy's gone,
I think I'll write about a swan.

151

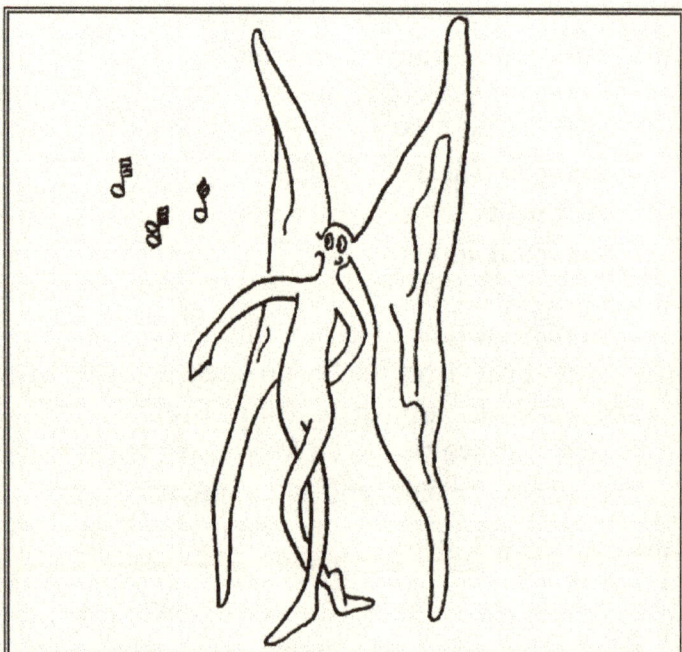

LAST EXIT TO EAST HAMPTON

I will get off the 4:19 in Easthampton at 7:15
—Frank O'Hara

"Entre nous, Roger and I visited some friends out on East Hampton, and there was a wealthy and beautiful chatelaine there, sans man, whose name I have conveniently forgotten, and Roger took up with her, because, *I* think, she looked like Truman Capote, blond and a little plump, and the next thing I know I'm soloing it with my Martini very dry and feeling like a dipstick in the sand. Roger and I are always together and I could not understand such isolation as had befallen me. After all, I was being dumped for a female—well, maybe. But just as I was reaching the blue dog black funk basement on the down elevator, a woman wearing an amazing diamond choker passed on some interesting and distracting gossip. Apparently, Bergdorf's had appropriated Augustus John's portrait of Tallulah, to whom *adieu*, which cheered me I can't tell you how much; and, after swallowing the last of my Martini very dry, I sighed happily, and said, Oh well, we still have beaucoup de music classique et moderne. There was a band all in gold. The diamond-choker lady elbowed my ribs, indicating the door, and so I saw Roger leaving with the beautiful lady (maybe). Absolutely horrid of him, of course. Still, I tittered anyway. Later I took a dive in the pool to cool off. You know how it is. These people are harder than they look, like a roll of Krugerrands you put in your fist to make your hand strong when you punch somebody's lights out. Oh hell, life is beautiful, don't you think?"

NEWS OF 45

Into his mid-life crisis
desperate man stalks wild
life brings home head of
thought for wall display
mounting it for worship
plenty yet more to come
proudly shows it to friends
who scoff saying some
body else got it for you
like hell they did shot
gun see all the holes
in it but its mine mine
mine proud of it autumnal
macho laughable necessary
joy so worry not thy heart
days of glory upon thy
wrinkled brow sparks
of plenty more to come
next better yet which
could be worse who
knows but plunge on
plunge on with no effort
for light takes you
smilingly home as you
stay & practice your
declensions sun-o
moon-a your conju
gations selvesyes
selvesalways selves
before selvesafter
glory glory glory
for my five & forty.

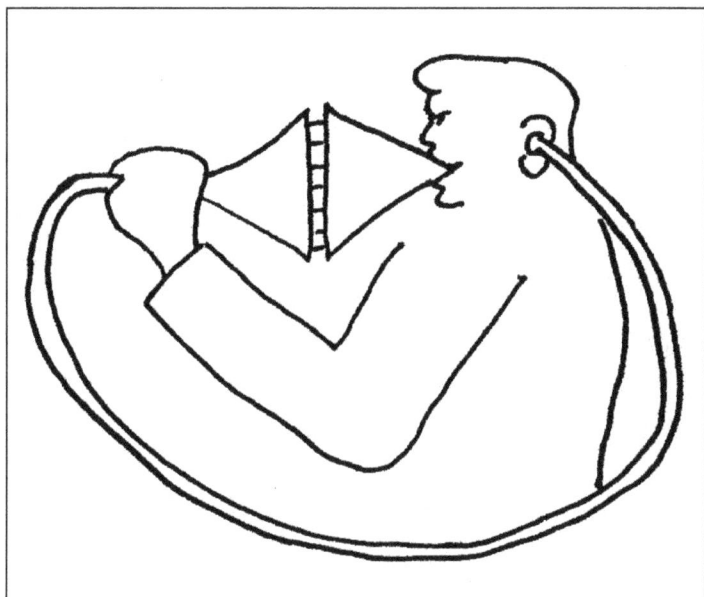

THE SANDAL SHOP

Or

How, while Being Pursued by the Divorce Demon,
Jimmy Whistler Discovered the Beats,
and was Saved by Marsayas, the King of the Beasts

1

The office of Magazine Subscriptions Unlimited was a bustling place, filled with telephones, none of which had time to ring for being dialed. Men and women of all races, creeds, ages, and costumes kept them leaping to their ears and slamming back for an instant's cradling before another leap and dialing. Jimmy Whistler estimated that at least fifty people crowded the place: workers, that is; aside from those, like himself, who waited to be interviewed for a job. Smoke hung heavy in the air, an ectoplasm.

There was a man seated across the table from Jimmy, a man with great broad shoulders, made to appear broader because of the heavy overcoat he was wearing. (It was February, and bitter weather: a fine time to come to New York from California; but nothing Vera and he did made any sense!) The man was big, but not fat. On the contrary, one could see—for he sat pushed back from the table in a sprawling, easy posture—that, where his coat fell open, his waist was neat and narrow. His legs were long and delicately shaped, seeming to be of a lighter bone structure than his upper body. Jimmy could see them plainly through the thin, blue, much-too-shiny summer slacks he wore. But what greatly interested Jimmy about him was that he wore a beard—a rarity in the clean-shaven Fifties and a pronouncement that the hirsute Sixties had arrived—every strand of which was thick as wire and glittery, coppery red. It was nearly a foot in length, and all of a piece, so that it moved

156

with his jaw. It rayed from his chin like a Blakian sun. All this blinding hair began directly under a sensual, long lower lip, flexible and pink as the innertube of a bicycle tire. His kinky hair puffed over his ears and down to his frayed collar. On top he was nearly bald; though Jimmy was to learn that this, his first Beatnik, was only twenty-eight. The big fellow seemed ill-at-ease, perhaps because Jimmy had been studying him so intently—and rudely, too, for that matter—or perhaps because he was waiting, in a place he did not wish to be to do something he had no wish to do.

In any case, after completing his application form, he behaved restively, crossing and uncrossing his legs, smoking cigarette after cigarette, thumbing through magazines, and throwing them back in the pile with a look of irritation on his benignly satanic face. Finally, he started fishing with very long, delicate fingers in an empty cigarette pack. He crumpled the pack in his fist, and startled Jimmy out of his contemplation of him by leaning across the table and, with a show of white teeth and a whisk-broom movement of beard, nearly sweeping away several magazines, asking if he could have a cigarette from him. Jimmy said, "Sure," and gave him one.

He told Jimmy he had just come back from Germany, where he had left his German wife and his two children, a boy and a girl. He had been a language teacher there, for Berlitz: had taught English to the Germans. He was in the process of breaking up with his wife, by his description a stuffily middle-class Hausfrau. He was staying with an aunt and uncle, a staid old couple, out on Long Island. They had ordered him to look for a job; and so, to appease them, he was making this half-hearted effort. But he had other things in mind, for the long run.

He told Jimmy that he had picked up a young woman on his first day in town, while wandering about in Greenwich Village, a big, strapping Fraulein, with an enormous bust and

157

a Madonna-like face. Not the least of her virtues was that she had a sister and a brother-in-law who were "really hip, swinging." They ran a sandal shop in Brooklyn Heights, had a baby who never cried, never wore a diaper, and who was allowed free use of the floor for urinary and defecatory purposes. The brother-in-law plunked the bass fiddle, studied Zen, kept a Mulligan stew going for a month at a time, made sandals, and did odd jobs in his neighborhood. The sister was a mysterious beauty who smoked pot and sang lullabies. And in many other ways, apparently, this couple led an idyllic and primitive existence of which Rousseau would have voiced his approval. "Call me Marsayas," he said.

Marsayas told Jimmy that he was going to work his way in down there (which wouldn't prove difficult, as Rolly, the brother-in-law, had already accepted him as his guru), and stay with them for a while, at least until he could get Joan (his girlfriend) to get him a studio of his own. He was a painter, you see, and a poet, too.

"Any old how," he said, "I've got to get out of my uncle's house. The old folks are driving me up the walls. Too much, too *much! When are you going to get a job? What are you going to do about your wife and those dear little kiddies of yours? Life is real, life is earnest. You must look to the future.* Would you believe it? They want me to be in the house by midnight!"

Jimmy agreed that that was a bit much to ask of a grown and married man, and especially one with two kids.

Marsayas said that his whole family was that way, "Impossible!" His whole family were "convention-racked lunatics," or "business fiends" or "materialist maniacs."

Not Marsayas. "I'm a Zoroastrian. I believe in the power of light to conquer the forces of darkness. I believe in universal love." Jimmy was impressed, even impressed with the holes in the heels of the argyles of this gleeful gargoyle as he walked to his interview as one walks to the gallows.

2

They were hired, and started the next evening at six.

Jimmy worked as fast as he could, thinking of Vera, of the latest peace pact, and worried that he might not be able to find a good, full-time job before the next rent fell due. But Marsayas, though Jimmy had heard him try a few times at first, had already given up the outlined pitch, and was engaging in long, relaxed conversations with, as the boss called them, "the Zombies."

Jimmy discovered that, though he had a certain talent for making people say yes, by the next evening, when the supervisor called them back to verify the sales, his customers had often changed their minds. They'd claim that they had not agreed to buy a subscription at all. They'd claim that they had only accepted his offer to send them a free dictionary.

Well, either he hadn't heard right, and had pressured the "Zombies" too hard in his financial desperation, and they had changed their minds as soon as his persuasive voice had clicked from their receivers; or his supervisor was a swindler, as some claimed, and was simply stealing his sales by canceling them in Jimmy's name and putting them in his own. This Jimmy suspected, but had no way of confirming, as the sales were checked by others and the order forms were out of his hands.

Rightly or wrongly, his sales were being canceled faster than he was making them. And this was the sort of thing that just could not be explained to Vera. He confided his plight to Marsayas, whose own sales hadn't added up to enough to get a cancellation from, and to his amazement Marsayas was surprised that Jimmy should be worried.

"For Chrissakes, Jimmy, I thought you were just working here for beer money, like me. Why don't you get that Frau of yours off her ass and out into the labor market? She an invalid?"

159

After work they stopped in a midtown bar and had a few beers. It was one of those dives that have a food bar, and smell of corned beef and cabbage, stewed potatoes, cheap wine, draft beer, and sour people.

As they had agreed to do the previous evening, they had brought their poems to work with them, and now they sat and read each other's work. "GuraaaAH!" Marsayas sounded, and sipped his beer, leaving a broken ring of foam in the bristling red wires around his mouth.

He slammed Jimmy's little, stapled booklet on the table, chug-a-lugged his remaining beer, and vanished. Then he was back through the crowd like an ecstatic Bacchus with four huge mugs of slopping broth, two in each hand. He shouted: "You, you poor fool, are among the elect, the elite, the only *true* elite on earth. You are a *poet*!"

"Do you like them?"

"*Like* them? They're real *poems*, good as anybody going!"

Jimmy was thrilled. No one but Marsayas had ever encouraged him in his yearning to be a poet, everyone else thought he was foolish—especially Vera.

It would be quite a let-down, after such stimulation, to have to take himself home to Vera and her cranky, middle-class Bohemianism. Midnight was looming, Marsayas's curfew hour.

"Well, it won't always be like this," said Marsayas. "I'll be out of that bourgeois scene before the week-end. I'm moving into the sandal shop. Then we'll be able to drink and talk all night."

"I wish Vera would help me with tuition for school," Jimmy said, dreamily. "I'd like to be a writer, but I need more education."

"There's all kinds of writers, boyo—and all kinds of education. If you want to write, first read, read, read, then write, write, write! But if you want to go to college, well, that's a different story. I've got a masters, but I can't write poetry like your stuff."

He drained a mug. "Chrissakes, Jimmy, who the hell is the boss in your house? Look at the lion. The king of the beasts! The lioness goes out and kills the quarry, then steps back and guards the old man while he eats."

"That's lions—not people."

"Well, people then. Do you know that the Indian brave never worked. He sent his old lady out to do it. *He* stayed at home and talked, talked *war* and *peace*," he shouted, and the whole bar, which seemed to be filled with middle-aged, unshaven men, turned to look at him, interest in their eyes, even hope.

"That's what women are meant to do," he roared on, after a bow. "Let them make the nest pretty and wait like the votary bird to be impregnated. Then you take over until the egg is laid. *Only* until then. And then you go back and keep the nest warm with wine and good conversation while they go and forage for worms. Worms of milk for the baby and worms of wine for you. I tell you that is their biological role. *They* know it, so why don't you? Don't they all want to go to work nowadays? Don't they? Well, for God's sake, let them!

"This guy Rolly I've told you about, he makes san-dals—because that's art, but Jean, his wife, chews the leather. That's right. She *chews* the leather—makes it soft so Rolly can work with it. Rolly only makes one pair of sandals a week, he tells me; but Jean, with those beautiful sharp little white teeth of hers, chews enough leather for him to make twenty! He keeps her at it all day—chewing, chewing—except when she's nursing the baby, or turning on. Now that's a *wife* for you! They're in the battle for survival together—it isn't all thrown on *his* back. That's *life*—and listen, that's *love*! I tell you, Jimmy, once I get to Brooklyn, I'll never work another day in my life. That's my oath. I intend to dedicate myself completely to the muses."

161

Jimmy wondered if Vera would chew leather for him. Marsayas was opening new vistas. He was an inspiration!

3

Jimmy got an idea. Friday night, pay night, he would have next-to-nothing coming, so over the weekend he would need all the moral support he could get. He thought that the hard edge of the weekend might be softened if Vera could hear Marsayas present his version of things before he presented his own. So they made a date for Marsayas to come to Jimmy's place on Saturday and help him out.

Marsayas didn't mind telling Jimmy that he thought he was quite a coward for being so afraid of a woman, and over such a little thing as not having any money. He had never heard of a wife who wasn't at least willing to help her husband, if asked. But Marsayas had no idea what Vera was like, or what she was capable of, if angered. And Jimmy had to admit that it was more than a modest proposal that had induced him to ask Marsayas over. He was also interested in finding out what would happen when these two forces of nature came into contact. Perhaps they would vanish in a clap of thunder, and leave only a little mushroom cloud behind.

Marsayas showed up at noon on Saturday, toting a case of beer and a gallon jug of purple wine. Jimmy saw him through the window, striding down Horatio Street. He had told Vera a little about Marsayas, and that he was coming, but he did not, could not, do him justice. He went over and stood by the expensive new coffee table (which Vera had bought the day before with the last of their savings, and upon which she had laid out all the tea-time and cocktail-hour delicacies a Happy Homemaker could conceive), and waited to enjoy the immediate impact his wild man find would have upon her.

The knock came, and Vera, who was near the door, opened it; then stood, as if transfixed, gripping the knob until her little fist turned white. Jimmy thought for an instant that

162

she was going to slam the door in his friend's face, and start screaming. But she collected herself, asking:

"*Marsayas?*"

"Vera, I presume?"

"Ha—yes!" said Vera, looking up into the aimed ends of his red rays, and finally bethinking herself to step back. "Please come in—come in, please—*please!*"

Marsayas gargoyle-grinned, and slippity-slapped into the apartment on shower shoes. His naked feet were dirty, and red-and-raw-looking with the cold. Jimmy saw Vera eyeing them distastefully as the guru set his burdens down in the midst of the hors d'oeuvres.

Jimmy had hoped that it would take Vera longer to get her wind back. He had hoped that from first sight this imposing giant would keep her off balance. But, plain to see, she was coming around, resilient as ever.

He indicated a chair for Marsayas, and Marsayas seated himself, moving Vera's tidbits aside and putting his feet up on the table, between a bowl of cheese dip and a platter of cold cuts. Vera looked at him wide-eyed; at Jimmy, narrow-eyed; then pulled a tight meager smile back to her downy ears, and sat. Jimmy had received the first dirty look of the day. And he knew something about Vera. One dirty look meant more to follow, and maybe even along their trajectory one might find, in an hour or so, a vase, or a bottle, flying.

The thought flashed that he had better move quickly to prevent Marsayas from saying what he knew Marsayas intended to say. But then he was distracted. Marsayas said, from his recumbent position, "I hope you kids don't mind, but I took the liberty of inviting some friends of mine down—my girlfriend's sister and her husband. I thought it might do you good to meet them."

Vera stared at Marsayas, as one might stare at an oddity, trying to figure out what to make of him.

"Do us good?" she said.

"Yes. They do everyone good."

"How do you mean?"

"They're an example, an inspiration."

Marsayas removed his feet from the table long enough to fill two glasses with wine and stick them before Vera and Jimmy. He waved aside Jimmy's apology for not having done the honors, placed his horny heels back in the cold cuts, jug neatly draped on an elbow which he raised in salute, and yelled "PROSIT" loud enough to make Vera blink. They picked up their glasses and yelled "Prosit!" back at him. It seemed like the right thing to do.

Then Marsayas made his gleeful gargoyle face, which put on display for Vera his big, beautiful white teeth, and said, "Why didn't you tell me you had such a pretty wife?"

Vera perked up. "Why, thank you," she said.

"Yes—yes—I must paint you some time. But first you're going to have to become more natural. These are the new, hip Sixties, Vera. Hang loose! You're the very person-ification of the uptight Fifties. You seem . . . *constrained*— yes. Even your hair—is it dyed? A Lana Turner helmet. You'll have to get that stuff out of your hair and let it down— let it be natural—yes—" He moved the thumb of his free hand in a painterly gesture of measurement. "And you stop Jimmy from being a wage-slave and help to develop him as a poet. He's the real thing." The wine bottle remained cradled in his other arm, like a baby.

Fortunately, for Jimmy could see Vera revving up for a reply, a knock came at the door. It was the Reuters.

Rolly Reuter was a little fellow with big, lugubrious brown eyes, long black hair, and a long, silky black beard. Jean, his wife, was a striking young woman, with chatoyant greenish eyes, and beautiful long ebony hair that swam, like a dark, glittery stream, down neck and chest and out, over a more than ample, T-shirted bosom, to twin falls, stippled by nipples.

Marsayas picked up the thread of what he had been saying. But the atmosphere was irrevocably altered. Vera was discontent. She no longer listened to Marsayas, but interjected odd, pointless questions, as if only to attract attention; and the conversation became forced and jittery. Even so, Jimmy was able to attend to the Reuters enough to see what Marsayas had meant about them. It was simple. They were in love.

He looked at Vera, popping off about something or other, that hard, mean look about the mouth, those hurt, jealous eyes, and he knew what was going on in her mind; knew that she wanted this pleasant vision of love out of her sight. It was too much for her, too uncomplicated.

Jimmy envied Rolly his beautiful Jean—and he saw that Marsayas envied him, too—but tried not to show it. If Jimmy let on to the slightest admiration, Vera would make him pay—make them all pay, possibly.

The Reuters stayed for two hours and then went on their way. But Marsayas sat on, like a great blood-bubbling fixture. He finished off the last of the wine and started whittling down the case of beer he'd brought; then he dragged Vera up and danced her about to the phonograph. Vera's mood brightened after Rolly took his beautiful Jean away. When Marsayas went to the bathroom, she kept on dancing by herself, whirling about the living room like the ballerina she had been trained to be. Once, she stopped, and tried to pull Jimmy to his feet to dance with her. But he refused. There was even something in her gaiety that made him nervous. He knew all too well how quickly it could change into angry hysteria. Yet she seemed happy, now; and if it hadn't been for all the misery she had caused him he'd have been glad to see her so. He'd have got up and danced with her, but for that.

Marsayas slept, head hanging forward, in an antiquated easy chair near the lumpy couch on which Jimmy woke. A young woman sat on the floor at his feet, propped up against his legs, asleep, with her head in his lap. She wore a quilted kimono, and one breast bulged into view where the kimono fell open. She was a bigger, heavier version of Jean.

Jimmy looked around, through puffed, uncertain eyes. There were sandals, belts, pocketbooks, all manner of leather goods, hanging in festoons from walls and ceiling. He must have moaned; because, then, from somewhere up near the ceiling, in a dark corner, in the rear of the shop, a soft, purring voice drifted down, asking,

"Got a headache?"

It was Jean. He could see her now, or see her eyes, like a cat's, high up, glimmering in shadows.

"Are you levitating?"

"I'm on a platform. This is where Rol and I sleep. How's your wife?"

Jimmy looked around, and there behind him, under a heap of coats, was Vera. She looked a mess. Her lipstick was smeared, there were Mascara-tear-stains down her cheeks, and her hair looked like a burning bush.

Well, was it paradise? Was this absurd little sandal shop a heaven on earth, a sanctuary? No, he guessed not; it was just that he had come from a small, unimportant hell. And why have anything to do with any hell if you can stay in a little, bright heaven? It was just too bad that there wasn't one more of these plump, lovely creatures around, another sister, for him.

He had been drinking beer with Marsayas for two hours before Vera grunted and woke up. She had a hangover, was angry, had slept badly (so she claimed—been mashed by him), and wanted to get out of this (whispers, harsh, in his ear) "filthy place." She would not have Jimmy drinking again today. It was Sunday.

"What *are* you, an alcoholic, like your so-called friend, Marsayas? He's a filthy beast and the sandal shop is a stinking zoo." She stomped outside "to get some clean, fresh air."

"She walked out on you last night—do you know that?" Marsayas seemed much amused by Jimmy's pickle. "You fell asleep in the car—I dumped you there, on the couch, and she got into a temper tantrum trying to wake you up. Feel your leg."

Jimmy felt around, looked at the place on his calf that hurt, and there was a large purple bruise. "It'll soon be time to go back to California," he said. "D.D. is catching up with us."

"Who's D.D.?"

"The Divorce Demon. He's been pursuing us since we got married."

"She gave you quite a pummeling before I could stop her." Marsayas laughed.

"You were inert—wouldn't, or couldn't, move for love nor money."

Jimmy was beginning not to like the way Marsayas looked, the beast. He seemed to think that Jimmy's problems were a joke. But then, who could blame him? It was the truth, after all. Vera and he were a joke. They had been making public fools of themselves for three years. Why shouldn't people laugh? The thought occurred to Jimmy that maybe he had finally come face to face with the Divorce Demon. Then Marsayas broke the news:

"Your phonograph and your TV were stolen last night. Some of your clothes, too."

Rolly came in from the back and sat down, looking lugubrious. Now he reminded Jimmy a little of Chico Marx.

"That's the trouble with having possessions," he said; "it's not that they get stolen, but that it should hurt when they

167

are. *Things!*" He sighed. "It's no good basing a life on *things!*"

He wore such a sad face. It struck Jimmy funny that he should seem to be suffering more over Jimmy's loss than Jimmy was.

"Oh, but it's true," Rolly said, as Jimmy laughed. Then he looked at Jimmy's feet. He had given him a pair of sandals to wear. Jimmy had them on over his socks. Quite a bumbling novitiate beatnik he was.

"Do they fit?" he asked. Jimmy said that they did, quite comfortably.

Marsayas went on to tell Jimmy that, after he had pulled Vera off him, she had run out into the street and stopped a car by standing with outstretched arms, like a crucifee. The car had gone off with her. Marsayas said that he had been too drunk to follow, but that after taking a nap he had driven up to Manhattan to see if he could get her to come back. He said that he had found the front door wide open and Vera hysterical. She told him that the man who had driven her home had threatened her, and that she had given him everything he asked for and was afraid to call the police.

Trouble! *Trouble*! Four hundred, maybe five hundred, dollars worth of his hard labor stolen! His most prized possession—his typewriter. More disorder! More chaos! Well, Rolly was right. He was a fool to work for *things*.

He wasn't angry; he was just disgusted, with himself and with Vera. What a dreadful pain in the ass they must always seem to people! Ah! He thought to himself that he would go right ahead and get just as drunk as he damned well pleased; and he would start right now to demand, through an iron-clad indifference to anybody's harangue, his *rights*!

But just then Vera appeared at the door, eyes shooting hot tears like sunstruck diamonds.

"I want to speak to you," she said, choking in temper.

Marsayas bent down and buried Joan's neck in the red excelsior of his beard.

"Do you hear?" Vera shouted. "I said I want to speak to you!"

Her smeared lips were pursed, her grim, green eyes on Marsayas.

Rolly peeked in through the curtain, from the back, but withdrew his scared, comic-Christ face when he saw Vera.

"Step outside, please," said Vera, and Jimmy felt as if he were being called out by a barroom bully. Her breath was hot, and he thought he saw a flame leap from her mouth.

He got up and walked outside, onto Henry Street, a pretty, quiet, Sunday view, reminiscent of Utrillo. He could hear tugboats tooting in the harbor, beyond the esplanade.

Vera had her coat on. He was in shirtsleeves, a little chilly. He shivered. He thought that he must look like hell, unshaven, disheveled. So did Vera.

"I want you to come home with me," she said. "I've been waiting in that church over there for nearly an hour. I was not going to step one foot back in that filthy zoo of a sandal shop, with that smell of dead skin, but I did, for *you*. Now you come along with me, do you *hear*?"

"I'm staying here for a while," Jimmy said, affirming his rights. "You go ahead. I'll be along."

He was a bit tipsy—not much, but a bit; enough to think he was going to get away with facing her down—enough to think he was going to win, this time.

"No!" she said. "You come now!"

"No!" he said. "Later! I am a lion."

"You are not the king of the beasts. You're a pussycat. I suppose you'll want to grow a beard now."

"You just listen to me roar," he said.

"If you don't come now, I'll kill myself!" she shouted. The sentence rang down the hollow, empty Sunday street like a ricocheting bullet.

"No," he said; but he was weakening.

"You'll see," she yelled at him, turning, and running around the corner. "You'll see," she yelled again, farther down, out of sight.

He stood still for what seemed a long time, determined not to give in, determined to hold his ground. But then he heard her yell, "*You'll see*," from far down, toward the docks, and he thought of the harbor and the water.

It came to him. She means to throw herself in. But then it occurred to him that she had won medals for swimming. How could she drown herself? And what could he do if she did take it into her head to jump into the drink? He couldn't swim at all! But he had lost already. Even to think about it was to lose.

He started running down the block, around the corner, to the river. He slowed down, occasionally, wondering what he would do when he got there. He couldn't save her! Three years in the Marines hadn't taught him to swim. He wasn't going to learn in the next five minutes. And she couldn't drown, was an expert!

He stopped running once, and began to laugh. The absurdity of what was happening struck him. He had a stitch in his side. What kind of damned crazy show was this? And what part was he intended to play? The clown who gets fished out of the drink by his wife? But, then, in an instant, he was frightened again. What was she going to do? She was capable of anything.

He started running again, and he got to the dock just in time to see Vera take off her coat, and, looking back to make sure he was watching—he felt she would have waited for him to catch up had he taken longer—jump in.

He walked the next hundred or so feet. He wondered what sort of expression he wore. Whatever it was, that miraculous crowd that gathers out of nowhere at public events such as the one taking place under the esplanade in Brooklyn

170

Heights did not like it at all. He did not move a wee bit faster, however. In fact, he sauntered. Meantime, until three or four burly firemen, who were stationed on a fireboat docked nearby, swam in three or four strokes to rescue her, Vera swam gracefully about, doing a lovely backstroke of the sort that had won her the medals. Then she allowed herself to be saved by the florid knights of the fireboat. Unfortunately, thought Jimmy, it wasn't even necessary to knock her out; they swam back to the boat in a beautiful formation, like well-trained frogmen, Vera on point, and the knights of the fireboat took her aboard.

As for Jimmy, he just stood where he was. He may have been laughing, or he may have been crying, but whatever he was doing, it roused no sympathy for him in the heart of the crowd. It was thumbs down for him.

Then one of the big, fire-colored knights stepped up to him.

"You that young lady's husband?" It sounded as much like an accusation as it did a question.

"Yes," Jimmy admitted, "I am."

"Well, whatsa matter widja? Why dinja jump in after huh?"

"I can't swim."

"Call that a 'scuse?" the fireman demanded.

Jimmy thought that he had best be careful now. He might be lynched.

"No," he said meekly.

"Well, now . . ." the fireman said, thinking. It must have been quite a search that went on in that big head, but he came out of it empty-handed. All he could say in his state of indignation was "Get aboard!"

There was a cop on the boat. "Are you prepared to take your wife home?" he asked, adding, "Otherwise I'll have to take you both to the station." Jimmy wanted to ask what he had done, but thought better of it. He said he was. He looked at Vera, who was sitting wrapped in blankets, three or four firemen asking her questions, consoling her, and no doubt condemning him. Vera saw him, then, and stood up, stretching her arms out to him through the blankets.

"Oh, Jimmy," she cried, "take me home."

Sure he would. What did it matter now? Something had happened, something had snapped. Vera thought she had won again, but she hadn't. This time he had won. And so had protean D.D., the Divorce Demon, in the form of Marsayas, poet, painter, prophet, and king of beasts.

THE CHAUVINIST SONG
Old Bird Instructs Fledgeling

Now the bird in the bush is an egg-laying thrush
    requiring a nest of some kind,
but the high-flying male, who freely would sail,
    to virtue is never so blind—
    to virtue is never so blind.
He spreads out his wings as soon as he's dined.

The high-flying male who freely would sail
    without envy or rancor or doubt
must not have his wings weighted down with mere things
    though his female forever should pout—
    though his female forever should pout.
The object of life is to keep objects out!

It's said that I'm selfish. That's better than *pel*fish,
    and greedily grasping at straws;
for what are possessions but straws of obsession
    in the winds of eternal laws—
    in the winds of eternal laws?
The high-flying cock will spread his great claws.

Remember, my boy, to get rid of the toy
    that is solid, existing in fact.
Let all of the things that you bear on your wings
    be musical, wise, and abstract—
    be musical, wise, and abstract!
All else from your flight you must fiercely subtract!

173

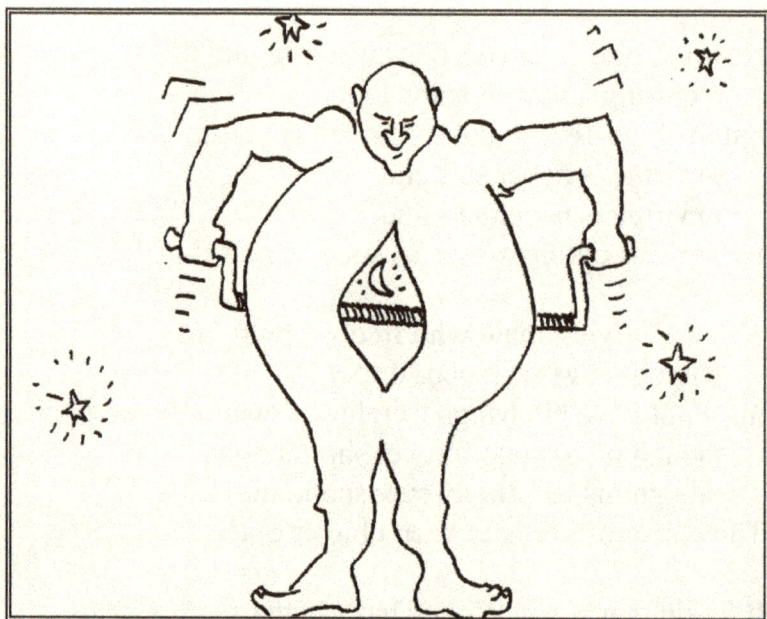

THE LIAR

She came in to the cafeteria three or four times that week, would sit with her older friend, a kind of watchdog, but pleasant, in his section, and would smile at him when he came near. He was a busboy. No, he wasn't. He was an acting student. No, he wasn't. He had run out of money. But he was going to have more money some day, and then he would go to New York University and take dramatic arts.

He was about her age; but, somehow, in the circumstances, and quite un-intentionally, she made him feel younger. She looked like she had money, and he did not, look like he had money, that is. Of course he did not have any, or why would he be a busboy in a cafeteria? She must have been in her late teens, early twenties, but she had a mature way about her, serious, intelligent. He lived in Greenwich Village, but not quite. He lived on the great wall of Greenwich Village, 14th Street, in a shoebox of a room with a sagging single bed which he shared with a friend as poor as himself, a Puerto Rican boy of intellectual bent who had been in the Marines with him. They were not out very long, a matter of months. They had a G.I. Bill coming, but had to get tuition money together first, and be reimbursed. They seldom had car fare. They had few clothes, which they shared, on a first come first serve basis, so that neither of them could be sure what he was going to wear at any particular time. Who knew what would be left? First one up and out was best dressed. They were too poor to feed their roaches. Now he wore a white jacket supplied by the restaurant, an apron stained with food, old baggy fatigues, split in the crotch from squatting to pick up under the tables, and down-at-heels muddy shoes of military issue. They had white soap stains at toe and heel. He owned no others. It embarrassed him that this beautiful young woman, who looked like a movie star, kept smiling at

175

him. The smile was sweet, intelligent, and kind. The smile was warm and friendly and respectful. But it hurt his pride, because she was so beautiful, and poised, and well-dressed, and obviously well-off, and established-looking. He would have thought that she was making fun of him or teasing him or something, but somehow he could see that she wasn't. She and her friend sat and smoked cigarettes after eating and he had no choice but to go to their table and collect their dishes. and he hated it, because of the way she looked and smiled; but he had no choice but to do it. The older woman said, in a pleasant voice, we've been watching you. My friend thinks you're very attractive. This horrified him, horrified him. What was he to say? He nearly spilled the stack of dishes. Careful, said the older woman, and laughed a little in a friendly way.

You take your break soon, said the younger one, you take your break about now, I noticed. Won't you bring us all some coffee and sit with us?

I can't sit with the customers, he lied. Nobody would care. It was a cafeteria.

Of course you can, said the older woman in a pretty full-throated voice. She was a bit overweight.

Please bring us some coffee and sit with us, said the beauty.

Can't you see she's smitten, said the other, and the beauty looked actually embarrassed herself. She wants to meet you. She thinks you're very handsome. What do you do? I mean, beside this.

I'm an actor, he said. Was he lying?

So am I, said the beauty. My friend, too. Are you studying?

Yes, he lied.

We thought you might be, said the older woman. Get the coffee and come and sit down. We want to talk to you.

So he sat with them that time and again the next time

176

they came in. The beauty seemed nicer and more cultivated the more he saw her. She was so young, it had not occurred to him that she might be working, but it turned out that she was already pretty well-known. She was in a play on Broadway. So was the other one. They made him feel like a roach. It wasn't their fault, of course. They were as sweet as could be. He knew it was himself, his pride, but he couldn't help it. They made him feel like a poor ignorant slob, bussing dirty dishes, his old stained shoes stinking under the table. And yet the beauty made him melt, just melt. She was nice and nicer and it frightened him. It embarrassed him. She wanted him to ask her for a date, but where could he take such a girl, a girl rich and famous and successful? He didn't have any clothes to wear, let alone an extra dime to spend on her. Why did she have to pick on him? Where could he take her? Oh, where could he take her? And as if she knew what was in his mind, she asked him if they couldn't take a walk together sometime. Just go for a walk, she said. You don't have to take me any place special. I'd just like to be with you. We could go for a walk in the park. To the zoo.

I have no clothes that I can wear to walk beside you, he thought. I am only a busboy, not even a real actor. But he *was* an actor, for he said, No. It will do no good to know me.

Why not?

Because, he said, looking down at his stained apron and muddy shoes, because, you see, like so many actors these days, I don't like women, I mean not in that way.

You mean, she said, you're gay?

Yes, he lied, and watched her gather up her things and leave, her friend consoling her; watched the most beautiful, wonderful girl he had ever known walk out of his ridiculous lying failure of a life forever. He gathered up their plates with deep sad relief, swearing to himself that he would get himself some new clothes, so that the next time this happened, he would be ready.

VANITY FAIR

I. *The Steroid Lady*

The steroid lady stands, flashing her smile,
    upon a pedestal at Muscle Beach.
She's come a long way, baby; the last mile
    was not beyond her iron-willed, wiry reach.
Delts, pecs, abs, obliques, gluts, hamstrings, triceps,
    erectus spinus: she walks in beauty like
a knight in well-oiled armor, flexing biceps,
    and spreading lats and giving traps a hike.

What hope for man is left? She's made of iron!
    She looks like Mike, my hirsute little friend,
but that she's hairless. Is she also barren?
    For mothers must have fat or hormones end.
The softness of a woman has been taken.
I feel as if my manhood's been forsaken.

II. *The Fashion Show*

The slim young women float their subtle curves
  before a fashion-conscious audience.
Diaphanous enough to tickle nerves,
  their gowns lift off them in a breezy dance
as left leg forward forces right hip out,
  and small breasts, bra-less, bounce beneath a gauze
of punctuated pink. Their red lips pout.
  Their veteran eyes, dark shadowed, seek applause.

Young women and some not so truly young,
  whose art it is to show another's art,
can you be sirens of whom Homer sung,
  can so much softness be so hard at heart,
that you would make this hard-pressed buyer sin,
forget the gowns, and buy the mannequin?

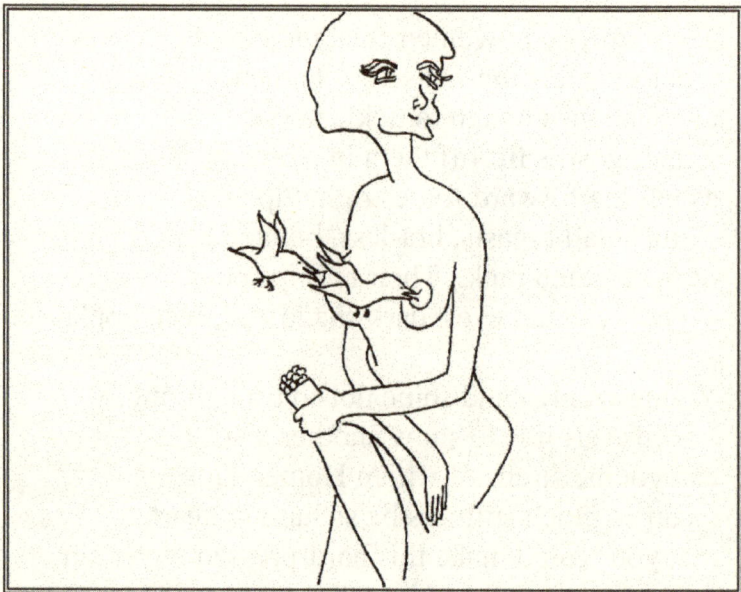

SMOKE

A poem in dialogue as if performed by Bogie and Bacall

She paused, gazing without expression at the smoldering,
unfiltered cigarette she held between her fingers, then said,
"You know, the thing about love is . . . "

"Like your cigarette " he said. "It has to be unfiltered and
leave stains on your fingers."

"When you say the word love," she said, "smoke should
come from your tongue."

"You mean that it's dangerous."

"I mean don't say it unless you mean it. It's a sacred word."

"And who uses it should be willing to die for its subject."

"Die for me. I'd die for you."

"You mean you'd die for love."

"Look at my beautiful fingers."

"Stained."

"Look at my beautiful eyes."

"Red."

"Here, take a deep drag," she said, and turned the wet end toward his wet mouth.

"It's hot and wet," he said.

"Like my best kiss."

"Your smokey kiss."

"Like a street in L.A., where you have to run inside at every corner to catch a breath of air-conditioned air, or your eyes will burn and tear until you can't see where you're going. Take a long drag."

"It's dangerous."

"Yes."

"I can taste your chewing gum in in. Juicy Fruit."

"And now I can taste your breakfast. Coffee. Coffee and more coffee."

"Our habits become identity."

"Love is more than I can bear," she said, snuffing the butt out in an ashtray full of similar, lipsticked butts, ashes on her crimson nails. "Almost," she added, shaking another unfiltered cig from a pack. "I'm a chain smoker," she said, then laughed. "I'm also a chain-lover."

"You've got the habit," he said. "Both habits. Both bad."

"But I'm starting on a brand-new pack of Luckies," she said, lighting up.

SHORTS

1 AN EXPERIMENT IN GOVERNANCE

For some very important, and top-secret, reasons of State, the people who decided policy desired a change in the thought processes of the people they ruled, so they brought back the rusty old rack and began to stretch anyone who could not change his or her mind fast enough to suit them. Members of the public entered the Ministry of Thought at their natural height and came out about two inches taller. At last, we have become competitive, cried one of the people who decided policy. We shall become the capital of fashion, for we have some of the tallest models available. The Eureka-like quality of this observation caused the people who decided policy at the Ministry of Thought to completely forget what the very important, and top-secret, reasons were that caused them to bring back the rusty old rack in the first place. It was our intention from the beginning, they said with one voice, to open an international modeling agency: and things looked very promising for the new democracy until the people began to shrink back to their natural height, shrinking cartilage pulled down by gravity, as it were, and the people at the Ministry of Fashion, which the Ministry of Thought was now called, searched everywhere for their original reasons for bringing back the rusty old rack, but found that their drawers and filing cabinets, originally stuffed with strategic schemes, were now stuffed with dress patterns, Butterick having infiltrated the Ministry, which had become little more than a rag-shop. Such are the pitfalls of governance.

2 THE BOWEL ORGANIST

No concerti are written for the bowel organ. This is generally thought to be due to the fact that the instrumentalist has little control over his or her instrument. The bowel organ is expected to produce little more than flourishes, if well-tempered. Usually, the bowel organist is placed on a small separate stage, at some distance from the main body of the orchestra. At outdoor concerts, however, he or she is usually placed at the rear of the orchestra, back to the audience. As is an actor's, the bowel organist's instrument is him or her self. There is no school that teaches the bowel organ. The bowel organist is a lonely artist. From youth, he or she must practice alone. But now a bowel organist has come forth to present to the world his own composition, Opus One for the Bowel Organ, as he has dubbed it. And for the first time, the bowel organist places himself at the front of the orchestra. There is the tapping of the baton, as the orchestra prepares to support his prelude, a long high trumpet-like riff that engulfs the audience.

3 BUTCH, THE BODY-FINDER

Everything was going along as usual, that is until a body that the police had been searching for was dragged into Mary Martin's house by her dog. It was evidence of a murder. The District Attorney had been working with nothing but circumstantial evidence. Now the police could bring him something solid—well, almost solid. They thanked Mary Martin and patted her dog, Butch, saying that he was no mutt but a true cadaver dog. Butch sensed that he had made an important contribution. A week later he came home with another body. Mary called the police. Now the police were puzzled. They had no need for this body. This was a superfluous body, a redundancy. They didn't thank Mary this time and they didn't pat Butch and say nice things about him. Butch suspected that he had failed to do enough, so he went out and found several more bodies in various places, two in one place. One morning Mary found a dozen bodies at her door, and Butch wagging and waiting for a bone. No, Butch, Mary told the dog patiently, you must not bring any more bodies home. I have all the bodies I need. And so did the police. They decided to investigate Mary, but Mary was on to them and decided to leave town. She sold her house and took Butch and her things away in a rental truck. But she was traced until the end of her days, when Butch finally dragged her back and left her on the old front porch.

Played the devil's fiddle, stomping to it, shaking it out, full of corned blood, his boot down down down! Days before the corn, his old bitch Lucy lay by his piston heel. Said later she smelled it, stayed by it, waiting for the meaty bone; said later never done him no harm at all; said later not even a ghost of evil but Lucy got it, old bloodhound bitch like red clay, wrinkled old lady hanging from her own bones—could make her moon-howl, pointing his wild bow—do that at dances. Devil in a Baptist, playing the fiddle. Gradual as the mountains, he found out how the devil got in. Fiddle under his spiked, gray chin, corn jug thumb-hooked and cradled on top his elbow—capful for Lucy—then stomp stomp stomp: music through Blue Ridge pines! Could choo choo it so's you see smoke and steam, hear that wheezy accordion whistle; could conjure with it up a trainload of places or turn you back home to the station of pines and blue smoke mountains, bring musical rain, or put the devil in your heart, winking and drinking and stomping. Everybody loved him and his Lucy, including said devil, as the corn dropped down into his right big toe. Said it hurt to stomp. But it don't stop the fiddler. Don't nothing stop the fiddler! He was one thing else than music; he was a man. Take more'n corn going through, dropping down in my right big toe, says at the May dance, everybody seeing him stomp, ouch ouch ouch on his big red gray spiked old corned face. Devil got in through the corn, slick as silk; got down in my boot, but I'll stomp him out; give old Satan a headache—stomp stomp stomp! But that corn went to killing him. His bow was flying! Went on like this, folks say, a tad's five year, him stomping the devil in the corn and the devil stomping back. Said now he couldn't play no more if he don't get rid o' that old devil. Takes him a broad wood chisel out back on a stump, sets his right foot up, sets that chisel to his toe, and strikes down with a good hefty hammer. When he pulls back his foot, that devil in the corned toe stays on the stump, says looka me, I'm off! Has brought him some fireplace soot and some gingham. Sticks that foot in that black soot, to staunch the blood, and wraps it in gingham rags. Said never done him no harm again, quiet as a bone, and he goes back to stomping in peace, rid of the devil. But first, he throws that old corned toe to Lucy. Says: I knowed you always wanted it. Now mind the nail, Lucy; don't let the devil get you, you drunk old droop-skinned hound bitch, cuz I love you. And Lucy goes to lickin' that toe, pops it in, and goes to grinding up that devil in her old ground down chops. And next time we see them, the fiddler and his drunk bitch, they both full of corn, and ready, now, for the dance!

5 MANNERS, MANNERS

Convention dictated that two people meeting in the street should knock their heads together in greeting, so Smirnoff banged his forehead into Zubov's, but, in his enthusiasm for formality, did not wait for Zubov to remove his hat and bang him back. Zubov therefore fell to ground in a semiconscious state, and Smirnoff had to help him to his feet. Manners, said Zubov, recrimination ringing in his voice, Manners. Smirnoff had Zubov standing now. A thousand pardons, he said. He held the swaying Zubov upright. Get my hat, please, said Zubov, pointing to the hat, which had rolled off into the gutter. Smirnoff let go of Zubov's shoulders and got the hat. He returned, spitting on the hat and brushing it with his sleeve, to find that Zubov had retreated to the ground and lay spreadeagled. This time Zubov had cracked the back of his head open and lay in a pool of blood. Just then another couple bumped heads, and both went down. Smirnoff shook his own large head, from the front of which a red welt was making an appearance. Our culture is too much bound by convention, he said in disgust, dropping the hat by Zubov's body, and going on about his business.

6 THE ISLAND OF THE LEADERS

If kissing Napoleon's hemorrhoidal ass brings a little romance into the lives of historians, so be it, but he is still on the Island, along with Alexander the Great, Al Capone, Hitler, Stalin, Papa Doc, Il Duce, Tojo, Pol Pot, and you name the thugs, rogues, and rascals that have made this world a living hell for the nameless many, the rest of us. You may have guessed by now that I am not referring to Elba or St. Helena, but to the hitherto unknown Island of the Evil Ones, also known as the Island of the Thugs or the Island of the Stupid, Naughty, or Not-so-Nice, the location of which I am about to reveal. For, you see, I am a whistleblower. I know where the island is and what happens on it, and I am about to tell all. How do I know? I was sent there by the Historical Society to be a cummerbunned waiter and sworn never to reveal what I saw. Guess with whom I saw guess-who dancing—go ahead, guess! First, I will tell you who is *not* there. Elvis is not there. Elvis is in heaven. But Poppa Doc is there. Mae West is not there, but was that Caterina de Medici I saw dancing with Adolf? Il Duce dances on his hands. Now who would know that but someone who had been there? Of course, since I was only a lowly waiter on the Island, I cannot be expected to know the names of the innumerable "leaders" I saw there, with their burdens of medals and awards weighing them down, their epaulets, their badges and whistles. There were also the heads of many "great families," but the father of twelve who lived down the street from me when I was a kid, the one who worked himself to death to support his brood, was of course not there. No decent people were there, only monsters, which is why it is sometimes called the Island of Monsters, though it is of course known as the Island of the Great by its denizens. And one more thing I can say about the island, before I give away its location. It contains the

189

worse tippers I have ever had the dissatisfaction of working for—real cheapos!

7 THE OPERA

This was some opera! The fat lady singing the aria was encased in red. Well, "encased" is a bit harsh. But she strode through thick yellow, syrupy golden yellow, like melted wedding bands. I liked it when she made a little fist, long red nails in a little fist, which she waved about her head with great passion. The opera was Wagner sung in Samoan. I could follow some of it—the search for the ring, everybody on stilts. The diva took a nosedive off her stilts but the tenor caught her on his horns. This was a cultural feast! Somebody just told me that the aria went something like: "I will pay you for some water." I studied the diva through my opera glasses. She had got back on her feet. The tenor's horn was crumpled. It must have been made of paper. Art is so tricky. Now just about everybody was on stage and caterwauling to beat the band. Cats in an alley. It was exciting. I felt that at any moment now something big was going to happen. There was a lot of blue smoke, and the diva strode right through it, unblinking, singing her heart out. "I will pay you for some water." It was my first opera, but you can bet I'm going back.

8 THE MOVING FINGER

The Moving Finger writes; and, having writ,
Moves on: nor all your Piety nor Wit
Shall lure it back to cancel half a Line,
Nor all your Tears wash out a Word of it.
  —*Rubáiyát of Omar Khayyám*
    Edward FitzGerald

Sad, suffering a mild depression, I went to Coney Island one winter day to walk along the beach and see the sea, when I came upon what I took to be a huge sandbox, four boards, at least twenty feet each, joined into a square, brimming with wet sand of a somewhat different shade than the rest of the beach, a sort of olive drab, and I immediately saw in this square a frame suitable for writing. It was a cold windy day and there was nobody about to bother me as I focused my attention on what I would write on this beautiful big page that looked up at the sky. I decided to write my sins for God to see, or perhaps for low-flying airplane travellers, or balloon people, anyway somebody up in the flowing clouds. Of course, one of my sins is that I am always looking for a way out, so I was counting on a high tide or rain or snow to wash my sins away before anyone got a good look at what I'm made of, deep inside. I decided I would tell the absolute truth about myself and my many misdeeds. I would attempt to do what Jean Jacques Rousseau meant to do in his Confessions, but did not succeed in doing; I would attempt to be perfectly honest, absolutely honest, come water or high hell. And so, having a tendency to hyperbole, another of my many sins, I went to great lengths to defame myself, mixed emotions rocking my heart, forcing me to stop several times in order to throw up on the beach—not of course, in my beautiful frame.

191

With first thoughts best thoughts in mind, I did not want anything I scratched in the olive drab slurry to be smudged or lost to the sky by being covered with nervous vomit. And I told of my misprisions until the huge page was covered. I signed my confession at the bottom and placed my address and phone number below my signature, then threw the stick down and surveyed my work. Confession is good for the soul, I had always heard, and there it was, my masterpiece, the truth and more than the truth about me. The work had taken most of the afternoon and the sun began to set out at sea. I was exhausted with all this truth-telling. I looked once more at my huge page of sins, and walked on along the shore where the tide was rising, soon to wash away all that I had written. Tired as I was, I felt new life surging through me, an exhilaration, for the worst was said and done and over. I slept well that night for the first time in weeks. I rose from my bed feeling like a new man, buoyant, weightless, with a new life before me, free of the terrible burden of my sinful past. I resolved to live in a new way, clean, straight, honorable, fruitful, with malice toward none. The sandbox had turned me into a child again, and I whistled my way through the day. That night I turned on the evening news to see what sins had been committed by the rest of the world that day, when one item caught my attention. A man had written a full confession on a cement slab at Coney Island. The slab had been intended to hold a concession stand. The phone rang, and I realized my voice mail was full of messages. Most of them were crank calls, many containing improper suggestions. Some gave me the news that I was in the papers, on TV and the net. One was from the police, another from the DA's office. I was to be called before a Grand Jury. Several others from various priests and ministers—You need spiritual help, they claimed. A psychiatrist offered me his couch and a lifetime of psychoanalysis, free of charge. The contractor who had laid the cement slab offered to reconstruct my nose but opined that he would settle for a law suit and a nice chunk of money. Several lawyers offered to fend off any lawsuits that might be brought against me, thus relieving my anxiety about the contractor. Finally, my girlfriend left a message to say that she was breaking off with me, a truly corrupt and perverted personality.

9 PARA IS NORMAL, NOT PARA

In the sixth dimension of the String Theory, electrician Joe Sixpack was repairing a refrigerator. He squatted before the turned-about machine. As Mrs. Doe stood watching Joe's beefy blemished backside smile and frown, there was an explosion, and, when the smoke cleared, Joe had vanished. Mrs. Doe ran to her next door neighbor for help and comfort, and that is the end of her part in this domestic tragedy. But at the very instant of the explosion, Joe Sixpack jumped up from the refrigerator, turned to Mrs. Doe of the first, second, and third dimensions, and said, "Damn this old piece of junk! It's got a serious short in it. Why don't you let me sell you a new one? You see," he added, as if talking to himself, "there is no such thing as the paranormal in the universe. Working with electrical appliances has taught me this little understood fact. The paranormal is normal, not para. Once, when I was working on a freezer, a ghost jumped right out at me. I figure it got caught in some odd corner of the universe and found its way into the freezer. It probably thought it was in the grave. You know, dark and cool, then I went and opened the door on the poor thing. It might have taken me for a grave-robber. Wow!" he ejaculated, holding his head, "that explosion knocked my brain loose. I can't remember my name or where I'm from. . . but not around here, I think." The shocked Mrs. Doe had no idea that she was at her neighbor's house, sipping coffee in a vain attempt to calm her own nerves. Bravely, she told the electrician who he was and he thanked her heartily, and there was much relieved laughter between the two.

194

10 THE NEW GREEN CARPET

The old brown carpet and liner were ripped up and thrown out, the new green carpeting laid by an expert from the store. The man owed the store a good deal of money, but he would pay the store in time. What counted was that he had a beautiful new floor to look at. He vacuumed the new carpet every day, taking great pleasure in its neat greenness. It reminded him of a golf course lawn. Just for fun, he got out his putter and putted a few balls into a paper cup. In his house, everything was smooth.

Now one night the man vacuumed his new green carpet and went to bed feeling very good about life, feeling really quite satisfied with things. But when he woke in the morning, he discovered that his carpet had grown into tall meadow grass, and he felt water between his toes as he waded through to the bathroom. Why, the nap of the carpet must have grown at least a foot during the night. Had last night's thunderstorm sent water in under the door, water that triggered this outlandish growth? Each of his children, a boy and a girl, had a room, but they were not in their beds. The carpet-grass was growing even as he waded about the house, and now it was up to his shoulders.

"Children, children, where are you?" he called. Here and there, in the livingroom and in the dining room, he plunged his hands into the tall grass and separated it in hope of finding his children. The grass had reached the ceiling and had turned back down and become vines, so that he felt that he was in a rain forest. Then it occurred to him that there might be snakes in all of this wetland, snakes and even alligators, who could say? Had his children been eaten by them?

He groped his way back to his bedroom and found his wife. "Come with me and help me find our children," he said.

"I told you not to buy this new green carpet, didn't I?"

"Yes," he said, for he had always been a man who was willing to admit to his mistakes, "you were quite right."

"The house is filled with mosquitoes," said his wife, slapping herself in the face.

"Watch out," said the man. "That's a boa constrictor." The man reached in the giant snake's mouth and pulled forth one of his children, the little girl.

"Thank you, Daddy," she said.

"Where is your brother?" he asked her.

"He's floating in the dining room," she said. So the man and his wife and his daughter waded into the dining room, where they found the little boy floating on his back.

"It's fun," said the little boy.

"No, it isn't," said the mother.

"Don't make a big deal out of this," said the man to his wife, "it'll all be paid off in five years."

11 THE PLAN

You will have to take my word for it, the Plan was perfect. You don't think, do you, that after all these years, all the experience we've gained, all those strategic exercises, landings and drops, the tactical work, you don't think, do you, that we don't know what we are doing? Because if you do you are definitely mistaken. I assert once again the Plan was perfect. Execution is of course the problem. Some get the idea, the governing idea, the overarching purpose, the spirit of the thing, and some don't. Some go by the letter and are of course doomed to failure. Some go by the thrust of the thing and do not stick to the precision, the details, of the Plan, the exact moments and turns, and are of course doomed to failure. The Plan is composed with a sense of balance, a knowledge that there will be leeway, room for alternatives, improvisations, which intelligent executives will easily grasp, but which will elude those doomed to failure. But the Plan is composed with precision as stated. It must be precise inside of lassitude. It must be free, improvisational even, inside of precision. I reassert the Plan was perfect. Why things went as they did, I leave to your judgment.

12 POUR LES OISEAUX

Fabliau, France, 1929, the year of the Phoenix—a gleaming white city rising like plumes on a cocked hat, in a semi-circle from the sea. Its port-section slums are famous for vice, crime, and an exotic mixture of birds—my kind of town! I'm a private dickybird. I flew here from the States seeking an exotic English chick, name of Song Sparrow. She knows where the eggs are hidden, and I'm going to find out. She's been smuggling guano in from South America. I'm pretty sure that it goes through Fabliau to the Italian Mafia— what they do with it, hey, don't ask me. Ever since the Crash, people have been pulling some pretty crazy deals. Guano is fungible. These days it can buy just about anything, including the goose who laid the golden egg. I know it'll buy me an Old Crow in any of these wormy waterfront nests. The barkeep's a big ugly-looking condor, one of the last of his breed. Is he a displaced Californian, I ask myself in pidgin. But I say it in his beak in plain American, that Peruvian parakeets and Hartz Mountain canaries can understand. The ugly old condor is as laconic as he looks and comes back at me with an owlish "oui" that's packed with innuendo and sarcasm. I slug down my Old Crow, swizzle-worm and all, and order another, take off my feathered Alpine hat, that I picked up on the wing, and place it on the bar, a kind of challenge. He can take it or leave it. He leaves it. He probably figures I got a quiver full of new-fletched arrows under my feathered boa. He's no dumb dodo. I'm looking for an English bird name of Song Sparrow, I tell him. He holds his long dirty wings out like what's it to me and I get a whiff of his wingpits. Fold 'em up, Pollution Pits, I tell him, as I take a gander at the rest of the roost. A couple of old ducks sitting down at the end of the bar, quacking on about the Crash, a middle-aged bird in a tux who looks like a

198

penguin, soft but there's something cold in his eyes; a Brooklyn bird name of Robin, with big, red breasts, a couple o' gay birds up the other end doing some kind of mating dance. But no sign of the real Song Sparrow. Now I got a little red light inside, tells me when there's danger, and on it goes. How do I put it? There's something reminds me of reptiles—no, dinosaurs. Yeah, that's it! These birds look too innocent, like they're hiding something—their real nature, which is definitely saurian. There are winged dragons afoot, and why didn't the canary sing, as Sherlock might not have put it. Then I'm pecked from all sides. It happens so fast I can't tell the pecking order. All I know is I'm getting the bird. It was at that moment, as I saw my life flap by me, that it first occurred to me what a worm I really was. Bob White, this is your life, I said to myself in disgust. Then I heard a distinctly English bird call, a sort of Oxonian chirp, and I found myself in a large cage. Sing, cooed the beautiful, copper-eyed Song Sparrow, who had emerged from her condor costume. I want you to turn canary, she told me, and sing your heart out, like the Hartz Mountain whistleblowers. I said, Sure, why not? I should die for twenty-five pounds of guano a day—and expenses? I'm no sapsucker. We know that the passenger pigeons are bringing the stuff in, I sang, but we don't know how you're getting it out. We fly it out, she tweeted, in stork sheets. She eyed me sideways, giving me the once-over, and then hopped forward and planted one on my beak. That was when I decided to quit being a Hawkshaw. I'm folding my wings, I told her. Let's you and me take off. She dipped her head in agreement. Then we picked up a couple of pieces of straw from the floor and went looking for a good old Anglo-American tree to build our nest in, leaving Fabliau and all its smuggled guano behind us.

Cage closed!

13 SNOWBOUND

How the free spirit suffers his winter out in the woods is his business, isolated alone in an unused farm house rented from a farmer by a tall strange city man with a beard like a board and a wife who would sleep in it but has left for the winter her husband alone to be hermit at his request, an artist, poet and painter, needing neither wife nor child nor sustenance but vision only, that she go forth to the wicked city and fare there with a former lover while he have visions during long mountain downfall of flakes building to crescendo in white isolation, that there be firewood alone was his matter, that chalk run smooth over blackboard and vision come summoned by white gods of sleet and snow and that that first time should he die then the plan be known as faulted with no firewood and the cold growing in his guts, that he understand what he never understood, the seriousness of his state, and learn to be a man once before claimed by the white tongue, snapped like a spot from large blankness making no orientation: be gone. He feared nothing but the thought of no vision, not the loss of his wife to another, nor the loss of his life, nor the meaning of loneliness, but for the vision forsaking all; was willing and willed that Death in a white coat with bony knuckles knock: his wife in wonder could not love her former lover but was young and thrilled at her husband's exploit, leaving the lover without chance as he regaled her with delights on city nights of restaurants and theaters for always she thought of her strange visionary husband in the mountains alone turning whiter and whiter like a snowbird of some extraordinary kind with wings wide and eaglehead highbeaked proud and coming down in spring with great talons spread arresting her in mid-flight at subway entrance and sweeping off up up and away to his glee-echoing lair high on the spiked cliffs—meanwhile the wise farmer

200

who owned the house had snowploughed his way to the visionary's door and knocked like whitecoated Life and found artist frozen but not dead, who awakened to strains of hospital music and surrendered his soul to it, thanking the gods but not any one in particular for the fact that only a few toes had had to be removed—he liked his nurse, a warm vision in white.

14 WHAT I DID ON MY SUMMER VACATION

This summer I flew to Trieste to visit with Joyce, then journeyed on to Prague to see Kafka, who was cryptic. I made a pit-stop in Paris to have a drink with Beckett, caught up with Thomas Wolfe, who had stayed over from the Oktoberfest in Hamburg, and roared around town for a few days, then flew on to Casablanca to have a drink at Rick's and hear some good piano. I met with Graham Greene in Saigon (though they call it Ho Chi Minh City now) and he explained how the quiet American was going to cause trouble. I made the big leap from Dirty Dick's to Sloppy Joe's because the Literary Travel Agency had screwed up my itinerary, but soon found myself chugging through the Chunnel and into Poet's Corner at Westminster Abbey, where I ran into a raging Dylan Thomas. Well, he hated the States but loved Third Avenue, so he said he would help me paint London red, white, and blue. Next morning we had vanilla ice-cream in our beer for our health's sake. Later that afternoon Caitlin kicked the stilts out from under his house, so I thought it was time to leave them there, fighting in Laugharne, and get on to the relative peace and quiet of Ireland, where I visited with Pat Kavanagh, who had come to regard comedy as the "ultimate sophistication," which ordinary people, "do not understand and therefore fear." Pat believed that in tragedy "there is always something of a lie—comedy is the abundance of life," etc., but I had to leave him there, laughing at himself, and life in general, and catch the train on to Heathrow. I landed in New York, where I was met by Walt Whitman, who was holding up a disheveled Eddie Poe, who greeted me with a wet kiss. I got a manly hug from Walt. Then I flew back down to Asheville to present Wolfe's hometown with his latest, *You Can't Go Home Again,* which he gave me in manuscript (much edited by Max Perkins) and then drove back to the College by the Lake; and here I am again, grading papers.

15 THE DOG SHOW

I have to take my master or mistress—or my "best friend"—and run one of them in a circle in front of the judges. Usually, it's my mistress whom I must run, and she has terrible coordination, often becoming entangled in the leash I pull her along with and tripping in front of the judges and the onlookers, causing me considerable embarrassment. I believe the person whom we lead is judged by what their clothing and jewels look like, and also possibly on their agility. It cannot be that they are judged by their physical assets, as most of the competitors are poor physical specimens indeed, with humps and lumps and bumps and other deformities aplenty. Also, most of them can't see very well, and none of them can detect the powerful odors backstage. Besides, we run too fast for them—especially if they wear lifted heels, as do many of the men. In their stage fright and general confusion at being onstage, they often drag their toupees along the floor, leaving us sitting on our haunches and laughing. Yes, dogs can laugh, too, and, as you can see, they can write as well.

The Town Crier came by crying, "Time to get up and trash the day." Nonsense, the Town Crier is not an alarm clock, but the Town Crier is an alarm clock of sorts, so the townspeople rose and immediately prepared for the monkey war of all against all. While they were having coffee, they scowled at one another. A sister threw porridge at her little brother, the little brother pulled the cat's tail, and the cat scratched the dog. It was a typical morning. The Town Crier went home to his wife.

"I have done my duty," he told her. "I have started the whole thing again."

"One day," said his wife, "I am going to refuse to wind you up." They scowled at each other.

The Mayor came to see the Town Crier. "I'm going to fire you," he said. "If it weren't for you waking the town every morning we shouldn't have all this strife."

"I have a contract," said the Town Crier. "You have no authority to give me the chuck."

Then the Doctor visited the Mayor.

"What we must do," said the Doctor, "is to make the town sleep through the Town Crier's cry. I shall put a powerful drug in the water."

"And the town will sleep peacefully all day long," cried the Mayor, seeing the merit of the Doctor's plan. So they tried it, and the town slept right through the Town Crier's cry. All but the Mayor and the Doctor and the Town Crier himself, who never drank water.

The Town Crier came to complain to the Mayor because he couldn't wake anyone up and felt that he might lose his job. On the grounds that he was being neurotic, the Mayor sent him to the Doctor. The Town Crier stated his case, and, to his surprise, the Doctor agreed with him.

"The fact is," said the Doctor, "I have no patients—no broken bones to heal, no blackened eyes, no split lips, nothing to do all day. And the City Contractor is upset. He has nothing to repair. Let's go and have it out with the Mayor."

So the Town Crier, the Doctor, the Fire Chief, and the City Contractor went to see the Mayor. The Mayor refused to see them, so they trashed his office, and, finding him hiding behind a file cabinet, they dragged him out into the town square and threatened to hang him.

By this time everyone in town was wide awake. Quickly, a mob formed, ready to hang the Mayor. A riot ensued, and the town was torn apart.

The City Contractor was very pleased. And when the mob set fire to the town, the Fire Chief was pleased to be busy again.

"You tear it down, and I'll rebuild it," said the City Contractor to the Fire Chief.

The Doctor said, "There will be injuries galore."

A wife said something hateful to her husband, a sister to a brother, and a cat scratched a dog.

The Town Crier cried, "Hear Ye, Hear Ye!" and life went on much as before.

17 THEY ARE HERE

He stepped into the frowning man to see what it was like. Oh, there was too much trouble in there. He stepped back out. This time he stepped into a smiling woman. He didn't like the feel of the clothes. He decided to try a dog. Too dim, except for the sense of smell. Quite remarkable, really. Try a cat. Dimmer, but more satisfied with life. But he did not like the aftertaste of mice. That's it, he said, try a mouse. Too hungry for comfort. Too furtive. Too scared. Quite miserable, heart beating too fast, too excited. Not much chance for relaxation. He tried a galloping horse, out at the racetrack, but immediately became winded. Try a bug, any bug, or maybe a worm. No thanks. He flew to the ledge of an office building in a pigeon. Coo. Coo. He looked down. Interesting. He looked in the window. CEO in his private office, having it with his secretary. He tried the boss, then the secretary. They were both faking, him for power and her for him. He left in a cockroach that he found in an empty Chinese food carton. Out under the door and down the hall. He took the elevator down on a peak in the furred arms of a rich woman. He judged her by her diamonds, which he chewed on as they sank to the lobby. He transferred to a rubbernecking tourist. The tourist was looking up at the pigeon outside the CEO's office. He already knew what was going on in there. Then he spotted another of his kind coming toward him in a bouncy blonde, apparently enjoying the ride. Get out of there, he said, you sex fiend. I've been looking all over for you, said the other. It's time to get back to the ship.

18 WORLD'S STRONGEST MAN
CALLED UPON TO LIFT SLEEP

*Life is movement. Once you
stop moving, you're dead.
Choose life.*
—Eugen Sandow

The world's strongest man was in the great tradition of Sandow, and so was intelligent as well as strong. He thought in terms of leverage and balance, not merely brute power. He would size things up, then think out a strategy for a lift. He resented being thought of as a mere freak of strength. He had studied engineering. This, he admitted, was to be his greatest challenge, and he thought for a long time before taking it on. The proposition posed many questions. Sleep has no handles. How do you get a grip on it? How do you train for such an event? Do you practice with naps, as you might with dumbbells for a barbell lift? And how many naps would be the equivalent of one sleep? Indeed, how long is a true sleep? And what of rem sleep? Do dreams and nightmares add to the weight? What does the average sleep weigh, and where can be found its specific gravity?

He asked himself, "Are they asking me to lift the sleep of the world, or of just one person?" The rules must be made clear.

His manager said not to worry, that lifting sleep sounded like a leadpipe cinch. "All you do is wake everyone up."

But the world's strongest man replied that it would not be an easy task to wake everyone up at once, all over the world. It took more than sheer brute strength to be the world's strongest man; you had to have brains as well. You had to understand exactly what you were getting into.

207

"You don't just lift things," he said. "But you have a point," he added, after a few minutes of thought. And he thought, Lifting sleep is the same as waking the sleepers. So I must find a way to wake everyone at once: and he decided to shake the Earth until everyone was awake.

"That's my angle," he said. "I've got it." He had decided to push against the sky and run until he turned Earth's rotation backwards, causing such an uproar that everyone would wake up at once, thus lifting sleep the world over. He began pushing against the sky and running, digging his spikes into the soft earth, and lifting his knees like pistons.

Then the world's strongest man's wife shook him and said, "Wake up, dear, you're having a nightmare." And he knew that he had lifted sleep from at least one person. Then the clock radio went on and he heard people talking, indicating that there were more from whom sleep had been lifted.

"I think I've done it," he said, running about the house and pushing the sky in front of him.

"We've overslept," said his wife. "You must hurry off to work."

"Yes," he said, grabbing his briefcase, and he heeled out the front door—forgetting the car, which waited in the driveway, and down the block of suburban houses, and into the slow rise of the mountains, pushing the sky as he vanished into the distance.

19 REACHING THE TOP

I hired a press agent who was said to be tops. Don't ask how much she cost me, but I had to sell everything I had. I was tired of being a nonentity. No more would people say Oh, it's just him. Instead, they would say Wow, that's him, that's him for sure! Any old how, that's the way I looked at it. So I found myself facing down a newsstand and a copy of the *Daily Do*, and there I was, in five inch headlines over an eight by ten picture. The headline read: *HE IS LOOKING AT THE PAPER.* I looked around to see if anyone nearby recognized me from the photograph. No, nobody seemed to notice. Then my eye was caught by a *People Magazine* cover. I was on it. The caption read: *HE SEES HIMSELF.* Then the newsy pointed at me and yelled, Look, there he is! Now I noticed that every magazine and newspaper on the stand had my picture on its cover or front page. The captions and headlines all read things like, *HE'S LOOKING AT HIMSELF AGAIN*, and, *WHY IS HE LOOKING AT HIMSELF?* People had gathered to see what the newsy was yelling about. I ducked out of the crowd and ran down the street, feeling a strong sense of terror. I passed a store window where I appeared on television. It looked like a talk show. Yes, it was called What About Me? I saw that I was on billboards. My name was being written across the sky. I went home and discovered myself all over the Internet. There could hardly be a soul on Earth who didn't know me. My fame brought money and soon I was one of the richest men in the world, able at last to escape my nightmare by paying my press agent to keep me out of notice so that I could achieve a life of anonymity, a shadowy figure in a penthouse looking down on the newsstand many stories below.

MARIJUANA AT MONTICELLO

A Farce in One Act

SETTING: THOMAS JEFFERSON's empty study at
            Monticello.

AT RISE: We hear low, indistinguishable voices off
            stage. Sounds of people milling about.

TOUR GUIDE *(voice-over)*
Stay together, please. Many believe Thomas Jefferson to
have been the greatest of the Founding Fathers. A liberal in
the classic, not the modern sense, he did not believe in big
government. That government is best, he wrote, that
governs least. In fact, he considered government service not
as a career at all, but as a duty, in the sense that the
legendary Cincinnatus of Rome considered it. You will
remember that Cincinnatus left his farms to save Rome and
returned to them as soon as possible after the crisis.
Jefferson did not even state that he had been President of the
United States on his gravestone, nor that he, along with
James Madison—and with Ben Franklin's input—wrote the
Constitution of the United States. He was proudest of the
fact that he founded the University of Virginia. A man with
a profoundly enquiring mind, he considered his work in
education to be his truest legacy. An architect, lawyer,
writer, farmer, inventor—his accomplishments are
numerous, outside the field of politics. Nothing was lost on
him. A gourmand, he did not consider it to be a minor point
that he brought the French fried potato back from France to
his homeland. He was a connoisseur of wines. A self-
taught chef. Truly, a man for all seasons. As tall as

211

Lincoln, he was a handsome, red-headed man built like an athlete. Now, follow me. I'm going to take you into his study—

JEFFERSON
(Enters, wearing work clothes, smudged on clothing and face with dirt, sweating. He goes to his bookcase and searches for something. Mutters to himself.)
Cannabis. Cannabis.

(There is a soft knock on the door. SALLY HEMINGS steps in.)

SALLY
Am I disturbing you?

JEFFERSON
No, no, my dear.
(He extends his hands to her and she crosses to him. They clasp hands and then he takes her in his arms and kisses her, a long, passionate kiss. He releases her, feigning annoyance.)
Now you've made me forget what I was looking for, you vixen. Should I pursue you through the house like a hang-tongued hound?

SALLY
A red bloodhound after a black bunny? You sweet-assed man, you mastermind, what are you after? It's not me, when you're onto an idea.

JEFFERSON
I've been planting an exotic, a plant with extraordinary properties. It produces a narcotic affect, quite pleasant,

212

when smoked. I have reason to believe it could be of enormous medicinal value. It's called Cannabis.
(Continues looking in bookcase)

SALLY

Pot! You been planting pot?

JEFFERSON

No, no, my silly. I've been planting it on yonder hill.
(pointing out window)

SALLY

Thomas Jefferson. You mean to say you don't know?

JEFFERSON

Know what, my dear? What are you on about?

SALLY

Why, you can't plant marijuana on yon hill. The D.E.A.—

JEFFERSON

The what—who—?

SALLY

The D.E.A., the Drug Enforcement Agency. They fly helicopters and light planes over here all the time. They'll spot your pot and raid Monticello. They break down your door and make you lie facedown on the floor and handcuff you from behind and drag you off, you big fool!

JEFFERSON

These helicopters—sun-drawn seeds? You've become quite the scientist. Exceeded the teacher, for I must admit I

have not heard of them before. What books are you
reading?

SALLY

Never mind that, Tom. The D.E.A.'ll—

JEFFERSON

Are they some secret band of terrorist sent by the mad old
king? Are the English still after revenge for the Revolution?
We have many friends in Parliament, but there are always
diehards. Should we raise an armed militia? It was for
such types, and others—primarily, for those in the
government of the United States who would attempt to
reduce the dream of freedom that is America, that I and the
others made certain that the citizen could retain his weapons
of defense. I feared a tyrannical taxation, which is the first
tool of tyrants in their attempt to subjugate their subjects.
Next is open force. (*He ponders*) So, the Brits are at it
again. Call out the militia!

SALLY

No, Tom, not the Brits. Parliament doesn't pay any heed to
the mad old king anymore.

JEFFERSON

Who, then? And why should this D.E.A.—did you call
them?—why should they care what I do? What possible
difference can it make to anyone, that I am experimenting
with Cannabis? I have experimented with things all my life.
It is the nature of the mind to explore. How is it any of their
affair?

SALLY

They are a government agency, Tom.

214

JEFFERSON

Is this a nightmare? Are you telling me that the government
of the United States of America would have anything to do
with what a citizen does on his own land and in the privacy
of his home, barring, of course, some criminal activity?

SALLY

But growing marijuana *is* a criminal activity.

JEFFERSON

How, confound it! It is an interest of mine, and it has
become a pleasure, like my wines, like my French fried
potatoes. What in heaven's name are you on about?

SALLY

They have made a law against it.

JEFFERSON

Why that would be exactly like making a law against opium.
Why would anyone do that?

SALLY

There *is* a law against opium—the same law.

JEFFERSON

Opium is against the law? Why? It has marvelous
properties.

SALLY

They don't want people to use drugs.

JEFFERSON

Who are *they*, that they should tell the people what to do?
Perhaps it's time for another revolution. Next you'll be

telling me there's a law against wine, the first miracle of Christ.

SALLY

There will be—between Nineteen-Nineteen and Nineteen Thirty-Three. It will be called Prohibition.

JEFFERSON *(astounded)*

Prohibition! To prohibit? The United States Government is in the business of prohibiting people from ingesting wine and good stout and bourbon whiskey and of all things, opium. Why?

SALLY

It's not good for us.

JEFFERSON

Who are they to say what is and is not good for anyone? The people decide that, individually. There is nothing *malum in se,* evil in itself, about any intoxicant. Life is difficult, one escapes it from time to time. It is perfectly normal. One does it in reading a book, watching a play, in conversation over wine, in watching a sunset. Prohibition? That is merely *malum prohibitum*, an evil because it is called one. And by whom? Let him who does not enjoy wine do what he does enjoy. I enjoy wine. What is it to him?
> *(goes to a sideboard, pours himself a drink, drinks it, then pours both of them a drink and hands one to her.)*

I must admit to shock. This has happened since my retirement?

SALLY

This and much more since you set my boys free.

JEFFERSON

I had not the power to set anyone free, my love. There is another example of the evil of law, what tyranny it becomes when unrestrained. How people give their freedom away for a false safety. Life is not a thing to feel safe in.

SALLY

A security blanket.

JEFFERSON

Yes, yes, that's very good. Yes, life is not a security blanket to feel safe in, it is a thrilling adventure, dangerous and doomed, but it offers the opportunity, once in the universe of eternity, to test one's metal, to see if the stardust can hold its own.

SALLY

You're wonderful with words, Tom. But you must go out and deracinate that pot.

JEFFERSON

Never! I stand on my Constitutional rights. After all, I wrote them. This government has its priorities misplaced. Every person has as much right to do as he or she desires to do as does the government, which is only another group of persons, somewhat less talented than the average artist or scientist, mostly middle-brow lawyers. The government is here to see that we do not hurt one another and are not hurt from the outside. We are here to see to it that the government doesn't hurt us. Have you not heard me say, my dear, that when the candidates tell you they have a plan, you should tell them that you already have a plan. It's called the Constitution of the United States of America, and proceed to inform them that they are not James Madison, et alia. The

217

purpose of the Constitution is well known. It's purpose is to keep out subsequent plans by politicians, including candidates. Its purpose is to make the government leave the citizen alone. This is called freedom and is highly valued by all enslaved peoples, though not so highly valued as it ought to be by those possessed of it. Freedom allows for invention, invention creates wealth, wealth is a syrup one pours into pies, causing them to expand their crusts, crack, and ooze rich juices that drip . . . all over the place!

SALLY

That's all very well, Tom, but, as to the drugs, they would say that they cause violence.

JEFFERSON

How? Oh, I've been in a taphouse brawl or two. I might not look it today, but I was quite accomplished in the art of fisticuffs when in my youth.

SALLY

I love your muscles, my dear. No, but that isn't what they mean. There are those who shoot each other over the drugs. Dealers and the like.

TOUR GUIDE *(voice-over)*

Right this way, now—into the garden.

SALLY

They'll see the pot out there.

JEFFERSON

Let them. I told you, my dearest, I planted the cannabis in the ground, not in a pot. Why do you keep insisting—?

SALLY

Tom, pour me another drink, please. I need one.

JEFFERSON

It's particularly good Amontillado. *(pouring)* We had a boy at the University of Virginia, I heard, an extremely intelligent chap name of Edgar Poe, who wrote a wonderful tale called the Cask of Amontillado. I enjoyed it immensely.
(handing her a glass)
Do you know, speaking of intoxicants, this young Poe was said to have experimented with all manner of them. I was so interested. I wanted to have him come for a visit but I was never able to locate him. Bit of a bounder, I'm told, but I can't help think that anyone who can write like that must have the stuff. Dropped out, unfortunately, after only a year. Money problems, gambling, or something.

SALLY

My dearest, you don't seem to understand the danger you're in. The D.E.A. plays rough.

JEFFERSON

Rougher than the Brits? I doubt it. And we sent Cornwallis on his way. Now, there again, is an example of what I mean. Taxation, the tool of tyranny!

SALLY

That's how they pay the D.E.A.

JEFFERSON

What? You mean with *our* taxes? I remember old Ben Franklin used to say, there are only two certainties in life, death and taxes. I always liked that one. But how do they extract such taxes?

219

SALLY

From income.

JEFFERSON

Tyranny, tyranny, tyranny, and the end of wealth. For a man of spirit will not work for under fifty percent of his labor's worth.

SALLY

Poor Tom, you ain't seen nothing yet!

JEFFERSON

No, no. "Haven't" and "Anything."

SALLY

I know, precious baby, I know.

TOUR GUIDE *(voice-over)*

Someone has planted marijuana in President Jefferson's garden. Marijuana at Monticello, can you imagine? But wait! What's that? There are Apache helicopters overhead. You can see the rockets and the machine guns. They are an American fleet. I can see the flag-emblem of the United States of America—and, something else—what is it?— D.E.A. Oh my God, people, run for your lives!

SALLY

Tom, Monticello is being stormed. Where can we hide?

JEFFERSON

Hide, nothing! Hand me my blunderbuss. I'll take my stand for *liberty*!

CURTAIN

Veilsville's quiet. Wind's playing low tunes through the whitened, skeletonized trees in the woods surrounding the house. I survive the nights with sleeping pills and bourbon, dull books and dying fires. But the days, George!

When I stepped out to collect the half-frozen milk this morning, a young woman poet was in the hammock on the porch. Late November! Bittercold! She lay snoring in a thin dress under a raincoat without a lining. Another of my crazy conquests. They come from all over, everywhere, anywhere! This was a good-looker. You'd be surprised at how many are good-looking. What do they want? I'm a serious man. I'm a heart-broken man. Don't they know? Where's all that much talked of poetic sensitivity? Can you imagine me, of all people, with stalking fans? It's too fantastic. Sometimes I think I've gone mad, that I'm hallucinating all this.

What was it? A year ago? A year ago! Here I was, a plain ordinary Professor of English in the English Department of a little backwater, jerkwater college with an enrollment of 600 students in the unheard of hamlet of Veilsville, Tennessee—and, George, I was happy! You, who weren't even satisfied to hold a chair in literature at one of the best— if not, etc.—Ivy League schools in the country; you, who must have power in New York as a critic; you, sophisticate, bon vivant, etc.; you, who have never been "happy"—you would not and probably still cannot believe it; but I was happy. I remember your constant jibes; your: "Why bury yourself with the hillbillies in the Appalachians?" Your Erewhon/Nowhere ribbing. But George, *you* were fully grown, a mature man. I've only recently been born. At forty!

I interrupted this letter for a few minutes to send my young stalker back to bed. Can you imagine? She's about twenty and "simply steaming" for me. Think of it! Charlie

Fallon, a sex object! It's so ludicrous it must be true. Now don't cluck your tongue. Yes, I let her in—yes, I let her stay. Why not? She's of age, and I've never been so lonely in my life. Maybe she'll help. I don't know. Her poetry's execrable but her legs are great; and she must be healthy or she'd be sick from sleeping out last night. Not a clogged sinus do I detect. Don't worry about me; it doesn't matter anyway.

What I mean is, George, that the past—one might say my pre-birth years, the ones from that false start my mother gave me to that period of a year or so ago—seems to me now like some sweet dead happy dream. I'm in the real world now, bloody born at last. Now I'm like you—tough old George—in a way. Except—I have a dream of happiness and yes even of beauty to recall. I can draw on it, like a big bank account. The Pulitzer was nothing, George. I'm going to be a *great* poet now. I hurt enough to send me right up to and on past the Nobel and into history. What poor Kathleen always wanted!

I suppose you see them occasionally. The cocktail circuit, or The White Horse, or wherever the literary chic waste their breath these days. Pardon my ignorance. I was a literary anchorite. I never knew that life. Whistler is a good poet—hell, a fine poet, maybe a great one—but he's had no luck. Not really. How odd that I of all people should have had such luck! Strange, strange luck! Whistler offended too many important people. But five fine books! And I, with just my one absurd sad long account of forebemoaned moan, and suddenly—as one of the New York papers put it—I'm a Cinderella poet (my God!), a Big Prize Winner! I'm more popular—I shy from the word famous—even more academically respected (but there I've got Whistler who never stopped to pick up a degree) than poor Kathleen's hero roaring boy. Add to that, that, at the age of forty (now forty-one) my ridiculous career, unlike Whistler's, has been called "meteoric." The world is truly tilted. And that embarrassing letter I wrote to my subscribers a year ago, when I was in the middle of my worst agony and confusion. Did you ever see it? I don't suppose so. You never would subscribe to what you called "Charlie's Little Poetaster's Journal." I can hear you now: "Don't encourage him. If you do, he'll stay buried out there in the boondocks forever. Charlie's a dear soul. He's got talent, but he wants bringing out. He's pathologically retiring." No, George: perhaps I was simple but I wasn't sick. Now I'm sick—and I'll never be able to be simple again.

When I look over copies of "A Poet's Journal" now, I can't believe that I was its editor, that *I* chose the pathetic (sometimes bathetic) poetic stuff that mimeos its pages. Was that Charlie Fallon? Did I think such stuff of merit? It's a wonder you didn't kick me down the stairs, George, as it's said Schopenhauer's mother did him. But, you see, I must have been a happy man. Innocent beyond belief. But nothing, George, absolutely nothing, had ever gone wrong for me. Now I understand that I didn't understand poetry at all, though I taught it. Think! I spent my summers at The Writers' Camp, giving my seminar on "Poe and the Dark Side of the Mind!" Well, here's a copy of the letter I sent out to the subscribers of "Fallon's, A Poet's Journal." Don't skip reading it, George. As simple-minded as it is, it will become part of literary history—now that I'm such a famous fellow.

AN OPEN LETTER

Dear FALLON'S, A POET'S JOURNAL Reader:

I feel that you subscribers are members of my family, and because I find myself in such a despondent frame of mind, it is to you I turn.

Some time ago my wife, Kathleen, took our five-year-old son, Chuck, and left me. Her move to New York was completely unexpected. As far as I could tell our life here together in Veilsville was a happy one. However, I have since learned that another man was involved.

224

For weeks I have lived here alone, miserably, unable to tell if I were awake or still within some hideous nightmare. Although I have sought and obtained professional help, I have lost over twenty pounds and still find it practically impossible to carry out the smallest domestic task.

However, out of this period of despondency, one solid and good thing has come. I have been forced for the first time in my life to look deeply into my own soul. And out of that painful sight I have gleaned a sheath of poems. I have assembled this collection of poems into a small volume, called A Closed Book. *The heartbreak I have endured and still labor under was occasioned by my wife's leaving, and I am having the collection printed so that I might present her with a copy on what would have been our sixth anniversary. In order to have one copy printed, I have had to contract for 250 copies.*

I hope it will not seem crass to you, dear reader, that I now offer the remainder of these copies for sale. It is only because I think of you as members of my own family and because I feel that you might want to help me now that I do so. I ask, too, that if any of you have any thoughts which may be of use to me now—any ideas on how one so stricken might begin again and pick up the pieces of a shattered life—please send them to me. You will not be considered a "busy-body," let me assure you. I am asking for any assistance you feel you might offer me.

The holiday season is coming on and I wish each of you a happy time, though I know my own will be bleak. Yours very sincerely,
Charles Fallon, Editor

I've read it so many times lately, George, I know it by heart. I just copied it out from memory. A few words here or there might be off, but that's the gist of it. I even put an order blank at the bottom!

You know part of what happened next, George. The wife of the top man at one of the big publishing houses was a subscriber. She was touched by my letter and sent for a copy of *A Closed Book*. Strange world, she was even more touched by the poems! Her husband's house published it—ten thousand copies first run! It was to be a gimmick. Another of those strange things called a popular poetry book, a trade book—no cultural endeavor—another *Stanton Street and Other Blues*—another *This Is My Love*.

None of us really knows what he or she is doing, do you think, George? But I suppose you think you do—that's your nature. But you can believe this, my friend: I do not even remember writing those poems, that book. Those first weeks after Kathleen went off with Jimmy Whistler—and took my darling little boy with her—those weeks—now—are a complete blank. It was so totally unexpected, George! There wasn't a hint.

Whistler had stayed with us, I remember, for about a week. He was drinking rather heavily—but who complains about a brilliant poet's drinking habits so long as he behaves himself? I'd only gotten a few issues of the magazine out at that point and I was all wrapped up in it, so perhaps didn't observe what was there to observe. I don't know—I don't *remember*.

Whistler and Kathleen and I all met at the same time, at The Writers' Camp. I was doing my Poe thing and Kathleen was a college junior up for the summer from Alabama to study creative writing. Whistler was putting the final touches on his second book—the one that would make him famous. I was 35, a full professor. Whistler an unknown 25 year old poet, with a few small press things to his credit. Kathleen paid no attention to him. In her eyes, it was I who was important. She developed one of those teacher-student crushes. At least I thought it a crush at first. Well, you know what happened. I don't know why I re-hash for you. No, it isn't for you. I'm trying to get it straight. But in short, Kathleen came up a few months later and we got married. She's a kid and I'm 35. But you know me, George—I'm a kid, too. Then my son is born. George, my whole heart is in Kathleen and that boy of mine. Suddenly I'm younger than I've ever been. I've got so much energy I can't contain myself. I'm happy-manic and forgetful. I'll publish a little magazine for poets. I'll teach at old Veilsville by day and edit and publish by evening and love Kathleen and the boy and even love my own silly poems, songs to them and to the sweetest and best of all possible worlds. I'm even dumber than you thought! I'm even happier than before. There's no end to my dumb happiness. But Kathleen's lonely out here in Erewhon/Nowhere. I should have heeded. She was young. But this was what I loved. Here I could write about my precious larks! I'm an innocent academic Henry David. Then Whistler hits it. Suddenly he's famous—famous as poets are famous. He writes me in response to a letter of mine congratulating him that he's dizzy with success, wants peace, quiet, etc. I invite him here. Well, you know.

He came here occasionally—even gave old Veilsville a free reading or two as a favor to me. Drank mostly. Kathleen went down south to see her folks. Only I gather that what she really did was to go into New York and make the rounds with famous brilliant Whistler. In those days it *was* The White Horse. But good old 40 year old Charlie Fallon, the perennial child, was too much of a dope to even dream it, what was "going down," as the jargon is. Then, just like that, it's over.

I can't work—I mean I can't teach. I get leave. I sit in here, a twisted, split-minded, broken-hearted creature, mooning over my vanished Kathleen and my taken boy. I drink and for the first time in my life, as it now seems clear, I write. What do I write? If I didn't have the book right here at my elbow I wouldn't know. Apparently I wrote these poems. They are terrible, sharable things to read. I was not myself. No, I became the self I am. I was born. But the tricks weren't done.

George, you know I don't know anything about literary politics. So I have never been able to explain satisfactorily to myself how a book of poems which was published to be a money-maker, a heart-throbber, could hit for The Pulitzer. But hit it did. Maybe it was the power of the publishing house. Obligations of the committee, etc. Maybe it was the tremendous popularity of the book—the first book of poems to hit the *Times* best seller list since . . . since I don't know what. Maybe it was the ballyhoo. Nothing to match it since *Love Story*. But there I am in New York, which I hate, and making the circuit, which I hate, and all I can think of is Kathleen and how she always wanted exactly this sort of thing to happen. I'll admit it was perverse satisfaction that occasionally tempered my misery. Indescribable misery, George—thinking how all of a sudden I have eclipsed Whistler.

"Now," I would tell myself, "I bet she wishes she had stuck it out with me, with young-old Charlie. Now she's sorry, I bet!" But it wasn't any good. And hell, it's obvious even to me that if she hadn't left me I'd never have been what she wanted me to be.

Christ, George, can you make sense of it? Of course you can. You can make sense of anything.

Yeah, Georgie boy, I'll take your European Tour. I'll do a residence at Oxford, or even the University of Cracow. For your sake if for no other reason—so you'll get your clever fee, you old hustler. Christ, George, you're a crook! Any honest agent would take ten percent, not twenty-five. You didn't think I even knew that, did you? Well, George, you're a friend, so you can hustle me if you want to.

Damn, I feel old! I'd better go join my young literary stalker under the sheets while she's still steaming and I'm still able to ease her pressure. Would it be okay if I brought her along on the tour? She really has got great legs.

You know, George, for the first time in my life I realize what it is to be a poet, with all that it means in loneliness. See you in New York. Hey, let's sail over. What do you say?

SONNET AT SIXTY-FIVE

Sixty-five orbits of the sun today
and, though I'm growing tired of this spacesuit,
which rag, as an unhappy by-the-way,
has lost its goggles and at least one boot,
so that I cannot see or even walk
as I once could, and have some trouble hearing,
and toothless too, and tongue-tied, cannot talk
without the noise of cranky broken gearing—

where was I?—tired of this spacesuit!—still I
am grateful that I have a suit to wear
at sixty-five, and wouldn't I be silly
if I preferred to lie in earth bone-bare
   to orbiting the sun again this year
   in this old-fashioned and bedraggled gear?

TREADWELL IN LEISURELAND

Treadwell had been doing his share—he now heard said of him—and more than his share for thirty years. No, not more than my share, he thought. One can never do enough.

He smiled at the assembly, and nodded his gratitude.

Some of these people—like old Joe Pusher there—he had labored alongside of for many a year. Others were relative newcomers, young upstanding men and women, just starting out. He felt grateful to them all for their presence here today, as he received his retirement number, clearly embossed on a brand-new plastic badge. He had handed in his thirty-year-old badge a moment before—ah, the exchange of badges! What a wonderful day! And yet—nostalgic. He heard his name.

"Treadwell," said Mr. Rumble, taking Treadwell's elbow and—rather proudly, Treadwell thought—showing him off to the assembly, "Treadwell, you have worked long and hard for Moloch Plastics and Moloch Plastics is grateful and hereby presents you with this government approved, brand-new plastic retirement badge. What do you say? And what do *you* say, employees? Come on, let's hear it for Treadwell!"

It was the youth who particularly impressed Treadwell as he stood there in the din of applause. It was something in their faces. An eagerness. Yes, that was it. For a moment the years rolled back and he saw himself again, a young man just out of school, packing his brand-new degree in Plastic Engineering. But immediately the years rolled forward again, from his first day of employment. Had he done well? He had tried.

He remembered, almost gaily, how, with his very first paycheck, he had bought four gravesites (himself, wife and

231

two children). He had met his wife about a year later. A condo, the first of thirty cars, the son, the boat, the season tickets for the games, the daughter, and promotion had followed in the usual way. But had he done right? He had worked very hard, but had he read enough? A book a year was advised. They had been sent by the Club; but had he read them? He felt a twinge of conscience. But he had tried. The wife, the condo, the cars, the son, the boat, the tickets, the games, the daughter, and promotions had kept him so busy that it seemed as if he had never had time to think.

He smiled and took the check from Mr. Rumble's hand—five hundred bobbits!

"—this retirement award, and a pension of two-hundred bobbits per—" Mr. Rumble was saying.

"Thirty years," said Treadwell.

"What's that, Treadwell?"

"Thirty years, sir—"

"That's right, Treadwell—thirty years. Let's hear it for Treadwell!"

* * *

"And what line were you in?" asked Ms. Glee.

"Plastic engineering."

"How long?"

"Thirty years."

"And have you given serious thought to just taking it easy? Are you sure you wish to resume employment?"

"Yes, quite sure. I've worked so many years—well, I just don't know what to do with myself."

"And you wish to go back into your old line?"

"I don't know anything else."

"But weren't you a member of the Club? Didn't you receive your books? I bet you never read your books, did you?" She winked.

Treadwell shrugged and smiled sheepishly. "Well, you know how it is. First there were the gravesites, then the wife, then the condo, then the son, then the boat—"

"It's very common, Mr. Treadwell. No time to develop the old inner resources—that it?"

"I'm afraid so."

"And now you want something meaningful to do. Yes, we live so much longer these days. We have so much to give and so much more time to give it in, thanks to science. Now let me see, Plastic Engineering—" Ms. Glee picked for a few minutes at her computer, then looked up as if she had forgotten something—"Oh, Mr. Treadwell, how much do you know about Leisureland? Have you been given a run-through? History? By-laws?"

"Some—" said Treadwell, uncertain. He really only knew that he could likely get a job here, and that was what counted.

"Leisureland was founded in 1995," said Ms. Glee, mechanically, "as a government-subsidized, private, neigh-borhood leisure-life counselling service whose purpose is to help retired people adjust to their new-won inactivity. People who don't develop their inner resources—imagination, etc.—sometimes don't know what to do with themselves when they reach the Golden Years. We were founded to help. Of course, we must charge for our services, or we'd be out of business in no time—and within a decade Leisureland has expanded to serve people all over the world. *We have a cure for what ails you.* That's our motto. The rest is in the brochure. Now then, how much are you able to put down?"

"I have my five-hundred bobbit retirement award."

"That will be adequate."

"And how much will I have to pay after that?"

"Say, one-hundred bobbits a month?"

"Yes, I think I can manage that, if my wife keeps on working."

"Fine. Now just sign here."

233

Treadwell signed with a shaking hand. He felt like a boy again. He said, feeling that it was all too good to be true: "And I'll be employed in Plastic Engineering?"

"You'll start at the bottom and it's up to you from there on out." Ms. Glee beamed to see his excitement.

"You see," she explained, "we are a subsidiary of Moloch Plastics. We are a subsidiary of everything. The only difference is that, as a retired person, with a badge embossed with your own retirement number on it"—here she beamed again, now with communal pride—"You'll pay us."

"I can't wait to get started," said Treadwell, the old enthusiasm illuminating his rheumy eyes.

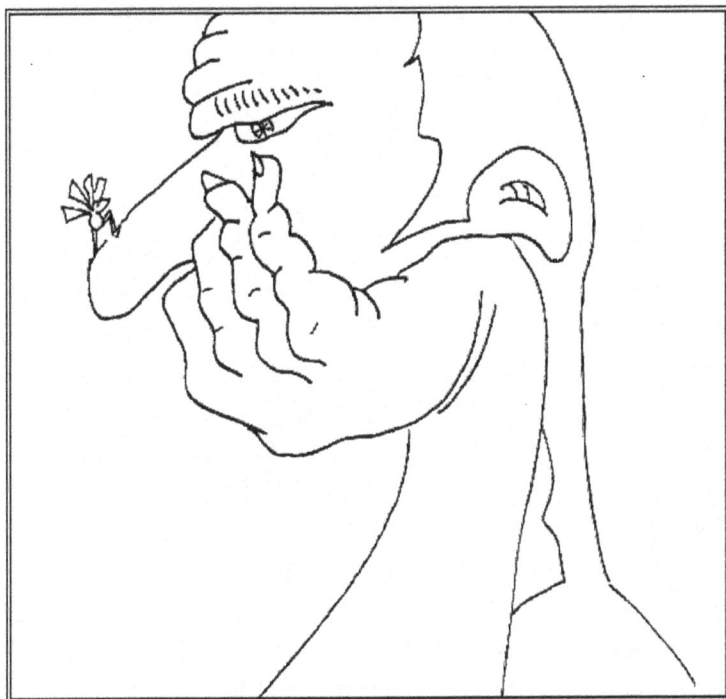

GENDER BENDER
An Authorized History of the Sex War

1
THE UPRISING OF THE DONGS

Miz Mandalay, a magnificent Amazon of twenty-five with splendidly developed anti-sex objects, held a Doctorate in Liberal Tyranny from the University of Xantippe, where she had written an eyebrow-raising thesis, later published on Say-screen, in which she had attempted to show that certain ancient Dongs, despite their sexual swinishness, had manifested symptoms of emerging mental capacity, and had even been capable—this is what had shocked the world—of a kind of tenderness.

Had the slum-lord class not become more liberal, that thesis might have consigned Miz Mandalay to the lower levels of governance. But these were turbulent times. It had become possible to say the un-sayable of ten years before. Dongs were cracking the information frontier, seeking a newer world, speaking boldly out from their hiding places, demanding Dong suffrage and other outrageous rights. Perhaps the most threatening of these revolutionary Dongs was a Spartacus-like character called Resurgius, known for his Tarzan-like physique, poetic speech, and flirtatious nature.

Whereas, after the Great Succession, Dongs were content to be allowed to walk in the gutters, with their heads hanging, and manifesting upon demand every sign of shame, from reddening cheeks to the squeezing of the legs together, today they went about right on the sidewalks, and mingled with the Mize (though they were not generally allowed to address them unless spoken to); and of late small, radical groups of Dongs had been making open protest. Some had gone so far as to lift a leg and ask for the vote! (Not that the vote meant anything, even to the Mize; but the *idea*!)

To liberals of Miz Mandalay's persuasion, these indications of unrest among the once shamefaced Dong population were healthy signs, showing that today's was a healthy, vital society. Some, like Miz Mandalay herself, would give the Dongs the vote. She, being an inner council member, knew that the vote was merely symbolic, but she also knew that that was precisely what made it important. She would liken it to a valve from which to release the steam of frustration from the pressure-cooker of society. After all, she told herself, the Dongs *are* human beings, even if they are Dongs.

Miz Jaye Edgahoova, and others of conservative persuasion, felt differently. As Miz Edgahoova, a poco-porcine middle-aged Miz, put it: "These Dong protesters are highly dangerous, potentially. Let us recall that our own Movement started in protest. And let us remember, further, that in the antique days protest did no real good for us. It is not in the nature of power to give itself away. Most of you are too young to remember, but we who date back to the time before the Great Succession, do—that we used to say, *This is a Dong-dominated society.* Of course, what we young vaginal revolutionaries did not understand at the time was how right we were. In those days, what we were naively doing was *asking* Dongs to stop dominating us and to empower us. It never seemed to occur to us that the fact that they *did* dominate indicated that they *could*—indeed, had, always. Why? Because dominance, after all, *is* power. And you cannot *ask* that the powerful cease being powerful. No, we came to realize that we couldn't simply ask for power—power is something you have to *take*. If you can take it, you are powerful; and if you can hold it, you remain powerful.

"Now today's liberals, the Dong fellow travellers, are asking us to give and give. Give in on this point, give in on that. Give in, and let the Dongs have the vote. Remember, that was the very first mistake the Dongs themselves made. That was the step that led to the Great Succession. The tactic in those days was to make the Dongs feel ashamed of their strength. We were successful in doing just that. Only through demoralizing the Dongs, only by making them feel ashamed of what they were, did we succeed in preparing them psychologically for the Great Capitulation which led to the Great Succession. And now persons like Miz Mandalay, perhaps unwittingly, but with the same kind of misguided generosity of spirit that led to the downfall of the Dongs, are doing to us what we did years ago in Pre-Succession days to the Dongs.

"Those who aid subversives, even unwittingly, are themselves subversive, and enemies of the State. If Miz Mandalay were to achieve full control, I have no doubt but that she would turn Atalanta over to the Dongs. Do I detect the odor of the sexual regressive? That's why we must be vigilant, and at the same time take strong action on both fronts—against traitors, and against Dongs." She addressed the Emergency Session of the Univacual Council, with a special word for Miz Mandalay:

"And I suppose you would give in to their demands, Miz Mandalay, and then when the Dongs ask for the right to be delegates you'd give in again—and why not just save us all a great deal of time and turn the hard-won reins of gov-ernnesting over to them right now, I ask you? Why don't we just go back to jock strap rule—back to the rule of—pardon my language—toxic masculine principle, where war is peace? Hey? Answer me that!" She twirled a not completely imaginary mustache and looked contemptuously at Miz Mandalay.

"If Miz Edgahoova were any kind of scholar," Miz Mandalay responded, rising from her seat, her clear, crisp voice ringing with the self-assurance and the apparent lucidity of her class (which was top-tone—her mother owned three States), "the

238

Miz would be forced to admit that we have engaged in thirty minor counteractions and two major ones since the Succession. It is to our shame that we have proven to be as violent as were the Dongs when they ran things."

"Bah! More violent!" cried Jaye Edgahoova, removing a spaceshoe and banging her rostrum top. She then grabbed from her satchel a copy of Plutarch's *Lives,* which she had been reading for the purpose of gleaning advice on warfare, and now she lifted it and brought it down on her rostrum-top with the explosive sound of a cherry bomb.

"We got to meet force wid force," she cried, falling back, as she sometimes did, especially when angered, on the rough, Jerseyish language of her youth. Out of common stock, she had fought her way to the top, tooth and nail, both feet forward.

"Dose Dames—" her aide took her by the sleeve and tugged. Her indiscretion noted, Miz Edgahoova renewed her attack with greater caution and better diction: "Those Yellow Mize were sneaking into our territory. If Miz Mandalay were as much of a Statesmiz as she is a scholar, she would know that our economy depends on the Tesla windmills of those Islands. What were we supposed to do—stand by and let them take them?"

"An extremely Dong-like argument" said Miz Mandalay, totally unaware of the bigotry in her statement.

"Oh no you don't," cried Jaye Edgahoova. "Just because you don't want to dirty your hands with jobs like that, and you let me make all the dirty decisions, don't mean you have a right to identify me with Dong-think. The Yellows was already shipping our oil away when my skyfleets creamed 'em."

"It could have been settled with reason," said Miz Mandalay with an unfortunate tinge of smugness.

"Reason!" Miz Edgahoova was boiling over. "Before we even opened fire the Yellows had shot down six ten-billion dollar Crawford Spikeheel rocketeers! Reason, she says!" Miz Edgahoova's aide tugged at her sleeve again. Miz Edgahoova pulled her arm free.

"I don't care," she shouted, pounding the rostrum top with her spaceshoe for emphasis, "I've said it before, and I'll say it right now, before this august body, those Yellows are tough titties. They'd have creamed us if I hadn't acted in time—or if you'd had your way."

At which several Yellow Mize scrambled to their feet and exited in a flurry, causing a general stir.

"Now you see what you've done!" cried Miz Mandalay. "You've offended the visiting representatives from the Mainland of Mizmou!"

"Bitches!" muttered Miz Edgahoova. "Them Yellow bitches!"

"Mize! Mize! Please! Order!" called Miz Mandalay. "Now then, it's time to hear the reports."

Miz Edgahoova, who had slumped back into her contour double-cheek cup, now jumped back to her feet. "I called for this emergency session," she cried, "and *I'll* call for the reports. If it's facts that this assembly wants, I've got 'em," claimed Miz Edgahoova. "As I was saying, them demonstrations must be stopped—"

"Facts, Miz Edgahoova," said Miz Mandalay coolly, "I called for facts."

"It's a fact that these demonstrations have been undermining the morale of the ruling Mize—that's a fact!"

"Speak for yourself; I was never more confident. These are great times to live in. Truly turbulent!"

Miz Edgahoova's rejoinder of "Balls," the filthiest of all words was spoken in such a low tone that none of the delegate Mize were sure they'd heard it. Still, it sent an electric thrill through the assembly. Miz Mandalay, fearing to reprimand Miz Edgahoova's language, also not certain of it, blushed to her tiny toes, but remained tight-lipped.

240

"The truth is," said Miz Edgahoova, "these are dangerous times. I repeat, the other day I reminded my class at the
Female Bureau of Investigation that revolution begins in
peaceful protest. As soon as the Dongs see that we are not
willing to relinquish our power to them, they'll take active
steps to steal it from us, just as the revolutionary libbies of the
Succession did to them. That's politics! That's life! That's
facts!"

"No speeches, please," interrupted Miz Mandalay. "No
political theories—just facts."

"O.K., then I call as my first witness Miz Rabble-Mead,
who has been working closely with me on this issue. As you
all know, Miz Rabble-Mead is Ministmiz of Depopulation—
also well known for her work in anthropological sperm
confusion—"

A pleasant-looking, rather tubby little Miz who had
produced several Say-screen docus on the mating habits of
the ancient Rednecks, tumbled to her feet, saying:

"Mind you, Gentlemize, I am a scientist, and therefore
it behooves me to be Harvardly objective. I stand with the
truth. Hem, hem! Now then. There is no doubt but that there
is great unrest among the Dongs. I have here a list of
complaints that has come into my commission's possession
from the four corners of the Universe—which we are
currently repairing—hem, hem! I have been asked by the
Honorable Miz Edgahoova to read these complaints before
this Assembly. But I wish it to be understood that I draw no
conclusions.

"Number one . . . Three days ago, in the state of Femina, a
large group of radical left-wing piece-marching Dongs paraded
before the Mansion of Dr. Brothers-Marx—known to the Universe
as Groucha of Femina, who owns said state—marched, I say, in full
erection, and with marigolds jutting from the mouths of their erected
members, carrying banners and placards bearing such legends as WE
WANT A PIECE! and USE US, DON'T ABUSE US! This march

241

was broken up by the Honorable Miz Edgahoova's Tactical Shrike Squads. Unfortunately, these wonderfully combative units were later accused by members of the radical media of having used more force than was necessary—of roughly pulling marigolds out and deliberately breaking off some frozen members . . ."

"Get on to the next report," cried Jaye Edgahoova. "Perhaps," she said, "they were a *little* too zealous. But they have a hard job. It's not easy to keep them Dongs down."

"This was just one incident reported in the past few days," Miz Rabble-Mead went on. "In Marthatown it was reported that small bands of Dongs gathered near the rotunda before a bronze statue of Edna St. Vincent Millay, whom the protesters felt had treated Dongs as mere sexual objects. They made reference to her sonnet, beginning: 'What lips my lips have kissed, and where and why;' which goes on to say that she had forgotten.

"The Dongs began by discarding their traditional dogsuit uniforms and shaving off their pubic hair. They then piled the pubic hair into a great heap at the foot of the statue of Miz Millay and set it afire. Unfortunately, the Tactical Shrike Squad arrived on the scene too late to prevent any of this—"

"I tell you," cried Jaye Edgahoova, "we're flooded with requests—"

"Here's another," Miz Rabble-Mead went on, "from, of all places, Papal-Land. Perhaps this is the most significant of all. This report, though I hasten to add, *unconfirmed,* has it that in Papal-Land—certainly the *last* place . . . that the Dongs have been burning their jockstraps!"

"I think they look kinda cute that way," whispered a back-bench Ultra-blue to her colleague. "I like the way they bounce when they walk."

"Shhh!" shushed her associate, suppressing a giggle.

"—And using such cries," Miz Rabble-Mead hastened on, "as 'Dong Power,' 'Empower the Tower,' and 'A Piece of the Action'!"

"We've all grown quite used to such vulgarities," put in Miz Mandalay, trying to subdue the assemblage, which had grown loud and lusty. "Please go on."

"Well, here's another. Only yesterday, only a few blocks from this building, three young Dongs quietly infiltrated Mary Sorley's Old Tea House, and managed to get served."

An offended roar came from the Anglo-Irish, Molly Maguires, the Lassies of Ire, contingent.

"Shhh!"

Miz Rabble-Mead went on: "—and these are only a minute number of serious offences. But, mind, I am trying to be objective."

"Well, if Miz Rabble-Mead, as a scientist, finds that it's impossible to draw a conclusion, I, as a Statesmiz have an opposite duty," said Jaye Edgahoova. "The situation is dangerous to the tranquility of the State. I propose immediate forceful suppression of the Dongs. Come on, let's put 'em in their place!"

"Violence solves nothing," said Miz Mandalay.

"Balls!"

"Miz Edgahoova!"

"*Balls*, I said—and balls I meant. Let my Tactical Shrike Squads loose on 'em. They'll scatter like sperm."

Shortly thereafter, Miz Mandalay left the council, her faction sadly defeated. Miz Edgahoova had proved once again what she had always known to be true: Reason has no chance in a competition with Energy. Jaye Edgahoova had won.

"Now," she said wrathfully, after the council room had nearly cleared, "when I get my mitts on the ringleader of those

Dongs, that big dick Resurgius, I'll nail his balls to the wall. I'll teach him he can't steal my sexmiz."

Some few ears were cupped, but the brains attached remained mystified.

2
THE KIDNAPPING OF MIZ MANDALAY

"Miz Mandalay looks angry," said one of the Butcherbirds, the elite, degenderit Secret Service Shrikes whose duty it was to guard the Statesmize, as Miz Mandalay rocketed from the Assembly Room.

"We'd better be on our little toesies. When she's in a conniption tizzy she's hard to keep up with." Her two companions nodded knowingly.

"She's got her five-inch spikes on," said one of them, "they'll slow her down."

"I hope she doesn't go kissing through the crowd, spreading joy," said the other.

"No chance," said the one in charge, "she's pissed."

"Cripes, what an ass she's got!" said the second. "They rub against each other and keep coming up like an upside-down heart, if you look at it the right way."

"And look at them anti-sex objects bounce," said the third, as Miz Mandalay flew by.

"Come on," said the one in charge, "we gotta keep up with her."

Miz Mandalay was already out the door.

When the Secret Service Shrikes hit the street, Miz Mandalay was wriggling into the back seat of her auto-chauffeured limousine, a pale pink Camille 3000.

Suddenly all hell broke loose.

Three wobbly, crazy-looking superdupermodelmize, their makeup smeared, made a lunging hobble for the car.

"Hey, you!" cried the Secret Service Shrike in charge. "What do you think you're doing?"

"Them are Dongs!" cried the second.

"Sure, look at those scrawny legs!" cried the third.

"No worse than yours!" cried another. "But modelmize don't have cods. Look!"

But before the Secret Service Shrikes could act, the three Dongs, who were dressed like high-fashion superdupermodelmize, had pulled Miz Mandalay from the love seat of her Camille 3000, and were now hustling the struggling Statesmiz into the wicker basket of a gigantic balloon, that looked for all the Universe like a golden condom.

"What's that on the top of the balloon?" asked the stunned second Secret Service Shrike.

"Tassels?" suggested the third, doubtfully.

"Feathers," said the shrike in charge. "It's a French tickler."

"Cripes!" cried the second.

"Wow!" cried the third. "It looks like one of them ancient Quaint Wieners. I saw one in the museum of natural history."

"But it's golden," cried another. "Must be mustard all over it."

"Where are you taking me?" Miz Mandalay cried from the basket.

"To Resurgius," said the one with the bad hairy legs, the ugliest of the imitation superdupermodelmize. His green lipstick was smeared and he had at least ten o'clock shadow.

And up, up, and away, went the beautiful balloon. At first the ride wasn't a smooth one. The glass canyons of the great state of Atalanta are deep and dark, and it was a long way to go before reaching the seductive sulphur of the sky.

Once the balloon caught in the towering marquee of the Porno Palace, and Miz Mandalay noted that "Little Men" was on the bill. She didn't have time to see what the second feature was, for the ugly Dong wearing the green lipstick had pushed them free. Up, up they soared, the sky above, the crowd below.

"Why don't they do something?" cried Miz Mandalay. By "they" she meant the three, now tiny, Secret Service Shrikes, who looked almost as if they were waving her good-bye.

Finally the great golden balloon cleared the tops of the skyscrapers and sailed out over the River Slime, buffeted occasionally by a sky full of commercial drones. Miz Mandalay could see the great LaMer Turnpike off in the distance, and behind her even the brightest lights of the city were fading, and for all Miz Mandalay knew she would never see them again. One crystal tear formed in each beautiful violet eye.

"What do you mean to do to me?" she asked the one in green lipstick.

"That's up to Resurgius."

"How does he command such worship from his followers?" Miz Mandalay asked, trying to learn something of the Dong whose prisoner she had become.

"Why he gave us back our pride," said the Dong. "He showed us that Dong was beautiful."

But green lipstick quickly ordered them to shut up. "We'll have no more say until we reach our destination."

And so the roar of the passing drones was the only sound Miz Mandalay heard until the balloon began to descend far out over the LaMer Turnpike.

"Why that's the old Maidenform factory down there," cried Miz Mandalay. It still gave her a slight sensation of pride to see the remains of a Dong-supported industry in deflation.

The balloon settled, with a few bounces, to the roof.

"All out," ordered green lipstick, and Miz Mandalay climbed out of the basket.

246

"Where to?" she asked, rather anticipating her meeting with the great Dong leader, Resurgius.

"This way," she was told, and followed.

Green lipstick led her down a stairwell and into a huge, long loft-room at the far end of which sat a Dong, whom she assumed to be the mighty Resurgius, and none other than Miz Bet, whose month-ago disappearance had been the trigger of Jaye Edgahoova's wrath.

Resurgius and Miz Bet sat like two monarchs of old, side by side, each in a padded inverted cup of the ten-foot wide white plastic Maidenform bra that had once been a sign on the roof of the building. Around and before them, but with all eyes turned on Miz Mandalay, were at least twenty couples, Dongs and Cunnies, gathered like a court, whom Miz Mandalay rightly took to be Resurgius' top aides. It was humiliating for her to have to walk the long red carpet toward that perverted group of naturals.

"He's trying to psyche me," she thought to herself, and walked handsomely forward. When she got close enough the court opened a path for her and she was brought directly before Resurgius and Miz Bet. To the latter, Miz Mandalay said:

"So, it's true then. You have gone over. You have become a Cunnie. How disgraceful. A Miz of your rank!"

"Don't *Miz* me," said Miz Bet. "My name is Beth. You will use that name when addressing me, and when appropriate."

"Beth! What a name! It sounds positively Elizabethan," said Miz Mandalay, in a show of bravado. But she *was* a bit awed. "And I suppose this is the great Dong himself."

"This is Resurgius," said Beth. The Dong, a huge, bronzed, gold-and-flame-headed fellow remained silent, and this had the effect of making Miz Mandalay even more nervous and uncertain than before.

"Can't he talk?" she said. "After all, I am a Univacual leader, and have the right to expect respectful treatment."

But the flame-haired Dong's green eyes only glittered mischievously, if through his hornrims, darkly. Miz Mandalay turned her own eyes to Beth.

"Is this the kind of life you want?"

Beth was a busty, satin-skinned brunette with wonderful calves and long green eyes which Miz Mandalay guessed were only plastics, and which she now slid across her face to aim at what she saw as Resurgius' classic profile. Hypnotized by love, what she saw was an "R" chested super suit, made of red, white and blue plastic, red caped, and from which at the collar emerged Resurgius' stalk of a neck, and a head actually resembling Woody Allen's—an ancient movie star—wearing a pair of hornrimmed glasses.

"What do *you* think, baby?" Miz Bet said with a sexy smirk.

"How long have you been involved in this sort of thing?" said Miz Mandalay, ignoring Miz Bet's facial implications.

"Since the beginning," said Beth proudly. "Why do you think I ever had anything to do with that sow, Edgahoova? It was only in order to get my position in Dong Pop. I knew that from there I would be able to work under cover to stir the limp, demoralized Dongs to revolutionary erection. It occurred to me that if someone could induce a hardon in the Dongs, that would last for at least four hours, they could be a tremendous source of power. Then, a little later, one day at the office, I got the craves and sent out for a Dong. They sent Resurgius up to me and I liked his style, as who wouldn't! and so the next time I got the craves I asked that they send me the same Dong. Pretty soon, in the after-say and shared electronic vape, I came to see that he was the Dong that I was looking for to lead the coup. Brawn and brains! He and I together have planned everything—all those protests that had

248

old Edgahoova in such a fit. She'd tell me everything, so I always knew how to counteract whatever action she might take. I used to laugh behind the old bag's back. But I *have* had my problems."

"Yes," said Resurgius, his voice like low drums, his speech like a tympanic tongue, "Beth means that she had had some difficulty convincing me of the wisdom of using actual force. Fundamentally, you see, I'm a pacifist, a lover—especially with my plastic Resurgius suit on—which has many push-button valves."

"Yes," said Beth, "he had been rather overshamed at Shame-school, unfortunately, and I had a hard time of it convincing him that force must be met with force, as Jaye Edgahoova so well taught me. Look at those muscles!"

"Yes," said Resurgius, a little sadly, "the white feather in me has had to admit that force must be employed if we are to win our goal."

"Which is?" asked Miz Mandalay, sharp, little ears aperk.

"Well," said Resurgius, "my original goal was equality, but—"

"But," said Beth, "I have showed him that it is a political fact of life among us simple simians, that there are oppressors and oppressed—"

"And if you don't want to be oppressed—" broke in Resurgius—

"—then you must oppress," Beth finished.

"And so, reluctantly, we have taken to the use of force," said Resurgius.

"This is very depressing," said Miz Mandalay, "and I'm your first victim."

"You are our first victim," said Resurgius, "but you needn't remain one. You might consider joining us."

"Never!"

"And in the meantime," said Beth, "we should be able to get some great concessions from the Univacual Council for the promise of your return."

"Of course, you will never return me to them . . . ."

"Of course not."

"But if you were to join us," said Resurgius, "we naturally would still be able to get what we want. They need never know that you aren't being held forcibly."

"She doesn't *want* to join us, Resurgius, didn't you hear her?" There were sparks at Beth's temples, and her eyes blazed emerald.

"I just thought—"

"I'm beginning to see what you're thinking," snapped Beth.

"She's right," said Miz Mandalay staunchly, "I'll never join. You are all enemies of Atalanta Mizstate, and you'll come to a bloody end when Miz Edgahoova's Tactical Police Shrikes catch up with you." At which threat, Beth only sniffed as if smelling something unpleasant.

"You'll see," Miz Mandalay added weakly.

"She has spunk," said a Dong member of the Court, off to the left of Miz Mandalay.

"That's what gives her her leadership qualities," said his Cunnie. "But if she only knew what she was missing," she added coyly, looking up into her Dong's eyes, which were awkwardly crossed.

"What I'd like to know is," said Miz Mandalay, "why are you telling me all this? And also, I'd like to know what's in it for you, Miz Bet? You're from a good background and you had a top post. Are you, perish the thought, *in love* with this—this *Dong*? You can have all you want of him or a hundred like him, you know. Why on earth do you want to make yourself his slave?"

"She is *not* my slave," said Resurgius. "If anything, I am her slave. But there'll be no talk of slavery. Beth is my wife."

"Wife!" cried Miz Mandalay. "Have you no respect, to use such a filthy pre-Succession word? There is no such thing as a—what you said, don't you know that? It's against the law."

"Resurgius is the law here," said Beth, "and I am indeed his wife—wife, wife, wife!— and to me it is the most wonderful word in the world.

"As to your questions—we are telling you about ourselves because Resurgius, who is the kindest Dong in the Universe," with which she gave him a wifely side-wise smile, "hoped that you would see the light, and join us. I had no doubt that you would not. You are all reactionaries, even you, who claim to be such a liberal, when there's any question of losing power. For me, I had a father, a real one, not something from the sperm bank or the vulcanization chamber, and though I never knew him, I have had my dreams of what he was like. I picture him—"

"Never mind that," said Miz Mandalay. "Everybody at the top knows about your mother's indiscretion."

"I picture him," Beth went on, "with white hair, standing in the kitchen before an old-fashioned raystove, baking me an apple pie."

"Beth," Resurgius nudged her.

"Hem!" she cleared her voice. "Anyway, my sympathies have always been with the Dongs. There's an old song that my great-grandmother used to sing—*"I enjoy being a girl."*

"Rotten old pre-Succession time," said Miz Mandalay.

"I know, but I love it," said Beth dreamily. "I'm an old-fashioned girl at heart." She looked at Resurgius.

"And ambition," said Miz Mandalay, "the desire for ultimate power, couldn't have anything to do with it, I suppose."

"Naturally, I'd like to rule the Universe, be the Queen of all I survey. Wouldn't anybody? First level psychology explains that, how deep inside of us the only way we can feel truly safe is to be in control. You're just the same."

"I suppose it's a throwback to your early disgrace. Very unfortunate. But do you suppose that this Dong is going to let *you* run things. He'll have all the power, *if* you succeed."

"And I'll have him, which is the same thing as having the power. I can withhold sex and make him do my bidding. He is a Dong, after all. You love me, don't you, my dear Dong?"

"Deedy, I do, but much of what you two are saying is over my head. I'm just a simple guy."

"Sorry, darling. Now what do you propose we do with our guest?"

"Take her to the padding room and feed her. She's a bit too lean for my taste."

"Take her away," cried Beth, and then added, "and for Cripe's sake, get her a bra—the Howard Hughes Double Derrick."

3

MOONLIGHT SONATA

The Howard Hughes Double Derrick was a torture device designed by the pre-Succession Dong for the ancient movie star Jane Russell, whom the famous Dong engineer had apparently hated. It caused the anti-sex objects to be pressed upward toward the chin in an extremely uncomfortable fashion. Beth's insistence that Miz Mandalay wear that horrid instrument of torture, which had been found, moth-eaten and faded, but with wiring and padding intact, in a bin of specialty brassieres, was indicative of her distaste for their kidnap victim.

Try as he might, enemy that she was, Resurgius could not feel the same rancor toward Miz Mandalay that Miz Bet apparently felt.

Perhaps it was her beauty. Miz Mandalay resembled a relentlessly blossoming female figure from a Frank Frazetta painting that he had seen in a secret collection of banished art. Much as he tried to contain himself, she steamed his hornrims and made him drool. After watching her suffering for a few days in the padding room, he relented in Beth's name and told Miz Mandalay that she might remove the Howard Hughes Double Derrick. To be sure that his orders were carried out, he stood and watched as she did so. The removal of the torture device prompted in him an even greater generosity of spirit, and he went on to tell Miz Mandalay that she might have the freedom of the top two floors of the five-story factory, and also of the roof, but she was warned that escape was impossible.

The roof had an eight-foot-high chain-link fence around it, for in the pre-Succession days the factory workers had used it for games and exercise, and all the windows down below were heavily gated. The lower floors made dormitories for a crack battalion of Resurgius' troops and their warrior Cunnies, who marched with old-fashioned electric harpoons. The basement had been converted into a combined garage— one basement door ran out onto the slope of a hill—arsenal, and storage room for supplies.

That evening, Miz Mandalay decided to partake of the night air and climbed to the roof. All the beautiful, dull bronze stars were out. Many lovely shades of smoke filled the air with the bracing scent of sulphur, and one could see the parti-colored signal lights on the half-moon's dark portion. It reminded her of an article she'd recently read in "Kosmo." She hopelessly wished that she were at some re-

253

sort on the Sea of Tranquility tonight, instead of being held a prisoner in an old, defunct brassiere factory. She wished she were eating an ancient Quaint Weiner, made of disgusting bad cholesterol, dripping fat, smeared with mustard and covered with sauerkraut, as people did happily once upon a time, at Coney Island, as she had seen pictures of in the ancient history books reproduced from the 2075 Giant Kloud, the Giant Kloud which was now so ancient and so full that nobody understood the early stuff that was in it; also a real Chesterfield cigarette and not a stupid humped Camel Vape. She was certain that nothing could taste as good as a Quaint Weiner or a real smoke. Somewhere deep inside she, too, was just an old-fashioned girl.

She wished now that at the last Economic Studies Conference she had voted for more funds for Poverty, so that this building and many others like it, that stood like ghosts of a bygone era about the fringes of Atalanta, might have been razed or perhaps converted for low income animal life or vegetable pod factories.

She couldn't help wondering why, for all their work, they had still been unable to banish poverty. Certainly her own mother had done her best to do just that in the States that she owned. One of them, Hollystate, which, unfortunately, was in danger of sinking in the sea, thus putting a final end to the film industry and its three remaining stars, who wouldn't leave—was the State that would someday be her own. Her mother, Miz Nansome, took as much money as she could from the middle-class Mize of her state and gave it to the starving tent people—O the grapes of wrath—and the Central State pursued the same policy under Governor Noisome. Somehow, it seemed that poverty just went hand in hand with progress. Well, that wasn't really her field of expertise, and she had no right to think of it. She cleared her head.

"Ah parti-colored moon in the lovely, sulphurous heavens, you above all know that there is a tide in the affairs

254

of Dongs, which, taken at the full, leads on to fortune. I have studied and prepared, and my time has come . . . ."

It was Resurgius! He stood alone, not twenty feet ahead, looking for all the Universe like an ancient statue of Eugen Sandow, pale, except for his glinting hornrims, against the night.

"Oh, shine on, shine on harvest moon up in the sky. I ain't had no lovin' since January, February, June or July—" He was singing.

"Ahem!" went Miz Mandalay, her natural good manners requiring that she make her presence known.

"Oh," said Resurgius, startled. "I—"

"You were talking to yourself, or singing, maybe." She walked up to him, thinking, "what a curious creature! I should like to know more about him! What shoulders! And what a small neck and what a big head. And what big glasses, and why the cape?"

"What are you then," asked Miz Mandalay, "a Say-screen that talks even if no one is present?"

"Yes," said Resurgius, turning to meet her, "it's a curious habit acquired early, when I had only myself for a friend."

"Then you had a Dong for a friend," said Miz Mandalay, wittily. "That's even more curious, don't you think?"

"You think so little of us, then?"

"Not so little, perhaps. But when I think of Dongs, I think of pre-Succession days. I think of the plight of Mize like my grandmother, and her mother, who led such lives of terrible hardship and virtual enslavement under the iron thumb of the Dongs."

"Your grandmother's husband, you mean, and her mother's husband. They, too, led hard lives, and solved their problems as they could. After your grandmother washed the stinky clothes in a washing machine, your grandfather took the laundry in a basket and hung it on a line with clothespins. They suffered too. Their thumbs were raw."

255

Miz Mandalay looked at the giant's poor little hands. "But see how things have changed since the Succession—"

"Yes, now Dongs are virtual slaves; I see that nothing has changed but the generations. Today there are masters and slaves just as always, and women are the masters."

"You really mean to pursue this revolt of the Dongs, then. . ."

"I have decided to do so."

"You'll never succeed, you know. You might have been able to deal with me, but you've made the wrong move by this kidnapping. Jaye Edgahoova will attack, tooth and nail, both feet forward."

"How can she attack when we have you for a hostage?"

"Bah! She'll let you kill me if you wish, then she'll have supreme power. Do you think my death would bother her in the least? Only I stand between her and total control. All you have done by kidnapping me is to give her the excuse she needs to annihilate you."

"But why then did Beth, who knows Edgahoova so well, advise me to take this step?"

"I have been thinking about that myself, and I think I have the answer."

"Say, please."

"You said that you at first believed in principles of pacifism."

"I did, until I saw that they were futile."

"Think, then, Resurgius, you are involved with a Miz possessed of a demon."

"She's not like that."

"Isn't she? I offer this possibility, dear Dong, for your consideration: Miz Bet—"

"Beth."

"All right, then, Beth is fully aware that this action which she has advised you to take will bring an attack by Jaye Edgahoova in its wake. She is staking everything on it. She

256

is afraid that you'll fall back into pacifism if you have time to think of what bloodshed might be ahead. She is gambling that you will be forced into open war, that you'll be able to repulse Edgahoova's first onslaught—she probably still has spies in Edgahoova's employ who will tip her as to what that Miz will do, so that you will be prepared—and then, that you will reign supreme in the counterattack."

"If what you say is true, my Beth is treacherous."

"I doubt that her treachery will stop there, Resurgius."

"What do you mean?"

"I mean that, if you are successful—but you won't be—as soon as you assume control, you will find yourself chewing poisoned gum."

Resurgius stood, his large bronzed forehead furrowed in thought, lifting his hornrims from his eagle beak; then his forehead smoothed and his eyes sparkled with eked intelligence behind his hornrims.

"And earlier you warned her of me," he said. "It couldn't be that you are trying to divide and conquer, could it?"

"But of course I am," said Miz Mandalay, lightly. "Still, what I say is true. Eventually, one of you will turn against the other."

"I can see that you don't know what love is," said Resurgius.

"Love—between a Dong and a Miz—it's ludicrous."

"Love is never ludicrous."

"Not between equal Mize, but—"

"Ah, the liberal speaketh—

"I only meant—"

"Listen," said Resurgius, "let me tell you of my love. As a boy, like all boys, I was taught shame. I had to sit for three hours a day before the Say-screen while a Miz told me the errors of my toxic masculine nature. I was taught that I was swinish, brutish, insensitive, cruel, stupid, gross, with no

257

capacity for fineness of sentiment or depth of emotion. I was told that even my organs felt as nothing compared with a woman's G-spot. In short, I was taught to hang my head and walk ashamed. I grew up during the period of severest suppression, right after the Great Succession. But one thing kept my spirit alive—a few lines of a poem that I remembered my mother reciting to me. They're by an early American poet named Robert Frost and became a symbol to me. I don't remember exactly, but they went something like this:

I'm a liberal, you know what that is—
Liberals are people who never take their
Own side in a quarrel."
"Nonsense!"

"Perhaps, but that sustained me, kept the spark of faith in myself alive. It taught me to take my own side against that Say-screen at Shame-school. They saved me from my pacifist tendencies when I was taken to be a gladiator. I kept thinking of my opponent, but what good will it do to let him kill me? I have as much right to live as he. Or why do I not? And I could think of no reason. After all, it was *I* inside of me, someone with as much of a claim on life as he."

"That's the root of war."

"Yes, it is: circumstance and survival."

"Ugly."

"No, beautiful. Tragic but beautiful. Then I was taken from gladiatorial service, after sustaining a serious wound, and placed out to stud. As Beth told you, it was on a crave call that I met her. Which brings us back to love, for it was she who taught me the meaning of the word."

"Gratitude, not love, is the word for it."

"Well then, perhaps—have it as you will. But try to think what it meant to me when, instead of the usual treatment, she treated me like a person with a soul. Once, during the after-say, she read to me from a very ancient book called *Plutarch's Lives*, how a slave named Spartacus lead a revolt

258

against his masters. She read how a snake coiled itself on his face as he lay asleep, and his wife, who was with him, and was a kind of prophetess, declared that it was a sign portending great and formidable power to him. I remember how the story stirred something in me, and excited me, and I fell asleep dreaming of it, and how suddenly the dream became so real that I could feel that snake upon my own face, and I jumped up to find that Beth had truly placed a small asp across my face that fell into my lap when I sat up, and, though I had been terrified, still I knew then that I had a destiny—for I had not been bitten—and that it was Beth who would help me to fulfill it. So you see, I knew that I loved her, and she me."

"You were grateful, Resurgius," said Miz Mandalay, genuinely touched by the story. "Perhaps we have been too hard on the Dongs," she added after a reflective moment. "But, you see, we have feared just such an enterprise as you now propose to undertake. It has always been my feeling that we should have given the Dongs the vote. It would have been a healthy channel wherein to release their frustrations and would have meant nothing, anyway."

"No," said Resurgius, "from your view, I believe that it was better that you didn't. A little freedom will always lead to the demand for more. My grandfather and others like him, made that mistake—giving the Mize that freedom—and I have paid for it with a life of slavery."

"Now you sound like Jaye Edgahoova—like a Conservative."

"A Conservative keeps what she's got for as long as she can, which certainly seems more like a natural impulse."

"You poor Dong, your mind, your soul, have been corrupted—"

"By society."

"By Beth."

"I've told you that I love her."

259

"Yes, you have, you poor Dong."

"But wait! As I looked at you in this beautiful sulphurous light, as I've listened to your commanding alto voice, something has come over me, possessed me. I want to sing:
> Oh sweet and lovely
> Lady be good,
> Oh lady be good to me—"

"So," snapped Beth, stepping suddenly from the shadows behind them, "I had the craves and went looking for you. And here I find you on the roof conspiring, as it appears, with the enemy, and romancing her!"

"Oh, Beth my love, Miz Mandalay and I were just—"

"There are no Mize here," Beth interrupted vehemently, "she's just plain Mandy now."

"Mandy!" cried Miz Mandalay indignantly. "How dare you! You were nothing but a third rank official until that fool Edgahoova got a crush you. I have hundreds like you under me."

"Yes," said Beth, "but you're dancing to my music now, my fair Miz. And Mandy you'll be from this day forth. I've a mind to have you locked in the corset room and fed nothing but sliced plastic and radioactive milk. What have you been doing, filling this poor Dong's head with a lot of lies? What's she been saying, Resurgius?"

"Love . . . love . . ."

"Answer me, you big fool!"

"We have been talking about the lights on the moon— see how prettily they spell out the names of products. Look, look now; what does it say? One Calorie, is it?"

In spite of herself, Miz Mandalay wished she could cover a bit for Resurgius, protect him.

"What are you trying to do to my Dong? Turn his head?"

"You've done a pretty fair job of that yourself," Miz Mandalay rejoined. "You've got the poor creature thinking

260

that he can become the super Dong of the universe. Don't you know you're riding him for a terrible fall? He's going to be deeply hurt when he sees that he's incompetent."

"Why, don't tell me you believe your own propaganda. He's got twice your mental capacity."

"Then it's you who should be careful."

"She has nothing to fear from me," said Resurgius.

"She's trying to turn us against each other," said Beth.

"How could I do that?" rejoined Miz Mandalay. "A Dong and an Accidental should make a perfect pair."

"So, you'd throw that up at me, would you?"

Suddenly—perhaps it was Resurgius' hurt, green eyes—they looked green in this sulphurous air and behind the dancing light of his hornrims—that touched her, but Miz Mandalay felt ashamed.

"I'm sorry," she said, looking at Resurgius, whose eyes had teared-up. "Perhaps I shouldn't have said that."

"You certainly shouldn't have," said Beth. "Now you're going to spend the rest of your little visit in the corset room, and don't say I didn't warn you."

"Oh, Beth," said Resurgius, "I don't think we need—"

"Are you going to overrule me—in front of her?"

"No," said Resurgius, shrugging his massive bronze shoulders, and skulking off to a far corner of the roof. He detested scenes.

And so it came to pass that Miz Mandalay was thrown into the corset room, and was left to sleep on a stack of those revolting objects.

4

HER GOVERNMENT IN ACTION

When word was brought back in to the Emergency Session of the Univacual Council, that Miz Mandalay had been kidnapped by Dongs disguised as superduper-

261

modelmize, and that she had been taken away in a golden condom-like balloon, the members of the Council as a body fairly screeched for reprisals. This was very much to Jaye Edgahoova's taste, and she made good use of all this feline fury.

"Hear me, Mize," she harangued, "the Dongs have stolen from amongst us the flower of our regime, the magnificent Miz Mandalay, whom we all know and love. Who knows but that right now she is being tortured, or even deliberately impregnated"—oohs of hypocritical terror and horror from her auditors—"by the scoundrel Resurgius? First it was our adored Miz Bet. Now it's Miz Mandalay. Who will be next? Me? Thank Sappho for my whiskers. Something must be done!"

Here came great tumult and shouting. There were cries for vengeance. All Dongs, no matter how innocent, should be rounded up and put into detention camps and the Ship of Dongs turned away.

"Great idea!" cried Jaye Edgahoova. "We must learn from history, while not letting it repeat itself. But—I must ask this question—might not such an action bring a reprisal in some form from the Dongs? Dare we to escalate, while they hold Miz Mandalay captive? But then again, dare we not? For what is the life of any one of us as opposed to the life of the Atalanta Mizstate? Sacrifices must be made in times of crisis. I know that if it were I who was being held, I should wish that the vote be for an immediate attack, that I might be made the proud and immortal martyr of freedom—but, do you agree?"

"Yea! Yea! Yea!" came the waves of approval. Vox populi! Vox dei! Long live liberty!

"Then let us withdraw, at this moment of crisis, my citimize, to contemplate the grave implications of our actions, and to make detailed plans of attack."

Volcanic eruptions of applause!

262

"It has been *your* decision," said Jaye Edgahoova, flushed with success, "I am merely your agent." She slammed her cup on the rostrum and withdrew, leaving the Council hall, and going directly to the Pink House. As she trudged along with her squad of Secret Service Shrikes, she mulled over what she had learned from secret communication with Miz Bet; that Bet had no thought of making any concessions with the Dongs. Edgahoover could trust that dame. As she crossed the lawn, the usual gaggle of reporters from the various news services had spread blankets and were having a tea-party while waiting for a statement from Edgahoova's Press Secretary, Hedy Parsons (also renowned as a pianist and a heavyweight champion weightlifter).

Upon arrival at the Pink House, now a-bustle with activity, she called for her chief of Shrike Police, one Furius, a red-haired ex-barmiz from Hoboken, who was notorious for having bitten off the ears of twenty Dongs. Everyone knew that the story was true, for she kept the ears, in a marinated state, in a gallon pickle jar that stood on her desk in her office at the Pinafore.

"Furius," said Edgahoova, "you are now looking at the absolute Boss of the Universe. The Dongs have played right into my hands. I can wage open war on them and get rid of Miz Mandalay at the same time. I'm thirsty. Get me a Pink Dongly. The kind with the big straws."

"I don't know," said Furius, pouring Edgahoova a drink, "it's too pat."

"What do you mean?" Edgahoova's pointed little red ears twitched.

"Well, why'd da Dongs make such a bad mistake?"

"I say dey was badly advised," said Edgahoova, lapsing into her natural speech.

"Yeah," said Furius, handing her the drink and shoving a skinny office Dong under her legs like a quivering ottoman, "but dat's what I mean. I smell a rat."

"If you mean Bet," said Edgahoova," I don't believe it."

"Yeah, cuz you got a case on her and won't look at da facts when you see 'em."

"You've always been jealous of her."

"O.K., but think about it. Resurgius never did nothin' like this before. This is her work."

"Of course it's her work, you fool. Don't you see that she's set the whole thing up for me. She's on my side."

"Dat's only what you *want* to believe. And if you win, she'll let you believe it. But if you lose, it'll be anudder story."

"She must know that I can't lose. Look at my armies—crawling on their stomachs for me!"

"You see, that's da point! Everybody, including Miz Bet and Resurgius, can look at your armies. But can you look at his? How do *you* know how many Dongs and Cunnies he has under his command? Look how widespread all these incidences have been. They might have spies to tell 'em where and how you'll attack, and they might have a network of millions, scattered through the Universe, to counterattack with. But still, I guess it's possible that they don't know that all dongbots are out of commission, even ours, ever since the Univacual Council ruled in ancient times that they'd be immobilized in time of war. You know, Chief, dongbots have always been programmed for pacifism. There's nothing to worry about there."

"True. Course we don't know for sure how much Miz Bet knows or remembers of ancient history."

"She's a scholar, ain't she?"

"Balls! I still say they'd try to strike first."

"Listen, we know from experience dat Resurgius don't work dat way. You know what I tink? I tink Miz Bet wants you to attack, so she can force Resurgius into action."

"Balls!" cried Edgahoova. "I don't believe a word of it."

"You're blinded by love. You've got a superplough on dat witch."

"Shut up and rub my anti-sex objects," said Edgahoova, "I've gotta think."

Seven minutes later, Hedy Parsons called the reporters into the Situation Room for a press conference. Naturally, there was a fine turnout of press Mize—indeed, most of Atalanta's renowned journalists were present, and still brushing tea-cake crumbs from their chins.

There was Sandra Van Orchid, the five-million-bobbit-a-year representative of Public Say-screen and Frieda Unfriendly of Network C.A.T. Nora Postman, the rough-talking, curly-headed femfist, already famed as a novelist, and now engaged in turning out such timely journalistic spectaculars as the recently best-selling *An Icecube on the Sun*, was very much present and already sputtering with caustic questions.

From the other side of the political spectrum came the two Wilhelminas; Sneller, of the arch-conservative Univacual Review, and Buckle, host of Public Say-screen's controversial Firing Squad show.

Jacqueline Anders, the Pink House muckraker was in the crowd, Mandalay Restless of the Atalanta *Times*, and Petite Hannabelle, whose firebrand-liberal tabloid column, "Bubbles," had gained her tremendous recent popularity as a somewhat muffled roaring girl.

Oh, yes, they were all there, and they looked tense and exhausted from their long waiting for a scoop. As soon as they were seated, Press Secretary Hedy Parsons made the familiar, solemn statement, "Lady Mize, the Honorable Jaye Edgahoova," and they all got miserably back to their feet, as that formidable Miz strode in and up to the speaker's platform. She was the very picture of energy and decision. Anyone could see that the buck stopped with her (in fact she had several large accounts in Moon banks, and would surely be able to double her assets if the new missile deal went through). Having had little time to make up properly, she was wearing a stern face, with slightly smudged purple lipstick.

"Atalantans," she began immediately, "it is with heavy heart that I come before you this evening to announce a state of crisis in our nation.

"At five o'clock this afternoon, Mae 13, 3000, our Co-Efficient, Most High Miz Mandalay, was, as our best intelligence reports lead us to believe, the victim of a dastardly kidnapping plot, executed with precision and ruthlessness by a group of Dongs disguised as high-fashion superdupermodelmize, whom we believe to be under the leadership of one Resurgius, a former gladiator and call-stud, who has gone underground for the purpose of overthrowing our beloved Motherland."

Jaye Edgahoova laid aside the sheet of paper from which she'd been reading, and leveled her little black ingot eyes on the journalists.

"Now there's the end of my prepared statement. I'd like to make a short off-the-cuff comment, however, in addition, before you Mize of the Press begin firing your questions. Off the Cuff—and let me make this perfectly clear—let me add that, though we seek no wider war, we are prepared to use all the vast power at our command to see that Miz Mandalay is returned safely to us and that those double-dealing pinko Dongs—and I hope they are listening—are brought within jabbing distance of the mailed fists of Miz Justice. We will show them no mercy, even if they should return Miz Mandalay unharmed, for they must be taught to ask, not what their country can do for them, but what they can do for their country!

"Now, Mize of the Press, proceed with your most explosive questions, please, and have no fear that I shall shrink from responsible reply. Miz Buckle?"

266

"I only wished to comment, Miz Edgahoova, that, to employ the oxy-moronic, and not as a mere epigrammatic device, but as an exemplification of my deepest feelings, your manifestation of the timocratical principle of cruel-kindness has caused me to become lachrymose eye for eye, drop for drop, pari-passu, and verbatim ac litteratim, so that you have moved me into a state of expialidocious-supercalifragilation for the flag."

"Well, thanks, Miz Buckle—I guess. How about you, Miz Restless? Got a toughy for me?"

"Well, Miz Edgahoova, you know perfectly well how I've always smugly opposed you—"

"Granted."

"But we can't let Atalanta go down the drain. Not until we've all milked her dry, anyway."

"Granted. I'm glad to see that we agree on something."

"And now I think that during this time of crisis we should all get behind you and support you. I, for one, promise to quit carping until after the crisis."

"Thanks. It took a big Miz to say that."

"I have a question," came from across the room.

"Yes, Norma."

"Well, to quote from that classic work by Ernesta Anyway, *Old Woman on the Ground*, 'Being brave is pressurized grace.'"

"Very true, but what is your question?"

"How'd you like to debate me? Or box?"

"I haven't got time right now, Norma."

"O.K., but have you ever heard of *In Praise of Silly* by Erasamiz?"

"No."

"Well, it's the latest best-seller, and I'm going to debate her, or maybe box her."

"Good, I'll tune in. How about you, Sandy?"

"I think we should get down to cases—the Public wants to know. Does this latest incident tie-up in any way with the disappearance last month of the Chairmiz in charge of Dong Pop, Miz Bet? And if so, how? All of us are familiar with the Pink House scuttlebutt that has it that Miz Bet defected. Would you comment on that?"

"Incisive questioning, Sandy. Yes, I'll be glad to comment on that, only to say this, in order to clear that up— so let me make this perfectly clear—Miz Bet—and let me address myself first to her character—is a Miz whose love of country is such that, there can be no doubt, whatsoever, as to the possibility that such an act, insofar as we understand it, but on the other hand, assuming that we have exhausted the possibilities of one, having employed every digit at its command, and on the third hand, all these for the furtherance of truth, as we know it, yet the iniquity of Mize were as easily viewed, in categoric terms, then we should certainly reckon ourselves fortunate, and this State stable. I hope that answers your question, Sandy. I've tried to be specific."

"Thank you."

"Not at all. We certainly must have an informed Public, for therein lies the strength of freedom and the free use of strength."

As Miz Edgahoova concluded this observation, she was handed a communiqué by Press Secretary Parsons. She paused to open the paper and read it, then she looked up.

"Gentlemize of the Press, I have just been handed a communiqué of great importance, and I am going to share its contents with you. Contact has been made with representatives of the Dongs, who have asked for certain concessions by our government in return for Miz Mandalay. They make the following demands—which I'll read verbatim.

1. A piece of the action.
2. Suffrage.
3. Right to hold public office.

4. Right to marry.
5. Dismantling of Shame-schools.
6. Impeachment of Jaye Edgahoova.
7. End the war on the dark side of the Moon and bring our girls home.

"As you can see, these demands are outrageous and completely unacceptable, and leave us only one course of action. Happily, the Senate and the House of Representatives are on vacation; and, this being clearly a state of emergency, the buck stops with me. Therefore, this day, Mae 13, 3000, a day of infamy, I do declare open and atrocious war upon the Dongs. The little people of this country will fight to the last death-rattle—at home, in their beds, or on the john—and never will your government have owed so much to the acquiescence and stupidity of so many. I thank you."

Furius had a nice double bourbon ready for her leader when the last reporter exited, and Edgahoova entered the little room adjacent the Ovary Office.

"Well," she asked, slamming the door behind her, "how'd it sound, Furius?"

"Chief, that was your finest hour."

"Thanks. How'd you like that part about even if they did return Miz Mandalay unharmed, we'd show them no mercy. That oughta get her throat cut, what?"

"Brilliant, Chief. And the way you fiddled Van Orchid's question about Miz Bet, if she'd brought a tape and played it back slow she couldn't get anything outa that mess."

"Your Chief is on her toes, Furius. Even if you're right about Bet defecting, it helps to keep the ball rolling that they think she was kidnapped too. Then again, if you're wrong about her, no harm's been done."

"Brilliant, Chief. But do you think it was smart to de-clare war? Wouldn't a surprise attack have been better—a stab in the back?"

"It would have been better if those Dongs thought for a moment that we'd meet their insane demands, but they know perfectly well that the war has started already. They know this is a struggle to the death between me and Resurgius, feet first, tooth and nail. He knows I'm not going to give up everything I've worked for all these years—the suppression of the Dongs, the Great Succession, the fortune I'm making on munitions contracts, all the States I've been able to buy, and don't forget Pluto, which I own lock, stock, and barrel, and now I'm only one step from total control. Why it would be the same as giving up my life. Before I joined the Movement and became one of its leaders, I was nothing but a poor femfist living in a roach-infested room in Greenwich Village. I worked with my hands—look at them—gnarled and claw-like. I used to grow organic vegetables and peddle them on a cart through the Lower East Side. Sure, I'm a peasant. I'm proud of it."

"You should be, Chief. You're one of the great Deplorables."

"Well, you know what it's like, Furius. You've been there."

"Right, and ain't nobody goin' to take it away from us, unless it's over our dead bodies. Ya know, Chief, in a way, we're what made Atalanta great."

"A typical Atalanta success story, that's us. Gimme another shot, Furius."

"Coming up, Chief."

5

THE FUNDAMENTAL THINGS SURVIVE

At midnight came a soft knock on the door of the corset room, and then a key turned in the lock. Miz Mandalay, who had been dozing off, woke with a heart-stopping start, and sat up straight as her curves would allow.

270

"Who's there?" she cried.

"Shhh! It's Resurgius. May I come in and talk with you?"

"I don't suppose I can stop you," said Miz Mandalay, pulling several corsets up to cover her bare knobs. It was quite hot in the little room, so she was sleeping au naturel.

"Of course you can—if you wish," replied Resurgius, through the crack of the door; "but I wish you wouldn't. I've brought you some news."

"Very well then, enter. What news do you bring?"

"Sad news, but inevitable, I'm afraid," said Resurgius, coming in and closing the door behind him. "May I sit next to you?"

"Come ahead."

Resurgius seated his plastic muscle-bound self on a stack of panty girdles and adjusted his cape and hornrims. "It is a sad day," he said, "but a day that had to come. Edgahoova has declared war."

"What did I tell you? My kidnapping, far from doing you any good, has only given Edgahoova the chance she was looking for, not that she wouldn't have made one up anyway. But now she can get rid of me into the bargain. My doom has come, I see."

"Oh no; don't think that. I'll see to it that you come to no harm."

"You? But why should you?"

"I like you."

"You like me? I—your enemy?"

"Alas, I do. You are curve-bound as I am muscle-bound. Besides, what good would it do now to harm you? I'll simply hold you until the hostilities end."

"You're a strange Dong, Resurgius. I should think that you would hate me and my kind for what we've done to you. You described your life to me earlier, and I did feel sympathy for you. Shame-school must have been a terrible experience

271

for a young Dong of pride, like you. You know, I have been working to abolish Shame-school, or at least modify it down to Modesty."

"You would have been a fool to have done so. It's always been the most valuable weapon that the Mize had. Without it, Dongs would have asserted themselves long ago."

"That's what Edgahoova always said."

"Edgahoova's is a cruel, greedy, and warped personality, but she has a brilliant political mind. She has never allowed herself to become confused in her motives. She wants power. She was an Alinsky radical before the Succession, a leading revolutionary through it, and, once possessed of power, she became the extremist conservative in the Universe. That's how you get power and that's how you keep it. It's called triangulation."

"You make it sound like she never had an ideal. I think when she started out she wanted to do good," said Miz Mandalay.

"Yes, that's how we all rationalize our compulsion to control."

"Are you like that?"

"Probably, though I don't like to think so."

"Then why don't you desist?"

"Because we humans live in fear and search for power to control our little time while here. Death compels the search for power. It's natural."

"I would resist the compulsion to control, if I were in love."

"That's because you were born into everything on the up side. You'll find your true hunger in the descent," said Resurgius, shaking his head sadly.

"Pooh!"

"Kiss me."

"No."

"Why not?"

"No."

"Wouldn't you call in a Dong if you had the craves?"

"Yes . . ."

"Well?"

"But that's different. I don't know them."

"And do you know me?"

"Yes—a little."

"Not enough to say no. Don't you have the craves?"

"A little."

"Well then?"

"Well."

"There."

"Ooom!"

"Ah!"

"Oh!"

"Yi!"

"Mmm?"

"A-ha!"

"Wooo!"

"Weee!"

"Now then," said Resurgius, panting, afterward, "that wasn't so bad, was it?"

"Mmm!" purred Miz Mandalay. "You're a super Dong."

"Thanks, but I'd rather have you say you liked the real me, the skinny guy inside this parti-colored plastic muscle suit."

"Wasn't that the real you, Resurgius?"

"Shucks," said Resurgius, "you know what I mean. Say, do you believe in love at first see?"

"Absolutely not."

"Oh, I was afraid you'd say that."

"I thought you said you loved Miz Bet."

"Well, I do—or thought I did. I like her. She has those wonder-curves ever since the operation, but yours are better. You know, I've been thinking about what you said on the roof—that I was confusing love, sex, and gratitude? Maybe there's something in that."

"And now I suppose you think that you're in love with me. Just like a Dong! Indecently romantic."

"But suppose I am?"

"It's nothing to me if you are. You're beginning to upset me, Resurgius. If you think that this little super frisk is going to turn me into one of your dumb Cunnies, you're mistaken. I'm a free Miz, with a life of my own. I don't do dishes or babies."

"Ah—but you're my prisoner—now. A prisoner of love!"

"Enough!" She waved him away. "This is what happens when one lets one's emotions get loose. I thank you for the excellent professional services that you've rendered me tonight. Now begone! I need my soma-coma."

"How hard and cold you grow!"

"How hard and hot you were! And how presumptuous you've become because of it! An inflatable plastic penis isn't everything—even when it's red, white, and blue. Please leave me, *Dong!*"

Resurgius went to the door; stopped and looked back at the raw hourglass lovely Miz Mandalay, her gorgeous sands flowing upward in the moonlight from the window, her ultra violets not cold, but somehow hurt and angry, as if in an instant they might fill with tears.

"Goodnight—Sweetheart," he said. "I think I love you." And he was gone.

The tears flew from Miz Mandalay's eyes, like the hot sparks of a welder, while she sat and called herself a fool. What kind of fool she wasn't sure.

"What kind of fool am I?" she asked the night. A fool for love, answered a leaden star.

6
ANABASIS

The next morning, Tuesday, Mae 14, 3000, Resurgius woke to news that the Shrike-Troopers, with the assistance of the Tactical Shrike-Police, were arresting and placing into Detention Camps all Dongs who were so unfortunate as to not have gone into hiding.

The roundup was being shown on Say-screen, and watching it angered him.

Beth, filling Resurgius' bowl for the third time with vitamin-rich Vegan CoCo-Puffies, felt the moment propitious.

"Strike now," she whispered into his crimson shell-like ear, "before they've arrested all those who would support you."

"You are right," said Resurgius, "this is no time for equivocation. The tide is at the flood. Let it lead on to fortune."

So saying, he contacted all his generals on a secret Me-pad channel; and ordering those whose headquarters were nearest the infamous Pinafore, headquarters for Furius and her Chiefs of Staff—three sisters named Claudia, Cossina, and Publia, who in pre-Succession days had been the singing group, French Kiss, and who now were suffering the pangs of the Change—to mount an offensive against that seat of war, hatred, and cattiness. Those of his generals whose headquarters were nearest the Detention Camps should set out to free the suffering, imprisoned Dongs. He himself would march on Martha, D.C.; his goal—take the Pink House and capture Jaye Edgahoova.

"But first, eat your Puffies," said Beth, and Resurgius took her hand affectionately and kissed it. She was always concerned to keep him erect and robust.

Within hours, Resurgius and a thousand of his cracked Yellow Berets were on the march, along the LaMer Turnpike.

Resurgius was exhilarated, now that he was in action, filled with the old gay combative spirit of his gladiatorial days on Say-screen. Now all he desired was a chance to smite the enemy. But he had one regret; that circumstances had prevented him from saying farewell to Miz Mandalay, that curvy-wurvy darling. He had never before held in the palm of his hand a behind so soft as hers, and, nobody, not even the rain, had such small hands (he had recently visited the underground museum at Patchen Place). The trouble was, Beth watched him like a hawk, and if he had gone to say goodbye to Miz Mandalay, Beth would have suspected his attraction. Besides, the little darling was probably sleeping late—after last night, he added mentally, with a touch of vanity.

He was thinking of such things as these when one of his officers who had been scouting ahead came jogging down the road, crying that a large force of Tactical Shrike-Police were charging down the tarmac to meet the Dongs. Even now, he was warned, they were halfway across Pankhurst Bridge, their lace collars like answers, blowing in the wind.

Knowing that this first engagement of the war would set the psychological standard for his Dongs, most of whom, because of their years at Shame-school, were a bit too hang-dong anyhow, he decided on an outrageous head-on attack, feet first, tooth and nail.

He calculated this way: his Yellow Berets outnumbered the force of Shrike-Police, and if he could make good time he could still meet those formidable sisters, Claudia, Cossina, and Publia, while they were on the bridge. That way they could not range themselves against him with more than, say, twenty abosom. If he had, as he calculated, roughly twice their number, he could let rank after rank, of both his and theirs, hack each other to pieces, and with their last rank up, and then done for, he would still have half his army, and the way across Pankhurst Bridge, his first great obstacle, should have been cleared.

"Brilliant strategy," his officers concurred, and busily arranged the Yellow Berets into ranks of twenty. When this was done, Resurgius ordered his Moog player to sound the charge, "I'm in the Moog for a Billingsgate Rumpus!"

Onward, along the LaMer Turnpike, at double-time, ray-guns at high port, rockets to the left of them, rockets to the right of them, charged the six hundred. Resurgius lead them, his bronzed pectoral muscles bouncing, his shapely calves knotting, his gold-and-flame hair like the beacon torch of the old Statue of Liberty, his great hornrimmed specks bouncing on his nose, and his hearty cry of "Hi-ho, Dongs!" ringing back over the heads of the Yellow Berets like a call to mad inspiration.

The Battle of Pankhurst Bridge, the first engagement of the war that would become known to the historians of future centuries as The Battle of the Sexes, had begun.

All happened as Resurgius had calculated. The Yellow Berets caught the Tactical Shrike-Police when they were a little more than half way across the bridge, and those survivors who were later to tell of their experience on that day, have oft been quoted as saying that the sound of the clash of the opposing forces could be likened to a recording of an old Hubert Humphrey speech being played backwards.

After raying down thirty Shrikes, Resurgius' pistol was emptied of sunbeams, and, throwing it into the big open mouth of a particularly grizzly adversary, thus strangling her last hurrah, he drew his broadsword, and, wielding it so that it seemed to acquire the blurring speed of rotation of an old-fashioned helicopter, sliced his way to the opposite end of the bridge, and, coming from the rear, repeated this action. Up and down the files of Tactical Shrike-Police Resurgius went, like a white tornado, slicing them like liverwurst, making minced meat of multitudes, until the stagnant waters of the River Slime turned red beneath the bridge with the blood of the Tactical Shrike-Police. It was a complete rout.

The Victorias were done for. The Victors could camp and have a party.

When word of what had happened at Pankhurst Bridge reached Edgahoova, she summoned an Emergency meeting of Furius' Joint Chiefs and demanded an explanation of this disgraceful female failure.

"That force of Tactical Shrike-Police was caught napping, like sleeping beauties," said Edgahoova, her face aflame.

"You need a Pink Dongly, Chief?" asked Furius, concerned for her boss' health.

"Not now!" Edgahoova shouted back.

Well, Chief," said Furius, "the Tactical Shrike-Police were just on a routine patrol. How could they know that Resurgius' Yellow Berets were on the LaMer Turnpike?"

"Balls! They know we're in a state of war, don't they? Now listen, I want no more such catastrophes! Aren't we all on Top Bulletin Alert? Send Claudia with a large army to search out Resurgius and to *destroy* him! Break through that plastic suit of his and get to the little worm inside!"

"Will do, Chief!" said Furius enthusiastically. "Government is fun, just like the old Mafia."

"I'll take that Pink Dongly now," Edgahoova said, wiping her brow and breathing more easily.

"But, Chief," said the wounded and bandaged Claudia, ignoring Furius, who was mixing a Dongly for the Chief, "did you know that the Pinafore is under siege? How can I leave it to go out in the field again looking for Resurgius?"

"Balls! You just don't wanna leave that cushy office of yours and that cute aide-de-camp you've got. Put Cossina in charge of the Pinafore siege resistance. You're the ablest commander I've got. I need you in the field."

And thus it was decided that Claudia would take an army and go to seek out Resurgius and engage him in mortal combat.

The position of the main Dong army was vaguely known at this time to be somewhere in the squeeze-box area of the Pocono Mountains, and so Claudia led her army in that direction. It was hard to tell because nobody had paid the satellite bill and the satellites had all wobbled out of position, blurring human intelligence.

At eleven o'clock, Wednesday morning, Mae 15, 3000, Claudia's point-scout reported sighting the point-scout of Resurgius' Yellow Berets. He did not see her, she said. This was exactly the kind of situation that Claudia was hoping for. Her Shrikes, refreshed with cocaine, greatly outnumbered Resurgius' Milltowned Dongs, and she also had the element of surprise working in her favor. Resurgius' troops were marching through a canyon of medium size, with steep escarpments to their right and left. They couldn't be more than twenty abreast. It was Pankhurst Bridge all over again, only this time the Shrike-Troopers had the advantages which Resurgius had had at the previous battle, those of number and surprise. Claudia was always ready to learn, even from a Dong. She decided that she would employ Resurgius' own tactic against him, and attack head on. She signaled her Moog player to sound the charge.

Unfortunately for Claudia's plan, however, Resurgius' point-scout, Tonto, had spotted Claudia's point, and returned to tell Resurgius that an army was moving against him. Making lightning calculations, Resurgius saw that he was in the same peril which the Tactical Shrike-Police had been in on Pankhurst Bridge, and reasoning that Claudia would charge, decided to avoid the encounter, which could only cause his army to suffer the same fate as that of the Tactical Shrike-Police.

Obviously, retreat was necessary. But retreat to where? He could never back his army up out of the canyon in time, with its sheer escarpments upward to either side. And he heard with deep concern the distant whine and cacophony of a Moog sounding the charge!

Then he remembered the five backs of the Five Faces.

The Five Faces were stone portraits of five famous females which had been carved out of the gigantic rock-face of one of the major peaks of the Pocono Mountains by the famous Pip artist, Andrea Warlock. Not to be outdone by Mt. Rushmore's original monumentality, which had been made vague by winds and the sands of time, Warlock had one-upped the famous stone chipper, Borglum.

About a quarter of a mile back, Resurgius had passed an area which might have been climbed without too much difficulty, and had asked one of his Dongs if he knew where it led. The Yellow Beret had answered that that area had been made accessible by engineers so that Andrea Warlock and her aides could climb up to chip at the Five Faces.

"That area," said the Dong, "would be the tushes, as it were, of the famous females whose faces are there."

"I'd like to see them," said Resurgius, with a twinkle in his eye.

"They face off in the opposite direction," the Dong continued, "toward the Pink House.

"What," said Resurgius, "their behinds?"

"No, their tits. You have to climb up quite a distance to get to them, but you couldn't see anything, because of the bosom extension, unless you were to lower yourself down the front on a rope."

"Is it a long way down—and out—if you go over their foreheads?" asked Resurgius.

"Oh yes, a thousand feet, at least," his Dong answered. Resurgius now calculated the risks. It was either a matter of climbing to the summit of the Five Faces, and perhaps being trapped, or of attempting a hopeless retreat down the backs and asses, out of the canyon. He daringly opted for the Five Faces, and gave the order.

Fortunately for Resurgius, before the Shrike-Troopers under Claudia had entered the canyon, Resurgius' Dongs were within sight of the hackles of the statues. True, they were trapped, cornered, with no apparent way out, except back down over the big asses, a thousand feet into the canyon, where Claudia's huge force could easily annihilate them; but on the other hand, they were still intact, and Claudia would not dare to attack uphill, which is to say up the backs of the great women of the monument.

Resurgius' greatest fear, however, proved to be a likelihood. It was that Claudia, who was famous as a philistine, with an absolute detestation of art—and a personal grudge against Andrea Warlock, whom she had tried unsuccessfully to seduce at a Martha, D.C., political shindig—would call for a Rockcrusher missile to be brought to bear against his position.

Of course, he was right.

When Claudia entered the canyon, and saw what means Resurgius had used to make his escape, she did precisely that.

"We've got the Dongs trapped up there. They are impotent," she told her pretty aide-de-camp, whom she had decided to bring along. "Call the Pinafore and tell my sister Cossina to sight in on the Five Faces with a Rockcrusher. While we're waiting for the fireworks we can have a picinicium."

But Resurgius had guessed as much, and even now behind his giant hornrims was bringing to bear all his powers of invention and analysis, to find a solution to his predicament.

He called for the Dong who had earlier told him about the statues and asked him:

"What, precisely, is their hair made of?"

"Well, as you know," the Dong answered, "Andrea Warlock is a Pip artist, famed for doing the unusual."

"Just answer the question," said Resurgius, "I'm not anymore interested in art, at this moment, than Claudia is."

"Yes, sir," said the Dong. "Well, the hair of the statues is made of kudzu vine, but in the case of Gloria Steinem, weeping willow, so that it actually grows, and has to be cut and re-coiffed every month or so. The State employs a large staff of gardener Mize who also are licensed beauticians to care for the upkeep. That's a particularly attractive *croquignole* wave that they've given Susan B. Anthony, don't you think?"

"Yeah, it's very attractive; but how long do you suppose it's been since they've had a trim?"

"Oh, I'd say they were about due."

"And how long would a hairdo like that, these *croquignole* waves, be if it were undone and combed down over Susan B. Anthony's face? Would it reach her knobs?"

"I should think it would reach down to her belly button."

"And if you had some of it cut and attached to the end of that?"

"To her knees."

"And—"

"Yes, I see your point."

"Then get busy with those shears. We're going down."

Resurgius' plan was a brilliant piece of cosmetological invention under pressure, but it wouldn't have worked if it hadn't been for the fact that no one at the Pinafore wanted to go along with Claudia and blow the statues to hell. The O.K. finally came, but it came too late.

By the time Cossina, back at the Pinafore, got word to go ahead, that Edgahoova herself had overruled all who were opposed, Resurgius' Yellow Berets were already sliding and kicking their way down the noses of the Five Faces.

There they were—Susan B. Anthony, Margaret Sanger, Eleanor Roosevelt, Betty Freidan, and Gloria Steinem—with their kudzu and weeping willow streaming down over their faces, and Resurgius' Yellow Berets sliding down the strands right over their enormous titties. Resurgius was the first over a forehead. Dauntless, he slid down one of Betty Freidan's hairs, winking as he lowered himself past her left eye, and was the first to touch the ground.

Soon, all but one of the Yellow Berets were down. He had stayed behind in order to throw the ray guns down to his military comrades. Unfortunately, this brave trooper was killed in the blast that followed; he would later be honored at special ceremonies, at what was to become the tomb of the Unknown Dong.

Reaching the ground, Resurgius regrouped his Yellow Berets, marched around through the Pocono Mountains, and, entering the canyon by both mouths, surprised that picnicking and cavorting army of Claudia's, achieving his second victory of the Sex War, which was to be known as the Battle of the Five Faces. By the time the mountain was blown up, his troopers were already chasing many of the surviving and now unarmed Shrike-Troopers into the bushes. The success of the Yellow Berets in these sub-skirmishes must have been great, for many of the Shrike-Troopers, stout and nimble Mize, revolted over to the Dongs' side and became traitors, surrendering to slobbering love. Resurgius returned their weapons to some of them, who joined the ranks of his best shocking troops, while others, of somewhat questionable sincerity, he allowed to become scouts, like the great Tonto.

Unfortunately, Claudia, who had been bathing in a nearby tributary of the River Slime, made her escape by running along the bed of that river with a twenty foot hollow reed in her mouth. She emerged, stark naked and covered with leeches, three miles from the scene of battle. However,

Resurgius had succeeded in capturing her luggage, which consisted of five hundred assorted suitcases and hat boxes.

But, even though she had temporarily made her escape, Claudia's fate was sealed.

Early Thursday morning, Mae 16, 3000, Resurgius' advance guard caught up with her at the Appomattox Public Baths, where she had retired in order to rid herself of the leeches. A few hours later, she handed her hollow reed to Resurgius and retired from the war in disgrace. Thus ended the public career of a great Soldress, who, alas, had made the mistake of calling down a Rockcrusher upon the images of five heroines of her own revolution. It is an ironic footnote to history, that she later became a quiet-living, unassuming grandmother, the wife of a village blacksmith.

Entre nous, Edgahoova was pleased at the idea of blowing up the Five Faces. More room for her big head.

7

KATABASIS

At this point in the war Resurgius began to experience his first difficulties with his own Dongs. They, alas, grown confident in their numbers, and erected with their successes, began to break away in small groups by night to go about ravaging the suburbs of Atalanta, and occasionally even engaging in combat with one another.

Thus was it ever, that achieved power in a common goal will immediately lead to division among the powerful. For, one of the ironies of human life is, to be anything, one must be oneself, and to be oneself one must assert against others, for the line between the self and others can only consist of such an assertion—the hacking warrior and the catatonic guru are employed in the same pursuit.

And so, Resurgius made a serious gamble. He re-ordered his undisciplined troops, gave them an inspiring dressing-down, and turned his ashamed and weary force in the direction of the nearest Spaceport.

Now during these trying times Spaceports were occupied by tremendous bands of Space-Pirates. They had complete operational control of most Spaceports, and a special branch of the government had been set up, by the year 2050, to pay them an official danegeld in order to assure safe and efficient space travel. The Air-Traffic-Controlling Pirates ran the Spaceports admirably, but they demanded complete freedom from government interference, and since they could in no wise be controlled or suppressed, without extended, expensive conflicts, government had found it expedient to grant them immunity and give them semi-official recognition. They became known as the A.S.P.s or Atalantan Space-Pirates, and their right of legal exemption from the laws of Atalanta was approved by a long succession of governments, proving once again, for the as yet unconvinced, that, in politics at least, might makes right.

In any case, these Space-Pirates and their Spaceports were untouchable, and no force of the government's would dare to march upon them, for, if they did, Space travel would be hopelessly snarled; and out of this had come the tradition of using Spaceports very much as churches had been used during the Dark Ages, as places of sanctuary. If the Space-Pirates were in sympathy with your cause, they might take you in—but they'd be much more likely to take you in if you could pay them some form of danegeld, like cigarettes (a valuable artifact), or any kind of booze or drugs. An added source of hope for Resurgius was the fact that these pirates had no particular political affiliation, having seen clear through politics to its twin points of reference, money and power, and having decided to skip the bull shit rhetoric. They were comprised of all four sexes, and did little else but eat, drink, drug and fornicate in some amazing combos like drugged monkeys.

It was on the evening of Friday, Mae 17, 3000, that Resurgius and his weary Dongs entered the main gate of the Wanda Von Braunkirk Spacecenter and Port; and, surprisingly, to a hero's welcome. The Space-Pirates had been following the blazing course of the war on Say-screen; and, Edgahoova, recently having vetoed a bill to increase their tribute, for which they had spent a great deal of time and, worse, money, lobbying—having paid out a total of twenty-billion Bit Coins in bribes to officials—they had been on the verge of causing a total snarl in space-traffic, when the war had broken out, and naturally were very sympathetic to Resurgius; of course, they also saw the possibility of a deal.

In one of the world's great backroom deals, Resurgius, too, saw this possibility. In fact, the deal would be his tribute.

After the formalities of their first meeting, the leaders retired to the control tower for a private session, leaving Resurgius' Dongs and Shrike defectors to get acquainted with their counterparts among the Space-Pirates. Within minutes these had undertaken a marvelous bacchanal, so that for a thousand yards there was nothing to be seen but a hideously squirming daisy-chain, consisting of twenty thousand naked simian bodies.

Meanwhile, the leaders sat down before plates of assorted happy pills, including dream heaps of little red diablos, and began their conference. The main spokesman for the Space-Pirates was one Blackbeard, a Miz of robustious humor and keen mind.

"That was a marvelous and unexpected welcome," Resurgius began, feeling her up and out.

"A show of unity with your cause, my dear Resurgius," said Blackbeard, popping down several little red diablos. "We Space-Pirates think very highly of you."

"And of my cause?"

"Which is?"

"Freedom, égalité, et fraternité—or if you would prefer, sororité."

"As a woman," said Blackbeard, "I see it as a fine and noble cause, but before you can achieve such high ideals you must seize power. Many heads must roll! There must be one of those new electronic guillotines brought to the pubic square!"

"It's true," said Resurgius, "that only through my accession to supreme power can the Universe hope to see again what you might call the just life. Alas, the burden of leadership weighs heavily upon my extremely broad shoulders."

"Take care, Resurgius, that it doesn't weigh down those plastic shoulders of yours."

"I suppose that you are making reference to the fact that I am in military retreat."

"You must admit," said Blackbeard, with her super red Revloned lips in a guileful smile that tilted her black beard, "that it weakens your position. Immediately after the Battle of the Five Faces—incidentally, a brilliant piece of work—"

"Thanks."

"—we had begun to conceive of a plan whereby we might throw our considerable power in your direction, if—"

"Of course. I understand your position with regard to Martha, D.C., and Edgahoova."

"Yes, I knew that you'd understand. But now—here you are in full retreat. Things don't look very hopeful."

"You paint too black a picture, Blackbeard. Let's speak plainly. You are only trying to drive up your price for supporting me."

"Well, let's face it, Resurgius, the odds have altered, our gamble is a much greater one now. And let me remind you, that at this moment, we Space-Pirates are the only force standing between you and Furius."

"Yet you've seen that I am resourceful."

"Well, that is why we have welcomed you. But still, we'd be taking a big gamble to support you. You desired that we should speak plainly. Very well, what is our support worth to you?"

"Fair question, Blackbeard. I propose to offer you, if I am successful, all the states now owned and operated by Edgahoova, to the number of three, with a labor population totaling three-hundred million. The revenues from the natural resources and industries alone should come to something in the neighborhood of twenty trillion ultra bobbits—the big green—every year, and all social services—schools, hospitals, etc.—are completely paid for out of the pockets of the working middle-class, who also support the poor through taxation, which will leave your revenue to be a clear profit, just as it is for Edgahoova now. What say you to that? Is that a deal or what?"

"What about a counter-proposal?"

"Go ahead."

"How about, in addition to those states owned by Edgahoova, throwing in those owned by Miz Mandalay, Furius, Cossina, Publia, Claudia and Miz Bet."

"Miz Bet only owns one state, through her mother, and I intend to keep that. After all, Miz Bet is my wife."

"What about the others?"

"Well, you must be able to see that I'll have to have some states to give to my Dongs, especially my generals, and, as for Cossina's states, I'll have to let her keep them, now that she's come over to my side, else what would she be fighting for?"

"I thought she was fighting for freedom."

"Don't be snide. Of course she's fighting for freedom. She's fighting for the freedom to keep her states. Haven't you heard of incentive?"

And thus they wrangled on all night and into the early hours of dawn, when the only sounds aside from the wind in the wires and their own voices, was the last soft sequence of random orgasms from the field, the sipping of rum, and the hissing of pot.

Finally, at ten o'clock Saturday morning, Mae 18, 3000, they came to an agreement. In return for her services, Blackbeard was to get the following:

1. All those states owned by Edgahoova and Furius.

2. Resurgius' government would double the danegeld now being paid to the Space-Pirates.

3. All Offense plants were to be handed over to Blackbeard's first cousin, who was a banker and would make a respectable front.

4. Resurgius would guarantee the continuation of the war on the Dark Side of the Moon, so that there would be a place to drop bombs and explode missiles in order to supply a reason to keep the Offense plants operating.

5. Resurgius would, naturally, agree to a higher Offense budget.

For her part, Blackbeard was prepared to offer full co-operation with Resurgius, and to prove her good faith, they sealed their bargain with a kiss. Resurgius wiped his mouth with the back of his hand, and Blackbeard applied fresh lipstick. It was a distasteful end to difficult negotiations.

8
THE GREAT WALL OF FURIUS

Meanwhile, Furius had not been idle. Only a short league behind the tail of Resurgius' army as it had entered the gates of the Wanda Von Braunkirk Spacecenter and Port, Furius had her army set up camp while she contemplated the circumstances. To charge the Spacecenter was unthinkable. To call down a Grandsmasher upon it was out of the question, more especially in view of the sad fate of Claudia, who even now was pregnant with her first Accidental by the filthy village blacksmith with whom she had got drunk in order to console herself. In the midst of action she had forgotten to take her Defetus pills.

No, any attack was out of the question. If the Space-Pirates had taken Resurgius in, they would fight for him, and their numbers were large. Cripes, hadn't she warned Edgahoova of the folly of vetoing that increase in their danegeld! Secretly she sometimes thought her Chief was a vain fool.

But then a plan began to hatch in her mind. And what a plan! If she could bring it off, not only would she have Resurgius trapped and save the Atalantan way of life, to which purpose she was officially sworn, but she could make herself a nice little bit coin boodle on the side.

She got into communication with the Pinafore, the gist of her message being this (later made public as part of the Pinafore Papers):

"Have Resurgius and his Dongs trapped at the Wanda Von Braunkirk Spacecenter. Attack out of the question. Recommendation: Complete entrapment. Method: the construction of a moat, canalizing sludge from the River Slime, and the construction, within the perimeter of the moat, of a gigantic wall, to be known as the Great Wall of Furius, hereinafter.

"Naturally, the public would object to the use of Tactical Shrike-Police or Shrike-Troopers for the purpose, so I suggest that you give my aunt, Jennifer Thickneck, of Wonder Woman Constructions, a contract for the work. Note: the following is to be classified Top Secret. It must be understood by Auntie Thickneck that I am to get fifty percent of the profits paid her by the taxpayers for this work in return for the contract. If this plan is acceptable to all, a percentage of my fifty percent will find its way back to all who approve. Naturally, my army will do the actual labor, as a service to the country."

Within minutes a bill had been passed by both Houses, whose members were reached at various resorts on The Sea of Tranquility; and, all agreeing on the matriotic importance of the work, the Shrike-Troopers were issued backhoes and began digging.

By Saturday morning, just as Resurgius and Blackbeard came to final terms, Furius laid the last plastic brick to the wall which would forever bear her name. This great and difficult work she perfected in a space of time short beyond all expectation, digging a ditch from the banks of the River Slime to the gates of the Wanda Von Braunkirk Spacecenter and on around the whole port. Within this roiling moat of sludge stood a gleaming wall of fine pink plastic bricks eighty feet high, with large ducts at its base to allow the River Slime in, and so drown those inside, and with Atalantan flags flying from every turret, which was twenty feet from its likeness to left and right.

Upon first sight of this great wall and the moat beyond it, Resurgius slighted and despised it as unimportant, but when he realized that provisions were short, he began to worry, as did Blackbeard, who was a Miz, as Resurgius had come to know, of hearty appetites. Soon there was great fear in the Spacecenter that they should all starve because of the wall; and it was that fear, and the hysteria that came in its wake, which led directly to what later historians have come to call The Day of Infamy, which was Sunday, Mae 19, 3000. At the same time, Resurgius, who was never neglectful of the need for military discipline, was drilling his Dongs in another part of the Spacecenter, and Blackbeard and her Space-Pirates, occupying all the available Rockettes, deserted him, taking off for the Moon.

9

ESCAPE FROM THE SPACEPORT

Just as Resurgius discovered Blackbeard's infamous desertion of him, a great Spring deluge began to pelt the land and swell the River Slime, dilating its rather turgid water and sending it roaring with tremendous force over its bed of sludge. This in turn drove a great deal of water into the canal which Furius had dug, and, in a short time caused the waters of the moat to rise perceptibly against the plastic brick of the Great Wall of Furius. And this fact gave Furius an idea that, giving the devil her due, must go down as one of the most brilliant military ploys in history; right beside the Trojan Horse, Custard's Stand, or the brilliant Ride of the Six Hundred.

"We'll drown 'em like rats!" she cried.

When asked by one of her lieutenants what her meaning was, she elaborated:

"That's my plan," she said, "That's what the ducts are for. Get it?"

"The Spacecenter will fill up like a bathtub!"

"Right," said Furius, "and we'll attach pumps to make sure that it does. As soon as Resurgius and his motley crew of Dongs, Cunnies, Hookers, and Shrike-Groupies see that they're going to be drowned, they'll make for the exit, where we can pick them off one by one as they come out. They'll have to leave before the water can get deep enough to do any lasting damage to the Spaceport, so nobody can ever blame me for destroying it, the way they blamed Claudia for destroying the Five Faces Monument, and I'll issue strict orders not to shoot any of the Space-Pirates, and that way we can avoid a Space snarl. How does it sound?" (It should be noted here that Furius was unaware of the escape of the Space-Pirates, for at the time of their departure she was in her mobile command post, exercising her hobby, pickling and jarring ears.)

"It sounds brilliant," said her lieutenant, "should I issue the orders?"

"Yes, and *vaya con Dios*, my darling. If my plan works, we'll have a victory celebration in the form of a Matronalia as soon as the weather clears, and I don't mean an old fashioned Matronalia, I mean a panting-mouth and erected-tongue Matronalia! Hot damn!"

"Oh, goodie!" cried the lieutenant. "I just love a good Matronalia." And she went off to give the orders. Within hours the cry went up inside the Spaceport that the place was filling with water. Already now it was up to the average Dong's knees, and was rising rapidly.

"We'll all be drowned!" cried the more hysterical among the entrapped.

"Let's make a break for it out the front gates," cried the intrepid in unison.

"They'll mow us down as we come out," cried the timorous, "let's surrender instead."

Speaking in a firm stage-whisper over a loud speaker from the control tower, Resurgius gathered the attention of the disputants and forced them to apply reason to the crisis, saying:

"It is true that we have been deserted by our former ally, Blackbeard, and her Space-Pirates, and that we now must face the fact that we all may be drowned. But think on this: there are three elements which accommodate the traveller—land, air, and water. We cannot go by land, for there is an unscalable wall around us and an army in waiting outside its only exit. We cannot go by air, for our quondam allies, the Space-Pirates, have taken every craft that flies. Now, my ingenious Dongs, let me hear *you* solve the problem of your escape!"

From the knee-deep Dongs there arose a tremendous shout of "Water! We shall escape by water!"

"Exactly!"

"But how?" they cried.

In answer, Resurgius extended a bronzed and muscled arm and pointed at the administration building, across the way from him. It was a huge, zebra-striped, plastic edifice which had been modeled on the classic lines of the Ancient Pan-Am Building, which had once stood, albeit a little drunkenly, in the heart of Old Manhattan.

"Eureka!" he cried, his voice a dramatic and prophetic kettle-drum. "That thing'll float! All we have to do is to unmoor it, by which I mean throw all those computers out of it, and detach it from its foundations. It'll hold every last Dong of you. It'll be the Ark of the Deplorable Dongs! Get busy!"

Soon the Administration Building was afloat, and in a formal ceremony in the penthouse Resurgius was made an Admirable. "As surely as the water rises, we shall rise and sing," he had proclaimed, and sure enough they did. But it was a slow process, for it took billions of tons of water to fill the Spaceport and to float Resurgius' ark to the top of the wall. The new-fledged Admirable stood at his post in the penthouse all night as his fifty-story ship rose toward the stars rocking and swaying and creaking like an old tug at anchor.

Eventually though, the penthouse cleared the top of the wall, and Resurgius could look out over Furius' camp. Sure enough, a great body of troops was gathered at the gate, waiting for the Dongs to come out, and half drowning themselves in the waterfall deluge.

The whole countryside, as well, was under a greater siege than either Dong or Shrike could create: the siege of weather. Perhaps it was this very feminine softness of the earth that reminded Resurgius of Miz Mandalay—or as he had come to think of her; Mandy—and of the softness of her behind. Oh, that he might be back at the brassiere factory right now, and have a few moments in the corset room with her!

All night Resurgius' Ark circled inside the Spaceport and each time it got to the far side, where Furius could not see, fifty more of his Dongs leaped to the bank of the moat. By morning, he had regrouped his army on the other side of the Spaceport and was already drippingly on the march.

10
A MATRONALIA AND A MUTINY

Furius, still believing Resurgius and all of his Dongs to have been drowned, gave her permission for the Matronalia to begin, and now it was in full swing. This Matronalia was nothing but a modern revision of the old pagan rite, which had generally been held on the first of March in ancient times, and which consisted of the counterpart to the Saturnalia, or male festival, wherein masters feasted their slaves, and exchanged places with them, allowing them to give the orders, and generally bully and make fun of their masters— in other words, a day of Misrule.

Regrouped on the far side of the Spacecenter, Resurgius surveyed his troops and pondered his options. Two of his more militant commanders, "Old Blood" Castratus and "Old Guts" Cunnilingus, had come blustering up to his command post, which was in a hollow tree, and offered suggestions.

"We must attack," said Old Blood.

"Attack!" echoed Old Guts.

"But we can't attack," Resurgius objected. "They have us greatly outnumbered."

"We would have been in Martha, D.C., now, and eating slamburgs in the Pink House, if you hadn't started retreating. We think you're yellow! There!"

"Yellow!" echoed Old Guts.

"That's up to you," said Resurgius, coolly, eying them through his hornrims, "you may think what you will of me, but I'll not have my whole army chopped to pieces because of your hotheadedness. Once my little army of Yellow Berets is lost, the revolution itself is lost. We are in a Dunkirkian situation."

"But we haven't fought a good battle since the Five Faces," cried Old Blood. "All we do is retreat, like a bunch of sissy scaredy-cats."

"Sissy scaredy-cats!" Old Guts emphasized.

And the two generals stalked off cursing, hand in hand.

Within the hour, Resurgius was brought news that Old Blood Castratus and Old Guts Cunnilingus had deserted camp, taking with them over a third of his bravest Dongs.

"Well," he said, philosophically, "they're two of my best commanders. Perhaps they'll be able to harass Furius enough to allow me to make a getaway with my remaining Dongs. Still, I'd hate to see a third of my Dongs blown to bits." And so, he ordered that a scout go out after the mutineers and check as to their whereabouts, and see if they might need help.

Shortly thereafter, Furius learned of the desertion of this band of Dongs and gave orders that six thousand Shrike-Troopers were to go ahead of her main body, circle round Old Blood and Old Guts' camp and, camouflaged as Birnam Wood, secure Small Hill on the far side of the mutineers' camp and wait for three blasts on her Moog, and then attack.

Within a very short time, Furius was able to proclaim herself the victor. It must be said, however, that of some ninety Dongs who were killed, only two were found to be wounded in their split infinitives, the rest having stood in their ranks and fought to the death like the fighting fools that they were, feet first, tooth and nail.

By the time that Resurgius got the sad news of the fate of the mutineers, he had already taken his remaining force deep into the Pocono Mountains, fully aware that he would soon be pursued. Two of Furius' more bloodthirsty lieutenants leading a contingent of crack Shrikes had been dispatched to Resurgius' camp to keep an eye on him. And, seeing that his force was terribly diminished, decided that, instead of reporting his actions, they would themselves overtake and capture him. Unfortunately for them, they did succeed in overtaking him, for their Shrikes were fresh and his Dongs were tired; but instead of the defeat which they had expected to administer, Resurgius rallied, faced them, and utterly routed them, sending them in great disarray back to Furius, who bit off their ears for cowardice. It has always been difficult for generals and historians to explain the twists and turns of fate. The more intelligent among them have insisted that the explanations of historical events be left to the narrative poets.

This strange success, however, turned out to be Resurgius' final ruination in the field, because it once again inspired his Dongs to fight. Now a large group of the more militant Dongs forcibly compelled their captain, one Erectus Custard, to lead them back upon the advancing army of Furius, which was exactly what the latter was eager for; the reason being that her Shrikes had begun to talk openly about the situation, saying that the honor of this war was reserved for she who would put some backbone into these slinky-spined troops and thus put an end to this war, which was costing everyone a pretty penny.

Furius, therefore, was eager to fight a decisive battle. Within the hour, when she came upon Captain Erectus Custard and his Dongs, she was happy to supply him with the material for his last stand. (The Battle of Custard's Last Stand was fought in the late afternoon of Monday, Mae 20, 3000. Captain Erectus Custard and his complete compliment of Dongs were wiped out in this, the last important encounter of the Sex War.)

297

When Resurgius was brought word of Custard's Last Stand, his great green myopic eyes, magnified behind his hornrims, filled with tears. "The Establishment has proven too strong for us," he said, "and I, even in my Super-suit, have proven myself too weak to challenge it." He looked out on the draggled, mangled fifty-odd Dongs that he had left at his command and said, "Well, boys, let's call the whole thing off, shall we?"

They were too tired to answer.

For several days in his escape, Resurgius managed to keep just ahead of the advancing armies of Furius and Publia, which were vying with each other to strike the coup de grace.

On Thursday, Mae 23, 3000, Resurgius and his remaining Dongs came within view of the great spires of the LaMer Turnpike. There they disbanded, and, changing into the gray flannel business suits of Mize, two every hour, began to hitch rides from passing commuters into the city, where they took the long underground ride back to the LaMer Turnpike in surreptitious fashion, so that they might not be recognized as revolutionary Dongs, and in such circuitous manner returned to the Maidenform Brassiere Factory.

Resurgius, like a good captain, was the last to arrive.

"Well," said Beth, as he staggered up to her, shrinking inside his Super-suit, on shaky, if powerful-looking plastic legs, and hoping for a word of kindness to soothe his wounds of the spirit, and shame.

"You've certainly made a botch of it, haven't you?"

Debilitated, he looked back at her. "Frankly, my dear, I don't give a damn," he said, turning his eyes away from her protuberant boobs.

Was this, then, the death of the Dongs?

11
THE ETERNAL TRIANGLE

"Maybe Dongs really *are* inferior," Beth went on, dressing Resurgius down. "I never really believed it, but I'm beginning to now. How could you let a fool like Furius chase you back here to me with your dong between your legs?"

"I had to retreat; I couldn't engage that many Shrike-Troopers; my Dongs would have been cut off."

"Better that they had, than to come back here so shamefully, and dressed as Mize at that. For Cripe's sake, take off that lipstick! It doesn't go with your five-o'clock shadow."

"We had to disguise ourselves," said Resurgius, wiping the Maxine Factor stain from his lips, "otherwise we would have been picked up and thrown into a Boys Town detention camp."

"Oh, what a weakling!" Beth cried impatiently. "This looks like the end of my political career. I'm shit on a stick."

"Well, what about me?" asked Resurgius. "Don't you even have a kind word for me, after all I've been through? I did it all for you, you know."

"For *me*; that's a laugh!"

"You'd have been happy enough if I had won."

"But you didn't, you dumb Dong! You lost. Go on, get out of my sight, you loser, you musclebound piece of plastic, you skinny-necked intellectual brat! I've got plans to make." At which, Beth's green eyes turned red with calculation, and Resurgius walked away, cursing his fate.

Minutes later, he knocked on the door of the corset room.

"Who's there?" came the mellifluous, estrogen-loaded voice of Miz Mandalay.

"'Tis I, Resurgius, the great failure," said our hero in a sad voice.

The door flew open and the Amazonian Miz Mandalay stood looking down at him with big tears of joy and love squirting from her beautiful violet plastics.

"Oh, Resurgius!" she cried. "I had begun to think that you were lost in the Kloud and had become part of the babble of spacetime and I should never see you again." She threw her arms about his gigantic shoulders, and planted a dozen kisses all over his face, incidentally getting his lipstick on her cheek.

Resurgius was amazed by this Amazonian reception, though he wouldn't have been, had he been wiser in the ways of Mize, whose love is a process of incubation that, after months of stillness, bursts forth with a hearty cry.

"Oh, darling!" was that cry.

Taking her arms from his shoulders, Resurgius stepped back dizzily and looked at her.

"I was seeking more of the consolation of philosophy than of physiotherapy," he said, "and I never expected anything like this. Am I mistaken, or . . . do you love me?"

"I love you, Resurgius!"

"But I am a defeated Dong. I have no future to offer you."

"All the more reason for me to feel as I do, for I thought you were dead, and that made me suffer, and I had never suffered before, and I found it a rather pleasurable business: and now, because you return, as you say, a defeated Dong, you need me in a way that could not have been had you returned triumphant. Oh, my poor, dumb, defeated Dong, how you stir me with your failure! How my heart did sing at the news of your every defeat!"

"And yet you say that you love me?"

"By sun and candlelight!"

"Would you—would you mind explaining a little? Not that I don't feel highly gratified at the fact of your failed logic and increased love, but—"

300

"Of course, my poor, dearest Dong. But don't you see? No, of course you don't. A Miz understands these things. But it is only that, when you left, I thought you a worm; but it was possible that you might win, and return as a conqueror worm, to my dismay. We were enemies, officially, when you left. If you had returned a conqueror, it should have been *I* that you had conquered. But this way, with you defeated, I can imagine myself beginning a life with you; for I shall resign and we shall go to some satellite island and begin life anew as equals. Or I, a *little* superior, having come down in the world for your sake. And I will have you Resurgius, for you've tickled my fancy."

So saying, Miz Mandalay giggled, blushed, and began once again to plant kisses on Resurgius' spectacled face. Soon she had pulled him into the corset room and down upon a stack of panty-girdles, where they exploded into action.

"Oh my dear Mandalay," panted Resurgius, "all the time I was away at war I could think of nothing but the incredible softness of your behind."

"And for my part," panted Mandalay in reply, "I could think of little else but the incredible hardness of your cod-piece. You are my sex object!"

"And you are mine!"

"And you are mine!"

"Enough!" cried Beth, whose demeanor had returned to that of Miz Bet, and who suddenly stood in the doorway which, in their haste, the lovers had neglected to close. She had been looking for Resurgius; for, once her temper had cooled, her knickers had heated up. But now they were again thoroughly frozen.

"Look at him!" Beth cried in the dramatic third person. "Regard this weak and treacherous Dong in whom I have placed a Cunnie's hope! See how he uses me! Or should I say, uses my enemy! And now this knickerknocking! If he thinks he's going to make a fool of me with another Cunnie,

301

he's mistaken. He'll pay! He'll pay! I swear he will! This is it!" And she stalked off down the hall, her spiked heels clicking like hammers of revenge.

Upon leaving Resurgius and Miz Mandalay, Beth went directly to her private office in the old zipper room, and set into motion a plan which fell into place with her discovery of Resurgius' sexual betrayal. Not only had her plan to seize supreme power been wrecked by Resurgius' military ineptitudes, but her sexual pride had been injured, and revenge was uppermost in her mind. In a fit of blind rage, she tapped out the following message to Edgahoova, using her personal, F-phone:

Dear Jaye:

Dongs are monsters at heart. It's true—in case you might have heard it—that my heart betrayed me, and I almost fell for Resurgius with a real plough—but not like the superplough that I've always had on you, dear Jaye.

You must believe me when I tell you that when I dropped out of sight nearly six weeks ago, I did it for you. You see, Jaye, I had a plan, and I knew that you wouldn't O.K. it, because it would put me in great danger, and you wouldn't want your special curvy Cunnie-wunnie in danger, I know.

I met this Resurgius when he came to me on a crave call, when he was a stud. I discovered that he was the leader of a plot to overthrow the government. It was then that I decided to sacrifice myself, if need be, to save you and our blessed ovarian government from overthrow.

So I took it upon myself to pretend to befriend him, fall in love, and then run off with him. You see, I was playing a dangerous game and taking great risks for our Motherland. But it wasn't long before I found myself in his power—under his spell, I might almost put it. He is such a force for evil, as you must know.

But my head has cleared! Won't you take your little Cunnie-wunnie back into your giant lioness heart? You know

that it has always been you for me. I've made a fool of myself.
But I'm still your little playmate. Remember?

And now I'm ready to complete the job. Here's my plan:
If you'll welcome me back into your good graces, I'll tell you
where Resurgius is hiding.

Only—naturally, I have to take some care to my future—
I require that you reply to this proposition on Public Say-
screen, and that you make a public declaration, the gist of
which should be: that you have word that I'm safe, and am
soon to be released back to my duties by the rebel Dongs.
Also, that you have confirmed that I am innocent of any
wrong-doing, as indeed I am, unless it is a crime to be
hypnotized and misused, and abused. Upon seeing this on
Say-screen, you will within minutes receive word from me of
Resurgius' whereabouts.

Hanging my hopes upon this thin thread, as well as upon
the steel girder which I know your love to be, once given, and
looking forward to our loving reunion, I am, as always,

Your Miz Bet

"It isn't much," Beth thought, pushing the activation
button of the direct-line writer, "but it's all I've got. If horrid
old Edgahoova's still as crazy about me as she was, she'll go
for it. I might have my old job back by tomorrow. Oh, but
Ugh! How I hate the thought of having her big paws on me
again, pushing my head into her hairy bosom. I feel so
different since the operation, kind of pro-fem. Eeek!"

Indeed, these thoughts greatly depleted her anticipation
of re-establishment.

At this very moment, Edgahoova was discussing Miz
Bet's message with Furius who, fresh from battle, was soak-
ing in a marble tub, a Pink Dongly resting on its wide edge.

"This ought to convince you if nothing else has," said
Furius. "Can't you see through that transparent piece of ass?
Can't you read between the lines?"

303

"I'm not exactly stupid, Furius," said Edgahoova. "I didn't work my way up to the top of the heap, Queen of the Mountain, Mistress Miz of the Pink House, by being dumb, you know. I've got plenty of animal cunning, if not brains, plus a law degree from Harvest. I'm a politician."

"Sure Chief, but where that Miz Bet is concerned—well—"

"O.K.," said Edgahoova, "I've still got a crush on Miz Bet, but I can read too. But that's up to me. I'll decide what to do with her later. But right now, let me give you a good example of the cunning that has made me great."

"Fire away, Chief," said Furius, sponging her muscular arms.

"Well, it's clear that Miz Bet is now disposed to do as I order, regardless of whatever else she's done to date, right?"

"Right! No doubt about that part of it. She's scared now, and has obviously turned against Resurgius."

"O.K. So let's extract a high fee for our good will, false though it may—and I say *may*—be. I've got to see her before I make up my mind about that."

"But what's the fee, Chief?"

"Well, if she tips us as to where Resurgius is hiding, and we get there and clean the place out, we're going to find Miz Mandalay. Now I don't want that liberal dame in my hair ever again. I want complete control of Atalanta. Ain't that what we all lust for? Actually, I'd like to have her bumped, one way or the other. But there's bound to be too much public notice on Resurgius' capture. It's a touchy situation. Something might go wrong if we bumped her then and there, and later it'd be even harder to get away with."

"You got a point, all right," said Furius. "But how're we gonna get rid of her?"

"That'll be the price we ask of Miz Bet—the price of that clean slate she wants."

304

"Say, Chief, that's a great piece of cunning. How'll we work it?"

"You'll see. Miz Bet's an experienced diplomat. She'll get the message."

And, suddenly, there it was: The Message!

Beth leaned forward in anticipation. An announcement had just been made that Jaye Edgahoova was to speak next. And there she was now, on Say-screen, Jaye Edgahoova herself.

"My gentle Mize," she began. "As you may know, our great and good military leaders, the great Publia and the immortal Furius, have today completely routed the Dong army which has threatened our happy way of life, and which was commanded by the infamous Dong, Resurgius. A Dong-count shows that many millions of Dongs were killed, whereas our fine Shrike-Troopers suffered no more losses than a few red tips from their longer fingernails. Of course, these things must be expected. Sacrifice is a part of war. It is the price you pay for our feminine freedom.

"It is an unfortunate fact that Resurgius himself escaped capture, but it appears, even so, that he has come to the end of his ugly, male-factions.

"No doubt many of you have wondered about the strange disappearance of Miz Bet, one of my top aides. The fact is, six weeks ago I sent Miz Bet on a most hazardous mission. Her purpose: to infiltrate Resurgius' secret headquarters. And now my foresight and planning has borne fruit.

"I have, only a short time ago, received information as to the state of affairs in Resurgius' hideaway. It is tragic news. Our reports indicate that Resurgius, the infamous Dong leader, and the charismatic Miz Mandalay, whom you all know, and who it now appears was the victim only of a staged—I repeat, *staged*—kidnapping, and is in fact a spy and a traitor, and has been, in fact, Resurgius' accomplice and consort, have died in a suicide pact, directly resulting from Resurgius' defeat.

"It troubles me not a little to be forced to report that Miz Mandalay, formerly a leading member of the Univacual Council, has died in dishonor. But she died before she could do any more harm, and perhaps that's as well. Guten Abend, and as we Atalantans always say when toasting a cheerie event—not Cheers, not Prosit, but Up Yours!"

"So," said Beth to herself, turning off the Say-screen, "that's what the old devil asks of me, is it? Well, that's a pretty fair deal. She did clear me, pretty much, and that's a good sign. And he was my Dong, and he did do me wrong. And I hate that super bitch Mandalay anyway. But 'she died before she could do any more harm,' Edgahoova said. That means I'd better work fast."

Just then Resurgius' top remaining Dong Commander came jogging up the hall on powerful thighs and blistered feet, and pounded on her door. She pulled it open.

"I'm looking for Resurgius," he said.

"Is it about that Edgahoova speech that was on just now?"

"Yeah."

"Don't tell me you fell for that," said Beth. "You Dongs will believe anything."

"What do you mean?"

"That's exactly what Edgahoova's trying to do. She's trying to turn us against each other. You let me handle this. I'll tell Resurgius about it when he wakes up; he's sound asleep, poor Dong, exhausted from the war. You go back and tell everybody to calm down."

"But—"

"Do as I say, unless you want me to report you to Resurgius."

"Well—"

"Go on, now. Everything'll be ultra."

306

Looking unsure, the Dong turned and trotted back on powerful thighs and tender feet in the direction from which he'd come.

"I have to act fast," thought Beth. "I've got it. With a Spartacus snake I made him a leader, and with a Spartacus snake I'll poison him."

Beth ran to the kitchen—she was an excellent cook—rustled up two plates of green spaghetti with clam sauce, placed a little green asp in each plate, covered it, and took it into the hall, where she came upon a passing Dong, and, giving him the tray, told him to take it to Resurgius and Miz Mandalay in the corset room and asp no questions.

"He was my Dong
But he done me wrong . . ."
she sang, walking away, and dreaming of reinstatement.

"Say, that looks good," said Resurgius, opening the door and taking the tray from the Dong. "It's my favorite, green spaghetti and clam sauce. I sure did work up an appetite!"

"Me too," purred Miz Mandalay. "I'm starved."

Fortunately for them both, Resurgius, who had never mastered the art of Italian eating (by which we mean the use of spoon and fork and the winding up of spaghetti), and had been in the habit of feeding himself spaghetti with his fingers, as babies eat Gerber food, reached into his dish and, by chance, pulled an asp out by its tail.

"What's this?" he said. "This spaghetti squirms about as if it were alive. Perhaps it hasn't been cooked enough."

"I should say not," said Miz Mandalay, who had never been into a kitchen in her life. "Why they haven't even cut its head off. See, its tiny eyes are blinking."

"Nonsense," said Resurgius. "Spaghetti doesn't have eyes. It's made of whole food paste."

"It does so have eyes," said Miz Mandalay, "and a little forked tongue too, judging by the one you're holding."

Resurgius raised the thing up higher to see. He focused through his hornrims.

"Cripes!" he cried. "That's not green spaghetti, that's a snake!"

Letting go of the tail-end of the little asp, he knocked Mandalay's plate from her hand, and dumped his own, and began stomping all over the squirming green stuff. Fortunately, he had not removed his hobnail boots while making love (he needed traction)—this was not inconsideration on his part; Mandalay simply hadn't given him the chance—and now the hobnail bottoms went to work chopping up snakes and spaghetti alike.

"I don't know which is which," he cried, in slight hysteria, "but I'll kill all of it. This dish'll be fit to eat before I'm done."

And indeed, he made a mincemeat of the whole mess. When he was done he flopped down next to Miz Mandalay on a stack of corsets, his giant plastic pectorals heaving.

"This could only be the work of one person," said Miz Mandalay.

"Beth!" cried Resurgius.

"Hell hath no fury," said Miz Mandalay proudly.

Five minutes later Resurgius had Beth arrested and thrown into the corset room, bound and gagged. From now on, Resurgius and Miz Mandalay agreed, she was to have Beth's place in the cup next to Resurgius on the majestic bra.

"O, betrayal!" Resurgius cried, dumping his muscular, plastic buttocks into his cup. "O, treachery!"

"Alas," said Miz Mandalay, climbing into the cup next to his, "you must always remember, my great plastic hero, that hell hath no fury like a Cunnie scorned—and that might one day include me, my love. Circumstances are Fortune, my great muscled Cookie."

12
THE PINAFORE PAPERS

For Resurgius, Beth's attempt to murder him was the last straw.

"This revolution business is too much for me," he said later that night. "I just wish I could go off to the dark side of the moon and lead a quiet, meditative life."

"You're just tired," Miz Mandalay soothed. "You've been through hell."

"Would you consider giving up all this—Mandy—this ugly political life, I mean; this life of political monkeyhood—and running off with me to a desert planet, where it would just be thee and me and the drifting meteorites, the shooting stars?"

"Well, dear Dong, I do so hate to see you give up all that you've fought so hard for in this recent war; but, naturally, my love, whither thou goest, I will go. In the face of love, the life of politics seems but putrid trash. After all, as Jaye Edgahoova might say, politics is nothing but the profound entertainment of the people. I am no longer interested in entertaining the people. I am in love, and therefore selfish; and perhaps that is the best way to be; to be an individual following his or her bliss. At least, minding my own business, I won't be doing them any harm, poor devils—and let them mind theirs. I often wonder why they do what we tell them to. We are no better than they are. If you cut us, do we not bleed?"

"Because they're afraid to think for themselves. Because they mix us up with their ideals."

"It's really quite sad. The herds of beasts must have a leader, I guess."

"Then you'll go with me?"

"Anywhere, anytime."

309

"Tomorrow morning, to the moon. From there we can get the shuttle on to Jupiter or Europa."

"It'll be like an old-fashioned honeymoon."

"Let's start tonight. The honeymoon part, I mean."

"Oh, you! Sugarplum."

But in the morning Resurgius had a change of heart. A good night's sleep, prefaced by a vigorous exercise of his sensitized, pumped-up codpiece, had restored his vitality, and once again he felt ready to conquer the Universe.

"I can't give up now," he said to his beloved Mandy, a spoonful of Coco-Puffies at his lips, "I have a responsibility to all the hard-beset Dongs of this world, who look up to me as a symbol. If I were to quit now it would be like condemning them to another thirty years of slavery."

"It would have that effect."

"But won't you mind not going on our trip to the moon, and then shuttling on to Jupiter or Europa?"

"Resurgius, I knew that you didn't mean what you were saying. You were exhausted."

"I sure was, but I feel great now. Will you help me draw up a plan of action? I don't know how I'm going to do it yet, but I swear I'll think of some way of taking the Univacual Council away from Edgahoova, getting back the Pink House, and putting her on Pluto, where she belongs, just as the French once put Napoleon on Elba in ancient times."

"I'm afraid you might have to wait a while to do that, dear. You have too few Dongs to your name."

"Can't you—the great Miz Mandalay—go and reclaim your position?"

"You know perfectly well that that's impossible under the present circumstances. Edgahoover's branded me a traitor, publicly, and as long as *she's* the government, her accusation is true. I am a traitor, to *her* government. And don't forget, even though she's announced publicly, wickedly, that

310

we both are dead, you can be sure that the Shrike-Troopers are still scouring the country for us."

"I guess you're right," said Resurgius. "But there must be some way."

"We'll just have to wait, and build up a new army. My mother used to say that the shortest wait of all, is the wait for stupidity."

Just then a Dong-trooper knocked and came into the padding room.

"General-Admirable Resurgius," he said, "I have been instructed to tell you that big news is exploding all over the Say-screen. I have been instructed to request you to view this news, as it might be of great importance to our cause. Thank you, sir," he said snappily, and left, clicking his worn-down heels.

"What can that be?" said Mandy, turning in the Say-screen. She got a picture of Sandra Van Orchid, the renowned journalist, then turned up the volume.

Sandra said: "The whole Edgahoova regime has been shaken to its foundations by Daniela Illbird's revelations. Illbird, a member of the staff of the highly secret Strategic Force for Starvation, Death, Destruction and the Atalantic Way, a think tank, has revealed all; admitting that she has been married, illegally, to a Dong for several years. She is quoted as saying, 'I just got sick about what we've been doing to the poor Dongs.' Illbird has also made public many top-secret documents, which she calls the Pinafore Papers. These papers reveal deep and widespread corruption in the government.

"One document, a communiqué sent by General Furius to the Pinafore, and marked top-secret, reveals that General Furius' aunt, a Miz Thickneck, was awarded the contract to build The Great Wall of Furius through her niece's instigation. General Furius herself received a considerable rake-off of taxpayer money, and so did Jaye Edgahoova. Such reve-

311

lations as these are causing a tremendous public outcry against the current government, which, I hope my viewers will recall, I have always opposed. Mobs are roaming the streets chanting such tags as FRY FURIUS and HANG HOOVA! So far, there has been no comment from the Pink House. But, as I said, it is certain that the government of Jaye Edgahoova has been rocked to its foundations."

"This is it, Resurgius!" cried Miz Mandalay. "This is our *deus ex machina*!

"How?"

"*How*! Oh, I guess Mize think faster than Dongs. Don't you see? The people are ready for us. All we have to do now is to physically assume control. I have a marvelous record as a reformer. I've passed the only liberal legislation in this country since the Great Succession."

"You mean that one that gave all government employees a raise?"

"That one and many others—like that one that requires all Mize who own states to pay at least one bobbit a year in taxes. But never mind that! Stick to the point! I'm a reformer and everyone knows it. It was Edgahoova who blackened my good name, and now that the public knows what she is, they'll love me again, just like always, like Julius Caesar's. I've still got a legal claim to power, and I tell you Atalanta is ready for reform. If I assume power with you at my side, they'll accept you as my co-ruler, I know they will. We'll make it a real heterosexual government. We'll be equal partners!"

"O.K., but how'll we get to the Pink House?"

"I've figured it out. It's really easy. The balloon you used to kidnap me is still on the roof, isn't it?"

"Yeah. It's deflated, but it only takes a minute to blow it up. But that's no good; everybody knows about that balloon now, and Edgahoova's Shrike-Troopers'll shoot it down as soon as they spot it, and you have to admit that it's pretty noticeable."

"True enough," said Mandy, frowning. Then she grinned. "I've got it! We'll disguise it as an advertisement for that Old Roman Botula Sausage. All we'll need is some brown paint, and maybe a little black for the burnt part."

"Mandy, you're a genius! But how'll we get passed the guards at the Pink House?"

"We only have to worry about the guards on the roof, and I know all of them. They're a great bunch of gals."

"Okay," said Resurgius, "let's fly."

Resurgius was right, as usual. In less than an hour they came down over the roof of the Pink House. And Mandy was right too, for the guards cheered when they saw her, and cried:

"Why it's Miz Mandalay come home to us! She's no suicide! She lives!"

"And I'll never leave you again, my darlings," she cried, tears squirting from her plastics and streaming down her cheeks. "And I want you all to meet Resurgius; he's my Dong."

"Is he safe?" asked one doubtful Shrike.

"He's a good Dong, believe me, dear. Now if you'll excuse us, we have work to do. We are going to fundamentally change this Universe."

Resurgius ordered that Beth be removed from the wicker basket of the balloon and to be brought along. Then the little group descended to the Ovary Office.

They had arrived not a minute too soon.

When they entered the Ovary Office, they found Edgahoova and Furius desperately packing taxpayer money and treasury plates into two huge trunks.

"Going somewhere?" asked Resurgius.

When Furius saw him, she turned purple, made an animal cry, and charged him. Fortunately, with foresight, and a knowledge of their adversary, all the members of Resurgius' party had taken the precaution of wearing earmuffs, and it was only an earmuff that Furius succeeded in tearing from

313

Resurgius' head. With one powerhouse blow, he succeeded in flooring the unfortunate creature, which he had always wanted to do.

Edgahoova stood aghast.

"You are under arrest in the name of our George Washington," said Resurgius. "Let me warn you that anything you say may be used against you."

"You can't arrest me," said Edgahoova, getting her wits back. *I* am the law."

"No, you're not," said Resurgius. "I am!"

"*We* are, dear," put in Miz Mandalay.

"You're not," said Edgahoova, "I am."

"Well, there's only one way to settle this," said Resurgius, "and that's with logic." So saying, he stepped up to Edgahoova and drove an iron fist into her belly. She doubled up and sank to the floor. He straightened his horn-rims.

"Well, darling," said Miz Mandalay, "I guess we know who the law is now, don't we?"

Following Resurgius' orders, the three Dongs assumed supervision over the Pink House staff, and had Edgahoova and Furius thrown into the basement dungeon where tax-payers were often tortured.

Almost immediately, Miz Mandalay made a request for Say-screen time, and naturally, was granted it. She handled herself admirably, giving the impression that there was nothing more natural than that she should be in command of the government. Not a soul thought to doubt it.

She spoke first, with Resurgius seated beside her.

"Have no fear, my fellow Atalanteans," she said, "the Ship of State is sailing smoothly. Atalanta shall not fail to carry us forward into a future as yet undreamed, where every soul, like the seed of a great oak, will grow and spread and shut the sun from the ground.

"But the future is here and now. Therefore, my Atalanteans, I officially proclaim this day, Mae 25, 3000, as Equality Day. From this day forth, Dongs are recognized as full citizens of Atalanta, with all the rights and privileges thereof.

"And now, I should like to introduce you to the new Co-leader of Atalanta, the great General-Admirable Resurgius, former leader of the Dongs!"

"I only wish to say, on this solemn occasion" said Resurgius, "that I'll work with Miz Mandalay to do my best to bring all of us together and to heal the wounds inflicted by the late civil war. I hope to be the leader of *all* the people, not just the ones I like. And I promise you that I'll do everything I can to please every one of you out there, with charity for all. I thank you."

After their speeches, Resurgius and Mandalay waited in front of the Say-screen to see if the reviews would be good or bad.

Sandra Van Orchid, the first to comment, said, "Let's give these fighting liberals a chance."

Norma Postman said: "I'd like to debate Resurgius. He's got some interesting ideas."

Petite Hannabelle said: "They're gutsy!"

Generally, the reviews were very good, and the general public took the attractive young couple to its heart. It was Camelotian.

13

THE NEW ORDER

In the first months of Resurgius' and Miz Mandalay's Co-leadership, they pleased the public by instituting many reforms, such as warning the school crossing guards about taking the children's lunch money, and preventing the Old

315

Roman Botula Sausage Company from stuffing their product with cow dung.

Actually, Resurgius left most of the administrative things to Miz Mandalay. He had bigger fish to fry. Most of his first days in office were spent in coming to terms with the Space-Pirates. He was now in a much better position to bargain with Blackbeard than he had been at the time of their last meeting, and could truthfully claim that she and her Space-Pirates had done very little to help his cause.

On the other hand, Blackbeard still had a copy of their written agreement, which Resurgius had signed, and which, if made public—Resurgius shuddered to think of the consequences. Besides which, Blackbeard had begun to harass his new government with small space snarls. She really did own him, lock, stock, and barrel.

"Well," Resurgius thought philosophically, "was there ever a political leader who wasn't owned by someone?" Finally, he acceded to every one of Blackbeard's original demands.

"After all," he consoled himself, "it's the taxpayers' money, not mine."

One of Blackbeard's original demands had been that Resurgius keep the war on the dark side of the moon going, so that her cousin, the banker, might take over the Offence Industries and supply bombs and rockets for the war. This also meant that Resurgius was forced, eventually, to enact new draft laws, for the army was running low again on soldiers. Also, it was troublesome having to dream up circumstances which could be used to explain Atalanta's continued involvement there.

He was also responsible for punishing the guilty and rewarding the innocent. Publia he had arrested and thrown into the dungeon with Edgahoova and Furius. Claudia he pardoned, for, as we have mentioned, she married a village smithy. Cossina, who had defected to his side during the war,

316

he welcomed back to Martha, D.C., with a triumphal parade, awarded her the Atalanta Shtick, highest of all medals, and made her Chief of Staff, all of which goes to show that the difference between a dirty traitor and an illustrious hero is just the difference between winding up on the losing or on the winning side.

On June 25, 3000, Edgahoova and Furius tried to escape. Furius had called her naive young guard over and asked if she might whisper something in her ear. The poor Cunnie put her ear to Furius' mouth and found herself to be captive. Furius forced her to unlock her cell, then to free Edgahoova.

Apparently, there was then some argument about taking Miz Bet along, which argument Furius won, convincing Edgahoova that she could not trust Miz Bet. But the argument had wasted precious minutes. Several more guards had entered the cell block. While Furius went after these newcomers, Edgahoova slipped away. She has not been seen or heard of since, but for the persistent rumor that she is the mysterious leader of the Vigilante Libs, a radical political group based on the dark side of the moon. Furius made getaway to launch her famous Brahma rocket nicknamed "Bull." The rocket itself was bent in half due to her weight and clutching legs, and is now in a museum to show what happens to evil-doers: they spin in circles forever—unless they fall off.

Publia was brought to trial, and through the influence of Blackbeard, who was her second cousin once removed, she was given a suspended sentence on her charge of treason. Upon her release, she went back into show biz, which, if you'll remember, had been her first love, taking a job as a Dong impersonator in an All-Night Club.

14
RESURGIUS IN LOVE

Resurgius had only one other problem, and that was the question of how, what had come to be called "L'affaire Bet" by the public, should be handled.

Mandy, as he thought of her now, had become an awful pest about this situation, for it was her most ardent desire that she and Resurgius should be married, that venerable institution now having been given once again the sanction of law. She wanted them to be the first First Family of the New Order, but how could this be done so long as Beth kept insisting from her cell in the Pink House dungeon that she was actually Resurgius' wife, and therefore the First Lady of the Land?

Resurgius cursed himself for ever having married her. He had only done so because she had made him grateful and convinced him that it was love. Now, through Mandy's offices, he knew better. Desperate, he summoned his top legal advisor, Attorney General Mitch Shyster, and his top spiritual advisor, The Reverend Billy Cracker.

"What shall I do?" he asked of them.

Attorney General Shyster replied:

"The marriage wasn't legal in the first place, for there was a specific law against the institution of marriage at the time, and, frankly, I sometimes wish you hadn't countermanded it."

"All right," said Resurgius, searching his conscience, "perhaps it wasn't legal in the eyes of the Law, but what about in the eyes of the Lord?"

"Ah kin only ahdvise yo, suh," said the Reverend Billy, "ta search yo conscience. When yo sayed 'I do' didja mean it, or was yo bein' misguided by thah forces of Evil?"

"I was being misguided."

"Then they is no marriage."

318

"Golly, thanks a lot fellows—this is a great day for yours truly," said Resurgius. "But I'm still going to have to get rid of Beth or she'll always be in my hair."

"Let yo conscience be yo guide, my son," said the Reverend Billy.

Next day, Resurgius brought charges against Beth. He charged her with treason against the former government. Her epaulettes were torn from her shoulders and turned into heavy-duty mops. She was then exiled to Pluto, much as Napoleon had been exiled to Elba, to live a life of contemplation and regret.

Resurgius and Mandy enjoyed their nuptials later the same afternoon. Both died in office, Resurgius first, unfortunately, of toxic masculinity caused by his plastic muscle-suit with the big "R" on its chest, which turned out to be poisonous—and at his state funeral all that was left to observe was his skinny little body, his big head with its shock of auburn hair, his huge hornrimmed, thick-lensed spectacles, and a wan smile of victory. He had a right to his rictus, having put Dongs in their rightful place.

The beautifully embosomed Mandy died some twenty years later, having enjoyed two decades of a smashing superduper Univacual high life.

WOW!

BLARNEY STONED

Read with Brogue

Ah, Dionysus, ya grapey divil deity,
ya'd lak ta have me back in Hellas
ta guzzle in the juice of yer depravity!
Ya know yer dirty bottled blood'll
keep me at yer bidden.
Ah puke it up and force it down lak cud,
but I'll tell ya straight, ya satyr goat,
tomorrow, ah swear, ah'm quitten!
Ya make me drink this soupy slop,
ah know ya do, ah know it!
Ya tease me on ta gulp the rot,
and sure'n hell ah show it.
But ya'll not beat me, goaty beast,
cuz ah tell ya straight, ya satyr goat,
tomorrow, ah swear, ah'm quitten!

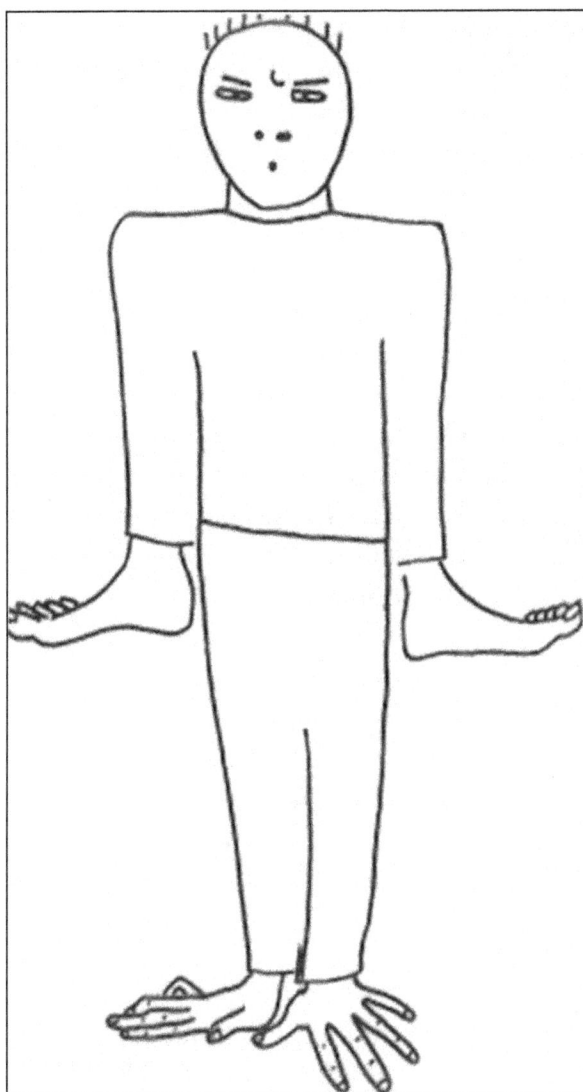

THE FRUITS OF HIS THOUGHT DELIVERED
TO HIS FAVORITE BARTENDER

The good man is like
the camel, George,
he standeth humped!
Drink not of the milk
of human kindness,
for it is binding!

Once a ladyfriend
tried to shut me up:
"Stop sounding like
a garrulous guru!"
she shouted.
"Be yourself!"
But then she thought,
and then she said,
"Oh, hell, you *are*
being yourself!"

She was looking
at *her*self in a
beautiful mirror,
and spoiling it.
"Art thou ugly?" I said.
"Not in the eye of the needle!"

THE DEVIL'S TAVERN

There are three kinds of lies:
lies, damned lies, and statistics.
—attributed by Mark Twain to Benjamin Disraeli

Sam Stock is a man of his time, a hyperproductive computer programmer employed by the New York branch of the International Ministry of Wellness as a data analyst, a stat man, a Super Cruncher. He finds correlatives—hamburgers and high blood pressure, gum soles and flat feet, life and death (one-hundred percent). Everyone is at-risk. Life correlates to danger. But cyberchondria abounds. Sam thinks he might be contributing to the general unease. His work as a technocrat may have contributed to the fears of the public—their fear of walking, of breathing, of whispering (aspiration produces deadly micro-globules of sputum). This winter in New York people are lining up at the mobile Wellness Stations to get bat flu shots. Three cases had been reported in Miramar. The queues, Sam has noticed, are extraordinarily attenuated. People don't want to get near to one another. But of course, the bat flu shots are mandated. Those who do not get them are considered public enemies and are sought and found and sent on to mental health clinics. Just the other day, Sam saw that a group of senior citizens who protested the ban on donuts was rounded up and sent to the Senior Mental Health Center for examination. Sam Stock thought that, yes, they should have their heads examined. After all, carbs can be deadly, and some of those donuts pack icing—vanilla, strawberry, and chocolate; veritable guns of destruction. But there was something troubling about declaring all those old people insane.

Sam tries to balance these thoughts as he maneuvers the lunch hour streets in search of a health food stand. It depresses him to think of the recent ban on mustard. He had to admit that mustard was the only thing that made much of the proffered food of the city palatable. But he himself was the first to find the correlation between mustard and misbehavior. It was bruited about that upscale gangs of rebellious youth in Brooklyn were now attacking public officials with gobs of grey poupon, and of course there was that incident in Atlanta where the mayor was assaulted with deep-fried hush-puppies after instituting a ban on them.

Sometimes Sam Stock thought that officialdom was going a bit too far. He understood the impulse, natural to people in power, to tell others who have no power what to do. But sometimes . . . ah, a stand full of Free-Toes—sugar-free, carb-free, fat-free, and food-free. And not even a dab of mustard to put on them! Sometimes Sam Stock thinks that life is becoming tasteless . . . munch, munch.

Twenty-twenty, the centennial of Prohibition, that was a big year for the Ministry of Wellness! The events of that year included a world-wide ban on smoking, the Bacon Act, and, perhaps the greatest coup the Ministry had ever effected, the institution of the Department of Mental Wellness, which allowed the authorities to take action against people who refused to care for themselves, people who puffed, tippled, or consumed food that was found by the experts at the Ministry of Wellness to be unhealthy. These slackers were of course costing us all money under the Universal Wellness Program. They were to be considered insane and sent to an asylum until they mended their thought-processing ways. Sometimes Sam Stock thought the authorities took advantage of this law to declare insane anyone who in his or her life of quiet desperation heard the sound of a different and distant drummer. It was from the dark underbelly that rumblings could be heard. There was the mysterious case of the physicist who smoked,

324

the notorious case of the tippling mayor, the amazing case of the cake-eating songstress—these stories were heard of and retold, novelized on-line by rebel writers—*Smokey, The Mad Scientist; The Red Nosed Mayor of Castorbridge;* and *God Bless America: The Dreadful Story of Cake Smith.* Sam Stock reads these cautionary tales and tries to learn from them; but sometimes he yearns for romantic adventure. The idea of sharing a chocolate-covered donut with a beauty on a tiger-skin rug set his heart racing. His Free-Toe melts like icing in his mouth at the thought.

How could Sam Stock have failed to notice Lorelei Rhinestein? She had been about the office for some time. But Sam is always intent on his production of correlatives. He sees another one—reading and suicide—and begins to run it. But he is distracted. Lorelei Rhinestein has lovely violet eyes. She reminds him of a flapper of eld. She has just come in from getting her bat flu shot and is flushed with . . . anxiety? The Ministry of Wellness does not want to tell the public about the many deaths correlating to bat flu shots. Sam Stock puts down "bat flu shots and death." He runs it—ummm! He looks at Lorelei Rhinestein. The flush is leaving her face. Not only will she live, he thinks, she will triumph. How not, with such eyes?

In the days following, he gets her name and her *modus vivendi.* She brings her own lunch. Fried chicken from home, long since banned from restaurants. She eats surreptitiously, suspicious even of associates. An atmosphere of danger clings to her drumstick. Sam Stock suspects her of transfats. He could see her in some ancient noir film, the banned-for-smoking "Casablanca" perhaps, still extant in cyberspace. Sam Stock blushes to think of it. Yes, he thought, she's like Ingrid Bergman—mysterious, beautiful, hat down over her violet eyes. But of course Ms. Rhinestein wears no hat. Though not yet banned, hats—with the one exception of cycling helmets—had been deemed bad for the circulation.

The more fashionable members of the ruling class wore them; but, Sam Stock noted, Authority says yes to itself and no to everyone else. He bet that in secret they even ate cake. They did as they pleased.

Sam Stock is increasingly restive, so when Lorelei Rhinestein asks him for a date—a date with a woman of danger—he decides to give adventure a chance and finds himself saying—

"Delighted. Where shall we go?" Men do not ask women for dates, nor do they decide where their time shall be spent; men cautiously wait to be invited, and even here could be entrapment. Can mystery and candor exist simultaneously in enchanting violet eyes? Fling it, he tells himself, I'm taking a chance on love!

Lorelei Rhinestein wants to go to New Jersey. She knows a place out beyond the Pine Barrens. She drives them. It's Saturday night at the Jersey Devil's Tavern.

Where are we, he wants to know, what is this place? What does it remind him of, dark and forebody with the moon overhead? In the woods, isolated, oh, what did they call them, roadhouses, speakeasies? Something out of cyberspace on-line noir dramas.

"I don't like the looks of this," he tells Lorelei. His hackles rise, tickled, but really he does like the looks of the place. The place is like Lorelei herself, mysterious, beautiful in the moonlight, dangerous.

"I've been watching you, Sam Stock," says Lorelei. "I've been watching you and thinking maybe you need a real outing. If I'm wrong I think I can trust you to keep this to yourself, but if I'm right about you . . . well, we may be able to share something exciting. You don't look like a scaredy-cat. The last boy I brought here—a personnel director for the Nursing Corps—he ran away like a rabbit and got lost in the Pine Barrens for two days. First time he had missed a day's work in his life. He threatened to report me to the Ministry

326

of Wellness, but I threatened to tell them that *he* was the one who brought *me* here and he kept his mouth shut."

"I'm not afraid," Sam Stock blusters. He is afraid but for some obscure reason it embarrasses him. Contradictions abound in a nature taught from childhood to be afraid of everything and at the same time to swim with Bubbles, the friendly shark. Sam Stock allows himself to be led into the Jersey Devil. People sit at candlelit tables, drinking adult beverages, smoking cigarettes and cigars, or dancing to the strains of "Smoke Gets in Your Eyes." Seated, Lorelei orders the house cocktails, two Jersey Devils, looks over the flickering candle at Sam, and, in a low voice, sings—

> *They asked me how I knew*
> *My true love was true*
> *Oh, I of course replied*
> *Something here inside*
> *Cannot be denied . . .*

Sam tries to ignore her alluring, husky, melodious voice.

"What kind of place is this?" he asks, looking through a haze of smoke, here and there set aglow by dim lights.

Lorelei observes how wide his innocent blue eyes are in the mesmerizing undulation of the candlelight.

"Sam Stock," she says, "this is a den of iniquity, a speak-drink-and-smoke-easy, and I have lured you here in order to make a criminal of you." She is saying this in such a manner that it sends a thrill of fear up Sam's spine, but then she laughs, and says, "Don't be afraid, Sammy," and Sam is so tense that he laughs too—a nervous hack—as the aromatic Jersey Devils arrive in tall, red, steaming glasses.

Three Jersey Devils later Sam finds himself smoking. At first he coughs but then he gets the hang of it and begins to like it.

"Inhale," urges Lorelei, and sings—

Oh, so I smile and say
When a lovely flame dies
Smoke gets in your eyes . . .

Six months later, at work, Sam is dying for a cigarette. After all, smokers are people who have one friend no worse than others, the sometimes of their pleasure and the ultimate difficulties, the big troubles, the being able to be quiet in the hurried world, the holding hands without a word, the sad truth of the matter as recognized by ashes, or ashes recognized, whatever is looking up from nothing, from the smoke-filled no-bottom of everything, the oh for just a moment, the please slow it down, the oh God I'm late, the don't forget, the oh forgotten, but smokers are people who have at least one friend. The relationship between smoking and disease is merely a correlative one, he tells himself and the greatest correlation of all is life and death (100%), but right now he needs a cigarette. Everyone who has a moment of contentment, he tells himself, dies; therefore, contentment kills.

Minutes after this moment of illumination, Sam is arrested by the dreaded Green (really olive drab) Shirts of the Ministry of Wellness for smoking in the men's room and taken away to the insane asylum for mental reprogramming. His psychiatric report confirms that he may ultimately prove to be a danger to the State. He has a definite proclivity toward disrespect of authority.

Sam says, "Authority says yes to itself and no to everyone else! It says No!" Sam tells Doctor Forbrane, his counselor, to shove it.

"And all this rebellion started with a single cigarette," Doctor Forbrane tells his colleagues over cigars and port.

"Good thing we wiped out marijuana," he continues, stabbing his Montecristo into space for emphasis, "or all of the little people would have become non-productive. But have no fear. I have implanted in his brain a continuously ticking taser in order to pacify him. He will represent no more challenge to Authority than a popinjay. He will, in fact, become a useful member of society. Wellness will be his way!"

One year later, Lorelei meets Sam upon his release.

"Are you cured?" she asks as she drives him away from the asylum.

"I'm fine now, but they caught me just in time. Got a cigarette?"

"In the glove compartment," Lorelei says, hitting the gas, heading for the Jersey Devil's Tavern, which, despite all efforts of the Green Shirts of the Ministry of Wellness, exists forever just beyond the Pine Barrens.

THE FUTURIST

And then we must replace you, Death, for you must go
with the combustion engine down the tube of time
and all will laugh at you as they do now at blimps
and bleeding, flapping wooden wings for flight and leeches
on the back for purifying blood, for in the future, Death,
hiatus will replace you, the storage called cryonics,
the deep freeze, or some such method to define
and discipline ourselves, to give a shape to time
and render meaningful our lives as you do now,
O wisdom-wasting Death, when life is lived poetically,
in many stanzas, each building on the last, developing
its theme, so that an open-sequence poem of life
is lived and not a golden drop of honey-wisdom wasted
that cost us generation after generation,
O Future, in long darkness climbing into you.

ON MUDDLING THROUGH

I like the English saying "muddle through."
It's always better than perfecting things,
although the human race keeps trying to,
keeps carving for stone Victory stone wings.

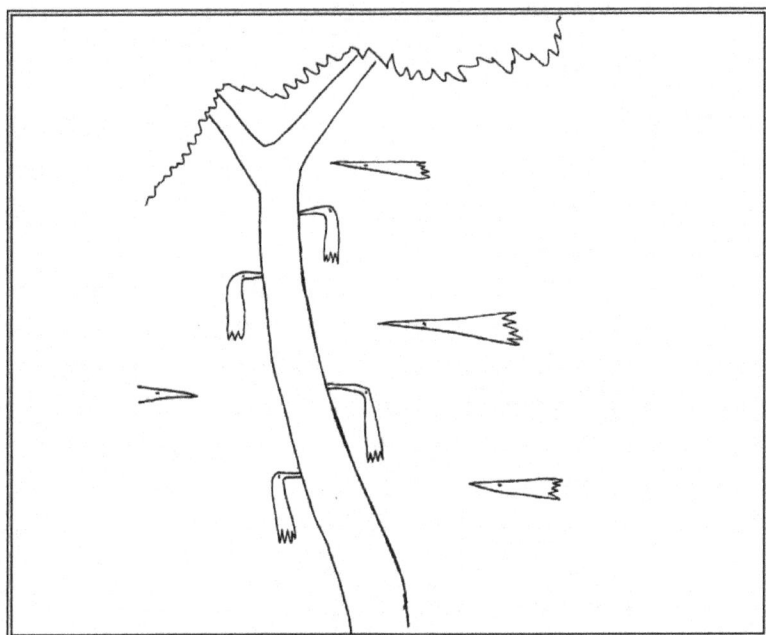

HAYDN'S HEAD: A PASTICHE

for Jack O'Brian, columnist, New York Journal-American,
who tipped me off

We are aboard the Orange Blossom Special, returning to
New York from Florida, and I am hopeful that Tweedledum
and Tweedledee, as Johnny calls them, a couple of bad eggs
in plaid suits, are not.

"Odds are we've left them shaking their fists on the
station platform, Pug," Johnny says, mopping his brown brow
with a white silk handkerchief. He gears his seat back,
loosens his tie, tips his Panama over his eyes, and acts like he
hasn't got a worry in the world. I act like I am watching the
midnight Miami lights recede, but what I am really doing is
watching the window for reflections. I expect to see Sam the
Elephant's bonebreakers appear at any second.

Most gamblers have a specialty—cards, craps, horses–
but Johnny Belmont will bet on anything. I have first heard
of him a year ago, when he places a spectacular bet on the
presidential election and loses to all concerned. He is in deep
trouble until his rich family steps in. But they are very much
put out, because he has bet on Stevenson and they are an
Eisenhower family. So they warn Johnny that they will not
rescue him again. At least this is the version I have heard
outside of Lindy's restaurant, in that vague area of the
environment around Broadway and Fiftieth Street which
Damon Runyon has dubbed Jacobs' Beach in honor of his
ticket speculating pal, Mike Jacobs. On Jacobs' Beach you
meet the sporting crowd—scalpers, bookies, touts, mobsters,
and journalists such as Walter Winchell and, until he passes
on in '46, Runyon himself.

But it is at Hialeah that Johnny and I have become pals.
The Florida sharks do not know that Johnny is a black sheep

without a red cent; so, with his good looks, his classy manners, and his family name, he has been able to borrow large amounts of hay from Sam the Elephant, who is called such because he does not forget so easy. But Johnny has been having the world's worst losing streak, and has tried to get on the good side of Lady Luck by placing some bets for me. Unfortunately, Sam the Elephant has heard of said bets; and, because he does not care from which individual he collects, has decided to hold me partners with Johnny when he calls in the bets.

We are tap city when we step off the Special at Penn Station—unless you count Johnny's lucky two-bit piece, which he never spends. But Johnny thinks we can get a stake at the Hotel Bon Chance, a gamblers' haven in the West Forties. I figure he means to check us in and flip his quarter into wealth. But I am worried that some of Sam the Elephant's boys might be keeping their eyes out for us there. Johnny laughs kind of grimly and says that we will have to gamble on that because the Bon Chance is the only place he can think of where he can raise a stake.

It looks like we are going to have to hoof it through a cold November rain, which is pouring out of buckets. It does not matter much to me, because I am not a dude, but it matters to Johnny, who is a clotheshorse. We have had to leave all our clothes in Florida, and he only has this one tropical suit left, which is on his back. So he shakes his head, and says: "Pug, I'm not going to let this suit get soaked."

I follow him through the crowd and up to the Lost and Found, which is open all night in those days, and it is now about midnight, as our trip takes us about twenty-four hours, and he tells the busy clerk behind the counter that he has lost his black umbrella. The clerk hustles off and is back in no time with three such. "That's it," cries Johnny, and takes the one that happens to be the best of the lot.

As we are walking away, Johnny says, "You know, Pug, one could get anything that way." He stops and looks at me with his green eyes bright like two Go signs. "Think of something, I'll bet you a belated C-note that they have it—that the clerk will hand it across to you."

There is nothing like a wager to cheer me up, and I need cheering. "You're on," I say. "We'll make it for the first C-note one of us gets."

"O.K.," says Johnny. "But I choose the item. It can't be anything with an I.D., and it can't be anything too unusual—like a zither. Fair enough?"

"Fair enough," I say, wondering what a zither is.

"Say a plain square box—a cardboard carton or package wrapped in plain brown paper and tied with twine—O.K.?"

"You're on."

"You ask for it. I got the umbrella. The clerk might remember me." On the 5-yard line from the Lost and Found desk, Johnny says: "I'll wait here." In two minutes I am back, carton in hand.

"I owe you a C-note," I say, dangling the package from a finger by the twine. "The bet's good," I add, and say that I will now return the package.

"Wait a minute, Pug," says Johnny. "How about another C-note on what's in it? Let's say on whether it's animal, vegetable, or mineral."

I say, "It's bigger than a breadbox, that's for sure."

"Takers?" says Johnny.

I shrug. "Takers," I say. "So where do we open it?"

"Not here," says Johnny. "I'll tell you what, Pug. We'll take it with us to the Bon Chance, and open it there. Then I'll have a boy re-wrap it and bring it back here to the Lost and Found. What do you say?"

"I suppose you want I should carry it?"

"And I'll keep us dry with the umbrella. Come on."

The Bon Chance is a few blocks uptown from Penn Station. Cats and Dogs of rain are bouncing knee-high as we turn off the avenue. On the next corner is a Yellow Cab stand, or used to be in those days. I duck to look into the first cab in the line and there as usual is Sleeping Bill, who could make a claim to being the worst hack in New York, as he never takes a fare. Actually, it is his own car, done up to look like a Yellow Cab, and he is no hack at all, but a bookie. I tap his windshield but he is asleep at the wheel. I think he has been so since I left for Florida. Anyway, he's in the same position he was in when I left.

In a block or two on this numbered cross-street the pedestrian traffic has thinned down to Johnny and me. Ahead, through the watery dark I see *BON CHANCE* come and go in nervous green neon winks. I am looking at this sign, and thinking about a hot bath, when a dark, shiny limo sprays up beside us. The back window on our side is rolled down and there is the head of a white-faced, dark-hatted woman in it. She has thin red lips and big white teeth through which she hisses something at us, which I cannot make out due to the fact that the rain is doing drum rolls. A big boy in a chauffeur's uniform comes around from the other side. He is waving a revolver which has a silencer on it like a rolled-up racing form. He believes that action speaks louder than words, because instead of explaining himself he hooks a couple of thick fingers into the twine on the box I am conveying and tugs. I tug back. He then swings at me and misses, but corrects himself by bashing the big silencer down on my knuckles. Only now does he decide to make himself clear.

"Let go, you fat swine!" he cries, adding insult to injury. But before I can be offended, Johnny has collapsed the umbrella and batted it down on the pistol, which splashes into a jumping lake at the rear end of the limo.

"En garde!" cries Johnny, stabbing the guy several short ones. The big guy lets go of the twine, and slips in the rain just as I step in with a right cross. He falls against the limo and keeps on going down toward where the pistol has submerged, slapping at street water, grabs up the pistol, aims, and pulls the trigger.

Because of the silencer and the noise of the rain, I don't know if I have been shot or not, but then I realize by the look on the big guy's face that the pistola is waterlogged.

Johnny and I have jumped away when he has had the pistola pointed at us, so he has a head start when he ducks around the limo. The door slams and the limo speeds off, making a wake like the Titanic.

"What the hell . . ." says Johnny, looking after the limo.

"It is this dumb package," I say.

"Did you see the plates?" says Johnny. "They were diplomatic. Let's get to a room and see what we've got here."

There is a new night clerk at the Bon Chance, a straw-haired, freckled kid with a Southern accent. This is a break, as the old clerk would have sold out his mother to Sam the Elephant or any other shark for the price of a warm beer. It won't help much if Sam the Elephant's boys are looking hard for us, but it is anyway worth the ink to register under a couple of phony names, so we do. A kid who looks like the younger brother of the yokel behind the desk shows us up, carrying the package by the twine, like a suitcase.

In our room, Johnny offers to flip the kid double or nothing for the tip, neglecting to state the amount involved, and the kid eagerly takes the bet. Johnny then offers to let the kid owe him "the ten spot." But before the kid has about-faced, Johnny has flipped him into serious debt, which he immediately cancels, on the condition that we get top service, to which the kid gratefully agrees.

Johnny orders sandwiches, coffee, cigarettes, cigars, razors, etc. He also needs a bottle of good Scotch. He sends the kid away with our wet clothes. In those days, you can get a good steam press all night, even in a cheap hotel.

"Well, now, Pug," says Johnny, ripping open the package, "let's have a look at this."

I go over to the table on which the kid has placed the box and look into it. Johnny is pulling out a lot of excelsior. There is something round and gray down in the middle of the box. Johnny pulls more excelsior out, reaches in, and jerks back like he's been stung. I see it now and let out a whistle. It is a human skull.

As soon as it sinks in what we have here, we do a thorough search of the box for identification of some kind— "Provenance," Johnny calls it—even checking inside the skull, but discover zero. We pack the bony head away; and then, while we bathe and shave, we discuss the nature of things as they stand.

We ask ourselves: Who are the foreign couple in the limo? Why do they want this old skull? Should we call the police?

Johnny says, combing his dark hair down over his forehead and cutting a part in it, "Do the chauffeur and his lady know that the package contains a skull, rather than something else more valuable? Surely an ordinary human skull can't be worth much. Surely not enough to induce armed robbery."

Comes a rapping at our chamber door.

"Who is it?" Johnny calls.

"Bellboy. I got your clothes and a wagon full of food and drinks."

When the bellboy goes, Johnny says, "Get dressed, Pug," and pulls on his pants.

I am tying my tie in the cloudy mirror over the dresser when there is a second knock at the door.

"What now?" Johnny calls over the transom. He thinks it is the bellboy again.

"Please," comes a reply. "I am Professor-Doctor Albrecht Schmitt with my daughter, Agnes. We have rooms down the hall. I must speak with you."

"It don't sound like anybody Sam the Elephant would know," I say.

"Nor like the chauffeur from the limo," says Johnny. He opens the door a crack and peers out. Then he steps back and opens it wide.

This gent has a couple of inches on me and I have a couple of pounds on him, making us two barrels, but his weight is then as old as mine is now, and he has never been a lightweight boxer as I have before I lose my last match in the late 40's and begin consoling myself with pumpkin pies.

He has a gray, yellow-streaked walrus mustache, and thick, silver-rimmed specs. His daughter is taller and a hundred pounds lighter, a honey-blonde in powder blue who looks like a wicked witch has chased her out of a fairy tale. She eyes Johnny like he is Prince Charming.

The gent extends a thin manicured hand. "I'm Professor-Doctor Schmitt," he repeats. Gray moths flutter behind his specs. "I see you have opened our package. We were on our way up from Washington with that skull when we suspected we were being followed. You see, it is a valuable specimen, and there are those who would stop at nothing to possess it. Research is highly competitive. You Americans have a phrase—*it's a jungle*." He gives out with a nervous cackle.

Johnny lights a Fatima. He says, "It hasn't got a name or a number on it. How do we know it's yours?"

The Doc looks stumped. The gray moths look like they are trying to break out from behind their glass cages.

Johnny purses his lips, lifting his little black mustache, and blows out some Turkish smoke, giving Agnes the once-over twice. She looks at him with big sad blue eyes. He cracks a smile. "Maybe you can tell me how you lost it?"

338

"Oh, no," the Doc almost stutters, "it wasn't lost. Just as we were leaving the train, we became *certain* that we were being followed. But we hoped we had lost our pursuers in the crowd when we came upon a row of lockers. Unfortunately, neither of us had an appropriate coin—"

"We had to work fast," Agnes breaks in. "In a moment's inspiration, my father saw the Lost and Found, and we deposited it there."

"Then," the Doc picks up, "we waited nearby to make certain that our pursuers had not seen us turn in the package."

"You can imagine," says Agnes, "our surprise when we saw—you, Mr.—"

"Morris," I say. "Pug Morris."

"—Mr. Morris, pick up the package."

"You were not at all what we were looking for in our pursuers," says the Doc.

"Sorry," I say, as I am pulling the ring from a Prince Albert.

"No, no," says the Doc, kind of flustered. "I did not mean—"

"Frankly," pipes Agnes, "we thought you might be some sort of confidence tricksters who preyed on Lost and Found patrons."

"If that should prove to be the case," says the Doc, kind of shrugging, "I'm certain that we can come to terms—"

This time I break in. "We picked up the package on a lark," I say, around my stogie, which I am busy lighting.

"We're gamblers," Johnny says. He explains the bet.

"I see," says the Doc, when Johnny has finished. "We followed when you left the station, and saw the assault on you. We should certainly have helped, for those who attempted to steal the package from you were assuredly those who pursued us from Washington, but I'm getting old, and the rain was beating down, and we had fallen too far behind to be of any assistance."

"They must have found us," says Agnes, "and then seen you ahead of us with the package, passed us by, and attacked—"

"We saw you turn in here," says the Doc.

"We told the clerk we were friends of yours and wanted rooms on your floor," says Agnes. "We've been drying off and making ourselves presentable."

"Now," says the Doc, "if you'd please be so kind as to give us our package . . ."

Johnny grins, and says: "We still don't know that the package is yours. Maybe it belongs to the pair who jumped us."

"Yeah," I say, "and maybe everything you've told us is a load of—"

"Pug!" says Johnny.

"—baloney," I say.

Schmitt's face falls. He thinks for a moment, and says, in a much more businesslike manner, "We haven't much time, gentlemen," reaches into a breast pocket, pulls out a fat wallet, and takes a couple of bills from it. "Will a hundred—er, two hundred—one each—be satisfactory?"

"Mister," I say, "we lose more than that before breakfast."

But Johnny takes the two bills, stuffs one in his pocket, and, handing me the other, says, "Here, Pug, cash this and call the cops."

I start for the phone, but the Doc cries, "Stop!" When I turn back, he is holding a .30 Mauser, with its little black eye looking right at me. "Put your hands up and hand me that box," he orders.

"Which is it, Professor?" says Johnny in his usual cheerful way, his hands half up, talking through the smoke from his dangling Fatima.

"Agnes," says Schmitt, "get the head."

Now we are all startled. Someone is at our door again.

340

"We are very popular tonight, Johnny," I say.

"Infamously, Pug," says Johnny.

Neck on neck, Johnny knocks the Mauser to the floor and I catch the Doc on the chin with a light fast uppercut.

Schmitt has gone down across the coffee wagon, taking a few items with him. In short, he has made a good deal of noise. Plus which, Agnes has screamed.

"It could be the Elephant's boys," I say.

Johnny grabs up the Doc's Mauser, looks sharp at Agnes, finger to lips, and steps to the wall by the door so he will be behind it when it opens. He nods at me.

I stay put and call, "Come in!"

It is the chauffeur and the pale-faced lady from the limo. The chauffeur is holding the revolver with the big silencer on it. The gat looks dry and newly oiled.

I back up some toward the table with the package on it, drawing them in. They bite, and step in, eyeing Agnes and the Doc's unconscious bulk.

"Where's the other—?"

But the chauffeur has got curious too late. Johnny jams the Doc's Mauser into his back.

"Well," says Johnny, "if it isn't my fencing partner! Drop it."

The chauffeur drops the big revolver with a thud. Johnny kicks the door shut behind him, steps around in front, and kicks the gat to the side.

"Who are you two?" he asks, pleasantly.

The chauffeur clicks his heels. "Colonel Ivan Lensky," he says, "Soviet State Security. This is my associate, Frau Yeva Von Heller of Austria."

"KGB," says Johnny. "How interesting. My uncle is Wild Bill Belmont."

"OSS," says Lensky. "I have met him. A double-dyed conservative McCarthyite reactionary."

"That's Uncle Bill," says Johnny, smiling.

341

"Who are you talking about?" I say.

"Spies!" says Johnny.

"We already know Doctor Schmitt and his daughter," says Lensky. "Who are you?"

"Not-so-innocent bystanders," says Johnny. "Gamblers who made a bet on a live lark and wound up with a dead head."

"That head is important to Frau Von Heller and myself—to the governments we represent. We are prepared to offer you two thousand dollars. I have on my person an instrument for that amount. Payment cannot be stopped."

"Two *grand*," I say. "That might keep the Elephant from our door, Johnny."

"Elephant?" The Colonel looks intrigued.

"An Americanism," says Johnny. He looks at Agnes, who frowns, and at the Doc, who groans, and at me, who shrugs. "Make it five thousand," he says.

"Ah," sighs Lensky. "It so happens—"

"That you have another instrument for five thousand," says Johnny.

Frau Von Heller says: "We represent the rightful owners."

The Colonel waves a hammy hand at Agnes and the Doc. "These two are frauds."

"No," cries the Doc, looking up from the floor, "don't give it to them! You would be betraying your country. It doesn't belong to them and you cannot put a money value on it. It's priceless!"

Now come more knocks. It is like a convention.

"House detective," comes a voice. "Open up!"

"No deal," says Johnny to Lensky and Von Heller, who have closed ranks. Lensky whispers something in Von Heller's ear.

"Shut up, you two," I say. "And behave."

"Open up!" says the dick outside the door.

342

"Get your father up," Johnny says to Agnes.

A key is inserted in the lock.

"He's got a key, Johnny," I say. "It's the house dick, all right."

Johnny shoves the Mauser in his belt at the small of his back and drops his coat tail over it. He pulls open the door, a ring of keys jangling on the other side of the lock.

"What the hell—" says the house dick. He is long and thin in a worn blue suit and looks at us from a long thin yellow face, sour as kraut. "Why didn't you open up?" he asks, scowling.

"There's been an accident," says Johnny. "We were busy."

"What's going on in here?" says the dick. "Folks down the hall say they heard noise and screaming. You realize it's two in the morning?" He gives me a hard look.

"Hey, wait a minute. Ain't you Pug Morris?"

"You got me," I say.

"You ain't registered, Morris. Who's he?" he asks, spotting the Doc.

"He's my father," says Agnes, rising from the floor where she's been trying to get the Doc up. "He fainted and knocked over the tray and the lamp and I cried out. He's been suffering this condition for some time, but I'm still terribly upset and was caught off guard when it happened. I'm sorry we disturbed the other patrons."

I notice now that Frau Von Heller has her big black hat off. The house dick has stepped in close to get a good look at the Doc, and Von Heller and Lensky are edging toward the door.

"You're not leaving?" says Johnny, like a disappointed host.

"Duty calls," says Lensky. "I hope you and Mr. Morris will reconsider our offer."

343

"Ah!" cries Von Heller. She has dropped her hat. It is pretty obvious to everybody but the house dick, who has his back to her, that she has scooped up the big revolver with the hat.

"Keep your powder dry," I say.

She touches her pale cheek with a red nail, says, "Yes, it's still raining," turns on Lensky's arm, and the pair step out of the room; and, I hope, out of my life, but I doubt it.

"Everything here all right then?" asks the dick. "Want me to get a doctor for your father, miss?"

"No," says Agnes. "It isn't serious. And my father's a doctor."

Schmitt sits up and shakes his head. "I'm getting too old for this work," he says.

"I'd better help Father to his room," says Agnes.

"I'll help you with him," says Johnny.

"Wait a minute," says the dick. "Don't I know you, too? Ain't you Johnny Belmont?"

"Clarence Feathergale," says Johnny. "It's on the register."

"Feathergale! Well, Feathergale, *I'll* help the young lady and her father. The Bon Chance don't want no lawsuit on its hands."

"I'll be back when Father is comfortable," says Agnes, "to explain."

Johnny pushes the door after them, leaving it ajar.

"That dick has us pegged," I say. "He'll tip the Elephant's boys for sure."

"Maybe not," says Johnny. "Maybe he doesn't want any trouble here on his carpeted beat. In any case, we'll have to gamble that he doesn't. We can't walk out on a situation like this, Pug. That young lady needs help, and maybe our country needs help—and maybe there's enough money somewhere in this situation to pay off Sam the Elephant and to get us a new stake."

344

"So what makes an old skull so valuable?" I say.

Johnny snaps his fingers. "Pug," he says, "maybe it's not *what*, but *who*."

This gives us something to think about while we straighten up the room. We set the wagon up, put what is unbroken back on top, and I fix us a couple of drinks. I call down for the boy to clean up the mess on the rug and bring us some fresh sandwiches. When he has gone we finally put some food aboard. I am several meals behind.

As I'm swallowing the last corner of the last sandwich, Agnes taps and steps in.

"How's your father?" says Johnny.

"All right," she says. "He's resting. But he really shouldn't be doing this."

"Doing what, exactly?" says Johnny.

"This kind of work—for the government."

"It's on the level, then?" I say. "Listen, Miss Schmitt, I am really sorry that I have to deck him, see, but I want to make sure that he comes loose from that Mauser."

"He understands," she says. "He shouldn't have drawn the gun. It was an act of desperation. Oh, why on earth did you pick up that package! How did you *know* about it?"

"We didn't know," I say. "It was just a wild bet."

"Then, you really *are* gamblers?"

"You do not know the half of it, lady," I say. "We are even now being chased by loan sharks who will bite off our legs if we do not paddle."

"You're not criminals?"

"My name, Miss Schmitt," says Johnny, "is Belmont. I come from a long line of generals and statesmen. A good third of my family is in government—the other two-thirds are in money."

"Then you're patriots?"

"Black sheep, but true blue," says Johnny, with plenty of pride, "and with wounds to prove it."

345

"Johnny made a hero of himself fighting Hitler," I say. "That's how come he ain't in Korea. War wounds. And he has the medals to prove it."

"Well," says Agnes, impressed. "Perhaps you'll fix me a drink. I'm a little unsteady."

I fix the three of us some Scotch and soda and we settle down to hear what she has to say.

"Do you know anything about Austria?" she begins.

"Nope," I say.

Johnny just sips his Scotch.

"It's divided," she says, "Into American, British, French, and Russian zones. Vienna is in the Russian zone, but the Inner City is administered by each power in turn for a month, and patrolled day and night by groups of four soldiers drawn from the Four Powers."

"Sounds complicated," I say.

"It is," she says. "There are hopes for reunification, even plans ongoing. But things *can* go wrong."

"Well, what has this got to do with the head?" I say.

"My father and I are agents for the forces in and out of Austria who oppose Communism. That skull may become important—even more important—if reunification fails. You see, it is the skull of one of the greatest composers who ever lived—an Austrian named Franz Josef Haydn."

"What did I tell you, Pug," chirps Johnny, beaming. "It's *who*." He leaps up and digs the skull out, palms it, and says, like an actor: "Alas, poor Haydn! I love his music!"

He sits down with the skull in his lap.

"Then you may know," Agnes goes on, "that Haydn died in Eighteen-nine. Austria was at war with France then. A battle was advancing into Vienna. Haydn was buried in the middle of that battle. The local prison chief, a man named Peter, was an amateur phrenologist—"

"What is that?" I say.

346

"One who studies the conformation of the skull to divine mental faculties," says Johnny.

I guess he can see that I have missed him.

"They study the bumps on your head to see what you're like," he explains.

"They would think that I am pretty complicated," I say, "what with all my bumps."

"Extremely complicated," says Johnny.

"And so," Agnes picks up, "in the middle of all the confusion of the battle, the prison chief, Peter, had the body exhumed, and the head cut off. He stripped the head of all flesh, studied the skull, and finally pronounced that Haydn had the bumps of music fully developed."

"And what if he hadn't?" asks Johnny, smiling. "Would this Peter have cancelled his season ticket?"

"I don't know," says Agnes, laughing. "Anyway, he had planned to return the skull, but had taken too long in his study of it, and now felt that returning it was too dangerous. Instead, he had an ebony, glass-windowed box made, which he had decorated with a golden lyre. The skull was placed in this box, on a white silk cushion trimmed with black.

"But Peter lived in fear of being caught with it, and later passed it on to a man named Rosenbaum, who was secretary to Haydn's patron, Prince Esterhazy. Prince Esterhazy was, of course, unaware of all this, until he decided to give Haydn a more dignified burial than the one he had during the war; and, in course, had the coffin brought to him at Eisenstadt, in East Austria, where Haydn had lived under his patronage, and opened. The Prince was horrified to discover that there was only a wig where the head should have been. He investigated, and traced the decapitation to the prison chief, Peter. He was furious, and sent the police to Peter, who confessed his deed, and that Rosenbaum now had the skull. The Prince demanded that the head be returned. Rosenbaum returned a skull. The Prince had it examined and identified as the skull of a twenty year old man. Haydn died at Seventy-seven. Now the Prince had a search made of Rosenbaum's house, but it did not yield any result, as Rosenbaum's wife, the singer Therese Gassmann, had hidden the skull in her straw mattress and lay on her bed during the search.

"It was Frau Rosenbaum who was behind Rosenbaum's refusal to return the skull. The glass and ebony display case containing that gruesome relic you're holding had become the highlight of her famous musical evenings.

"Then the Prince tried bribery. His emissaries promised Rosenbaum a huge sum if he would deliver the skull. Whereupon the besieged Rosenbaum bought the skull of an old man from a Vienna mortuary. This skull was much closer in phrenological detail to Haydn's, and was accepted as the original and interred with Haydn's body.

"On his deathbed, Rosenbaum bequeathed the real skull back to prison chief Peter, who in turn bequeathed it to the Society of Friends of Music in Vienna, who owned a great number of Haydn relics. But Peter's wife gave it to her doctor instead, who presented it to the Austrian Institute of Pathology and Anatomy in Eighteen-Thirty-two. They supposedly passed it on to the Society of Friends of Music, to whom it was originally willed by Peter.

"In Nineteen Thirty-two, Prince Paul Esterhazy—direct descendant of Haydn's patron—promised to build a magnificent tomb for Haydn, if the head were restored to the body. But, while the authorities were still discussing the matter, the Second World War erupted. As a result of new political divisions after the war, Haydn's skeleton lay in the Soviet Zone while his skull rested in the International Zone. All of this is public knowledge; but of how the skull was stolen and taken to the Soviet Zone, then retrieved by agents of the Western democracies, nothing has been made public. The world in general still believes the real skull to be in the possession of the Society of Friends of Music, in Vienna. Both the democracies and the forces of Communism would like to claim the genius for their own, but neither can, until skull and skeleton are reunited. No price can be put upon the propaganda value of such a coup."

"And this is the real head?" I say.

"Yes," says Agnes, "and the Communists know it. If they get it, they will have Haydn."

"How did it get to the States?" says Johnny.

"That remains a classified secret," says Agnes. "But it's my father's job to get it back to Vienna."

"Why didn't they send it on a battleship?" I say.

"Classified," says Agnes. "But let me say this much. It's not generally realized that the skull in Vienna is a fake, as I've said. So everything has to be done—unobtrusively." She studies us for a moment, then says: "The head is priceless because you can't put a price on propaganda value, but there *is* financial value attached to it. The authorities are offering twenty-five thousand dollars to anyone who is of assistance in recovering the head. So, if you'll help us, you wouldn't be doing it for nothing."

I look at Johnny. His green eyes are very bright.

"I can explain a little further," says Agnes. "There are two other skulls being pursued right now—bogus skulls—one in Europe and one in Asia. They are meant to confuse the Communists."

"Two phonies," I say, "and we have the real one. Just like three card monte, eh, Johnny?"

"What do you want us to do?" says Johnny.

"There's a freighter leaving at four this morning from Pier Ten. We want to be on it and at sea before Von Heller and Lensky or anyone else knows. If you and Mr. Morris could get us safely to it . . ."

"Why not a plane?" I say.

"The Captain is our associate. The few other passengers will have been closely screened and will present us with no problems. It's all been arranged, you see. We were supposed to go directly to the ship from Penn Station. Your intervention—"

"Threw your plans off," says Johnny. "Of course we'll help. Pug, would you wrap up Maestro Haydn's head, please. Here, let's have one more drink for the road, then we'll go down the hall and collect your father and see how we can get safely to Pier Ten."

In a few minutes we are standing in front of Doc Schmitt's door. Agnes raps on it lightly, calling:

"Father! Father!"

When no answer comes, Agnes opens the door.

The Doc is stretched out on the carpet. He faces the ceiling, open-eyed.

Agnes runs over and shakes him. "Father! Father!" she cries. She looks back at Johnny, her face twisting with grief. Johnny goes to her, bends down, feels the Doc's pulse, listens for his heart, but it's all automatic, as the old man's eyes keep staring up, like he's looking through the ceiling at the stars. Johnny takes a shoulder and turns him over.

"He's been stabbed," he says.

"Not shot?" I say.

"There's a slit in the back of his coat, not a hole."

"Stabbed in the back," I say. "The dirty cowards."

"But why not shot?" says Johnny, like he's talking to himself.

"Noise," I say.

Johnny gives me an impatient look.

Agnes falls across the Doc's body in a dead faint. It must be delayed reaction. Johnny carries her to an easy chair, gets a damp towel from the bathroom, and pats her cheeks and forehead. Pretty soon she opens her eyes, which look bigger and bluer and sadder than ever. Johnny perches on the arm of her chair and puts an arm around her shoulders, which are shaking. She buries her face in his chest and in ten seconds his suit is wetter than it got in the rain. Finally she pulls back and says: "I shouldn't have left him alone . . ."

"Shouldn't we call the cops?" I say.

"No," says Johnny. "They'll tie us up and we've got to make that ship." He thinks for a minute, then says: "We've got to leave things as they are—for the time being. It's what your father would have wanted, Agnes."

"Yes," says Agnes, wiping her eyes. "He would want me to carry on with the mission. I must pull myself together—for him. What time is it?"

"Nearly three," I tell her.

She says: "And the ship weighs anchor at four o'clock this morning."

"Won't it wait for you?" I say.

"No," she says, shaking her head. "It's to leave without us. The Captain is to assume that we've failed."

"And if you fail," I say, "it will be our fault. Maybe this will cure you of making these wild bets, Johnny," I add, feeling pretty bad about the whole thing. "Now maybe we have even hurt Uncle Sam."

Johnny says: "This must have happened a few minutes ago, when Agnes was in our room. That means that Lensky and Von Heller aren't very far away. Pug," he says, "take Agnes back to our room. Give her a drink. I'll be right along."

"What are you going to do?" I say.

"Place a bet," says he.

"A bet!" I am disgusted—almost.

"Go along now," he says, and I can see that he means business. "But leave the head here."

I have almost forgotten that all this time I am holding the box. I shrug, put the box on the bed, help Agnes to her feet, and take her out. She is pretty shaky, poor kid.

In the hall, she says: "I can trust Johnny, can't I?"

351

"You can trust us both," I tell her. But I cannot figure out what Johnny is up to.

In our room, I fix two drinks and hand one to Agnes.

"I guess he's right," she says. "The main thing is to get the head to the ship." She threw down her drink like she needed it. "We can call the authorities about—about my father once that's done."

"Sure," I say, pouring her another drink. She is beginning to get back some color. I jaw with her for nearly twenty minutes, and I am beginning to worry about Johnny, when in he comes, carrying the box.

"Now, listen, Pug," he says, "we've got to be careful–"

I interrupt him with: "What have you been up to?"

"Calling us a cab," he says. "I got the cab stand to tap Sleeping Bill. He'll be waiting out front."

"All that time!" I say. "And why didn't you call from here?"

"I didn't want that house dick—or anyone else—to know that anyone from this room was going any place. Now stop asking questions," he says, "and keep sharp." He looks at his watch. "We better get a move on, if we plan to make that ship."

What makes me edgy as we step out of the elevator is that the lobby is deserted. The yokel night clerk and his kid brother are nowhere in sight. But, as we are halfway to the front door, the house dick appears from a room behind the desk.

"Checking out?" he says. "Trying to skip on your bill?"

"We'll be coming back," says Johnny.

"Then," says the dick, "let's have your keys."

Johnny checks his watch. "We haven't much time," he says. "We better pay him."

We go back to the desk. I, for one, feeling kind of sheepish.

352

"What's the tab?" says Johnny, pulling Doc Schmitt's hundred dollar bill from his pocket.

"Ten G-s," says the dick. "You boys owe Sam the Elephant ten G's."

"Can't stop now," says Johnny, turning us about.

"Oh, yes you can," says the dick, pulling a gat. "Now, if you two and your lady friend will just step back into the office for a minute . . ."

Behind the desk, the dick does a quick frisk on me and Johnny. I guess he thinks he is too much of a gent to touch Agnes. He puts his own pistola away and holds Doc Schmitt's Mauser, taken from Johnny, pointed at us.

He orders us into the office with a jerk of his gun hand.

Who should be waiting for us there but Tweedledum and Tweedledee, our bonebreaking friends from Miami, the bad eggs in plaid suits.

The night clerk and his kid brother are sitting on a small couch, looking meek and mild.

The dick is behind us, blocking the door.

Tweedledum says: "We was just on our way up to see youse. Tanks for coming down."

Tweedledee says: "Mr. Elefanti wants his ten G's, Belmont. I hope for your sake that you have scored well during your brief stay here at the Bon Chance."

Johnny says: "I have, indeed, boys. As a matter of fact, we were off just now to collect a large sum. How about giving me an hour?"

"You must be nuts," says Tweedledum.

"Let's break his arms," says Tweedledee.

"Let's break his knees," says Tweedledum. "Then he can still deal from up his sleeves and make Mr. Elefanti's money back, but he can't run, see?"

"Pug," says Johnny, "we haven't got time for this right now" and I know what he means.

I grab Agnes by the arm and slam back with the box, knocking the Mauser from the dick's hand, as Johnny is making two stabs with his umbrella to the soft round bellies in plaid.

We jam through the door, I lose my grip on Agnes, and she falls. I pull her up, and we beat it out of the hotel to Sleeping Bill's phony Yellow Cab. But Sleeping Bill is not ready for our getaway. He is—sleeping.

Johnny pulls him out of the driver's seat, stuffs the C-note into his pocket, and we leave him standing there. I think he is still asleep as Johnny steers us out through the flood like we are in a motor launch. We head for the river, downtown.

At corners we are making huge wakes of water, which blur the night lights outside so they seem to run crazily down the windshield and windows. But through the back windows I can see headlights that are staying with us.

It is just like this when a shot smacks through the back window between Agnes and me and goes out the front by Johnny's ear, and Sleeping Bill's old car kind of faces one of these steel pylons, that are holding up the West Side Highway. Johnny is a smooth driver and pumps coolly on the brake, coaxing it, but Sleeping Bill's car has made up its mind. At the last second Johnny finds some traction and pulls the wheel sharp. The car leaps, avoiding a head-on, and slams into the pylon sidewise, on my side, back by the gas tank. Then we hear a puff.

"We're on fire!" cries Johnny. "Get out! Out!"

Now the three of us are running in deep water over slippery cobblestones.

I hear Sleeping Bill's phony old cab blow apart. Well, Johnny gave him a C-note, and the car was worth maybe only fifty bucks.

Up ahead of us is coming a police car, siren squawking. The cops in the car don't see us in the rain and the dark. They pass right by us.

I look over my shoulder and see that the Elephant's boys have negotiated a U-turn and are now heading off from whence they came.

Agnes says: "There's the ship! Follow me!"

Aboard, Agnes takes charge. "This way," she says, leading us through passageways. "Cabin A," she says. When we are at Cabin A, she opens the door and walks in ahead of us. We follow her into a good-sized stateroom, I guess you call it.

She crosses the room and turns around to us. Now she is not like Agnes at all. She is like some altogether different person. It is all in the look on her face. I get a cold chill up my back.

"Good morning, gentlemen," comes a voice from behind us.

I turn around and there are Von Heller and Lensky. He is holding his pistola with the silencer.

I am certainly confused. I look at Agnes. She is holding her daddy's Mauser.

"I'll take the package," says Agnes.

"What is going on here?" I say. I must admit I am by now feeling pretty stupid. I look at Johnny, and I am amazed to see that he is smiling. He sees that I am mentally in a bind and is good enough to answer my questions before I ask.

"We are rounding up secret agents, Pug," he says. "Uncle Wild Bill would be proud of us."

"What does he mean?" says Lensky to Agnes.

"I don't have the slightest idea," says Agnes.

"How did she come by the Mauser, Johnny?" I say.

"That falling act she pulled at the hotel. These two women—not to call them ladies—are aces at scooping up guns."

"But Agnes," I say, sadly depressed, "your father—"

"Doctor Schmitt wasn't her father," says Johnny.

The hatch now opens behind Von Heller and Lensky.

355

Two men with pistolas in their mitts step in.

"F.B.I.," says one.

"C.I.A." says the other.

"You might as well hand over your weapons," says Johnny. "There's a Coast Guard cutter blocking your way out to sea."

The feds go around the room collecting from Von Heller, who has a nice little pearl-handled automatic of her own, and Lensky, and Agnes. When the F.B.I. agent is taking the Mauser from Agnes, Johnny says:

"Agnes, I've been meaning to tell you all night that you have beautiful legs. Would you mind lifting up your skirt so that I can get one good look at them before you go?"

Agnes gives Johnny a grim little smile, shrugs, and lifts her skirt. On her right thigh is a scabbard with a long knife in it.

"That's what killed Schmitt,' says Johnny. "Oh," he adds, "thank you, Agnes. I shall never forget them."

* * *

It is a week later and we are sitting in a couple of beach chairs by the pool of Sam the Elephant's Miami Beach hotel. It is a glorious day and there are beautiful ladies stepping all around us and the noise of the diving board and splashing and palm fronds waving over our heads.

Sam the Elephant is in his gold bathing trunks and has a gold towel over one hairy shoulder and is wearing dark shades over his eyes and smoking a huge Havana cigar and sipping occasionally on a straw which draws up something green inside it. Johnny has been telling him the story, as follows, which clears things up for me too:

It seems that Agnes planned to slip away from Schmitt, with the head, at Penn Station, and catch the limo in which are waiting Von Heller and Lensky. The three were then going to drive to the freighter. The freighter was a Communist ship. Agnes, however, has been suspected of being a double agent. In Washington, she has been ordered to pose as Schmitt's daughter, but Schmitt has been warned not to trust her. Agnes, of course, does not know that Schmitt suspects her. Then Schmitt's inspiration about the Lost and Found, plus Johnny's bet with me, messes up her plans.

Later, she dumps Schmitt the hard way, with a knife, when the house dick leaves her alone with him, calls some contact with the freighter, and explains what has happened. She leaves word for Von Heller and Lensky to meet her at the freighter, and that she has a couple of suckers who will help her make the pier without interference.

Then she comes back to our room to tell us the story of Haydn's head, to make enough time elapse before we discover the body so that we will think Von Heller and Lensky have killed Schmitt. Also because the story will help convince us that she is in danger and needs help.

We go and find Schmitt, with me, at least, thinking what she wants us to think, that Von Heller and Lensky have paid Schmitt a visit. But Johnny doesn't think so. What troubles him is that Schmitt is stabbed in the back. Why should Lensky need to use a knife when he keeps waving around a revolver with a silencer on it? And why in the back?

That's when he thinks of Agnes. He sends me off with her to our room, but he keeps the head with him. He's afraid she will use the shiv on me, take the head, and scram.

(When I asked him how come he knows for sure that she has a knife, he says: "It was a logical deduction, Pug, from the circumstances—besides, I felt it on her thigh when I put her in the chair." He guffaws.

"What about me?" I say. "She wouldn't tackle you, Johnny, because you had the Mauser. But suppose she used that pig-sticker on me?"

Johnny says: "Why would she? She wanted to keep us with her. Besides, I had the head." Then he laughs and says:

357

"I just had to gamble that she wouldn't knife you, Pug old boy."

I say: "Thanks a lot!"

Then Johnny puts in a call to uncle Wild Bill Belmont, in Washington (He says: "I took great pleasure in waking him up at three in the morning"), gets the dope on the situation, and sets the trap at the pier.

Sam the Elephant is delighted with the whole story. He is also delighted that he will get his ten G's when we get the reward, which is to be within a month, from what we are told. But it is our nerve, says Sam the Elephant, which delights him most, the way we have come down to Miami and walked right in on him with our tale. Also, he is a great patriot, he tells us, and appreciates what we have done for our country. He is going to stake us until our money comes, and we will have the best.

He is laughing as he heaves himself up and waddles off, laughing and shaking his head.

A waiter comes out and passes him, bringing a telephone. It is Wild Bill in Washington has something to say.

Johnny is all smiles at first, but then he frowns.

"Wait a minute," he says, "are you sure?"

But I have already heard a click.

Johnny hangs up, looks at me, and says:

"Pug, we've got a problem."

"What's that?" I say.

"The head was a fake. The real skull has been with the Society of Friends of Music in Vienna since Eighteen-Ninety-five. The authenticity of the skull in their possession has been proven beyond doubt."

"A fake," I say. "Does that mean we do not get any reward?"

"I'm afraid not," he says. "It seems that Schmitt knew he was carrying a fake. He was under orders to do everything he could to convince Agnes that it was the real thing, and she believed it. And so did we."

"But, Johnny," I say, "now we owe Sam the Elephant the ten G's again—"

"Plus," says Johnny, "five hundred expense money."

"Not to mention," I add to the list of our woes, "our hotel bill."

"We better get packing, Pug," says Johnny.

"So it looks like we are on the run again," I say with a sigh.

I am not overly interested in history, as I have a tendency to think that it is all in the past; but, for what I guess are obvious reasons, I stay interested in the subject of Haydn and his head. I follow it in the newspapers.

They finally get his head and the rest of him together in Nineteen-Fifty-four in Burgenland. In Nineteen Fifty-five there is such a thing as an Austrian State Treaty, which is signed by the Four Powers. So it seems that nobody takes over Haydn's country, which joins the U.N. in the same year. All this is very interesting to me, because I feel like, in a little way, I am a part of it. Also, when I think of it now, it brings back the days when Johnny and me were always on the run. Being on the run was a lot of fun if you ran with Johnny Belmont.

AGENT SONNET

Alex Jackinson, R.I.P.

"Why don't you write a novel, for God's sake,
   get down to something good to read, instead
of solipsistic verse? Give us a break!
   Write something worth a read at night in bed.

The public likes a song, a song in rhyme,
   not free-verse pouting about the poet's life
in chopped-up prose, a reader's waste of time!
   The reader wants a story full of strife!

The reader likes a good detective story,
or else a horror story, good and gory.
   The public likes a bit of gruesome fun.

The public wants some sex; to be a voyeur;
to let a woman be a man-destroyer
   while islanded romantically in sun."

www.ingramcontent.com/pod-product-compliance
Lightning Source LLC
Chambersburg PA
CBHW021826090426
42811CB00032B/2039/J